"Why do bad things happen to good people? That question has haunted humanity for centuries. In his new commentary on Job, Dr. David Allen shows that in the crucible of suffering, we can learn to trust God more deeply. In his darkest days, Job came to view life and the Lord in a new light. He learned to trust God in the midst of his pain, and then he lived to see his life restored with hope. Dr. Allen masterfully maneuvers through Job's suffering and shows us how to navigate through the negativity of our own lives. This commentary gives fresh insights into one of the oldest and most pertinent books of the Bible. I highly recommend it."

Steve Gaines, pastor, Bellevue Baptist Church, Memphis, Tennessee

"The message of Job is vital in a world of suffering and sickness, but the book is long and complicated, and many readers find it difficult to understand. Enter David Allen's excellent exposition, where the message of the book is clearly unpacked. Allen doesn't leave us only with an interpretation of Job, but he also shows its relevance and application for life in today's world. I expect many pastors, Sunday school teachers, and laypeople to turn regularly to this accessible commentary for help in interpreting the book of Job."

Thomas Schreiner, James Buchanan Harrison professor of New Testament interpretation and associate dean for Scripture and interpretation at The Southern Baptist Theological Seminary in Louisville, Kentucky

"Dr. Allen has given us a remarkable book on Job. We see in it Dr. Allen's rare combination of the scholar and the preacher. He gives us scholarly exegesis and interpretation as well as sermonic word pictures, rhetorical devices, illustrations, and applications. I can find only one thing wrong with Dr. Allen's commentary on Job: He should have written it before I attempted to preach a series on Job!"

Jerry Vines, pastor emeritus of First Baptist Church, Jacksonville, Florida, and two-term President of the Southern Baptist Convention

CHRIST-CENTERED

Exposition

OT / COMMENTARY   FEATURING

AUTHOR David L. Allen
SERIES EDITORS David Platt, Daniel L. Akin, and Tony Merida

CHRIST-CENTERED

Exposition

EXALTING JESUS IN

JOB

HOLMAN®
REFERENCE
BRENTWOOD, TENNESSEE

B&H Publishing Group
Brentwood, Tennessee
All rights reserved.

ISBN: 978-0-8054-9740-3

Dewey Decimal Classification: 220.7
Subject Heading: BIBLE. O.T. JOB—
COMMENTARIES\JESUS CHRIST

Printed in the United States of America
2 3 4 5 6 7 8 9 10 • 27 26 25 24 23

SERIES DEDICATION

Dedicated to Adrian Rogers and John Piper. They have taught us to love the gospel of Jesus Christ, to preach the Bible as the inerrant Word of God, to pastor the church for which our Savior died, and to have a passion to see all nations gladly worship the Lamb.

—David Platt, Tony Merida, and Danny Akin
March 2013

AUTHOR'S DEDICATION

To those who have suffered and asked "Why?"

To those wounded healers we call preachers who have preached to those asking "Why?"

To those who have asked "Why?" and then discovered that is the wrong question

To those who asked the right question—"Who?"—and found their answer:

Him

TABLE OF CONTENTS

ACKNOWLEDGMENTS

No author is an island. No author stands alone. To that innumerable throng who being dead yet speak, whose brains I have ransacked, I owe a debt of gratitude. To those still in the land of the living, two deserve my sincere gratitude. Danny Akin, my friend for forty-five years, invited me to participate in this project. We share many common bonds, none stronger than a commitment to Christ-centered exposition. Finally, no greater debt do I owe than to Dave Stabnow, whose kind encouragement, sharp eye, and helpful advice have been a lifesaver for me in writing this volume.

SERIES INTRODUCTION

Augustine said, "Where Scripture speaks, God speaks." The editors of the Christ-Centered Exposition Commentary series believe that where God speaks, the pastor must speak. God speaks through His written Word. We must speak from that Word. We believe the Bible is God breathed, authoritative, inerrant, sufficient, understandable, necessary, and timeless. We also affirm that the Bible is a Christ-centered book; that is, it contains a unified story of redemptive history of which Jesus is the hero. Because of this Christ-centered trajectory that runs from Genesis 1 through Revelation 22, we believe the Bible has a corresponding global-missions thrust. From beginning to end, we see God's mission as one of making worshipers of Christ from every tribe and tongue worked out through this redemptive drama in Scripture. To that end we must preach the Word.

In addition to these distinct convictions, the Christ-Centered Exposition Commentary series has some distinguishing characteristics. First, this series seeks to display exegetical accuracy. What the Bible says is what we want to say. While not every volume in the series will be a verse-by-verse commentary, we nevertheless desire to handle the text carefully and explain it rightly. Those who teach and preach bear the heavy responsibility of saying what God has said in His Word and declaring what God has done in Christ. We desire to handle God's Word faithfully, knowing that we must give an account for how we have fulfilled this holy calling (Jas 3:1).

Second, the Christ-Centered Exposition Commentary series has pastors in view. While we hope others will read this series, such as parents, teachers, small-group leaders, and student ministers, we desire to provide a commentary busy pastors will use for weekly preparation of biblically faithful and gospel-saturated sermons. This series is not academic in nature. Our aim is to present a readable and pastoral style of commentaries. We believe this aim will serve the church of the Lord Jesus Christ.

Third, we want the Christ-Centered Exposition Commentary series to be known for the inclusion of helpful illustrations and theologically driven applications. Many commentaries offer no help in illustrations, and few offer any kind of help in application. Often those that do offer illustrative material and application unfortunately give little serious attention to the text. While giving ourselves primarily to explanation, we also hope to serve readers by providing inspiring and illuminating illustrations coupled with timely and timeless application.

Finally, as the name suggests, the editors seek to exalt Jesus from every book of the Bible. In saying this, we are not commending wild allegory or fanciful typology. We certainly believe we must be constrained to the meaning intended by the divine Author himself, the Holy Spirit of God. However, we also believe the Bible has a messianic focus, and our hope is that the individual authors will exalt Christ from particular texts. Luke 24:25-27,44-47 and John 5:39,46 inform both our hermeneutics and our homiletics. Not every author will do this the same way or have the same degree of Christ-centered emphasis. That is fine with us. We believe faithful exposition that is Christ centered is not monolithic. We do believe, however, that we must read the whole Bible as Christian Scripture. Therefore, our aim is both to honor the historical particularity of each biblical passage and to highlight its intrinsic connection to the Redeemer.

The editors are indebted to the contributors of each volume. The reader will detect a unique style from each writer, and we celebrate these unique gifts and traits. While distinctive in their approaches, the authors share a common characteristic in that they are pastoral theologians. They love the church, and they regularly preach and teach God's Word to God's people. Further, many of these contributors are younger voices. We think these new, fresh voices can serve the church well, especially among a rising generation that has the task of proclaiming the Word of Christ and the Christ of the Word to the lost world.

We hope and pray this series will serve the body of Christ well in these ways until our Savior returns in glory. If it does, we will have succeeded in our assignment.

David Platt
Daniel L. Akin
Tony Merida
Series Editors
February 2013

Job

Introduction to Job

Thomas Carlyle called Job "one of the grandest things ever written with pen. . . . There is nothing written, I think, in the Bible or out of it, of equal literary merit" (*On Heroes*, 49). Many have fallen under the spell of Job's artistic brilliance, moving pathos, and dramatic suffering. Many writers have used Job as the basis for their plots, including H. G. Wells and Archibald MacLeish in his one-time Broadway hit, *J. B.* (McGee, *Poetry*). More than a museum exhibit, Job is a living, breathing, book (Stewart, *Message*, 27). Job "offers a rare peek through the keyhole of eternity" (Yancey, "Fresh Reading," 143).

Job is a book easily translated into the language of our own circumstances. Sir Walter Raleigh is reported to have said of William Wordsworth, "To know him is to learn courage." To get to know Job the person is to learn courage, not to mention patience, as the New Testament authors speak of his character (Jas 5:11).

Everyone understands and no one questions when people suffer for their own evil choices and decisions. Everyone knows when we do wrong, we pay the consequences. But a time comes when most people realize there is often no correlation between the amount of wrong we commit and the amount of pain we suffer. In fact, often it is just the opposite. What do you do when you are doing everything (or most everything) right, and suddenly everything goes wrong? That's what happened to Job. Job was just sitting there minding his own business and serving God faithfully when all hell broke loose in his life. Job did not take his sufferings piously or quietly, nor did he seek a second opinion from outside physicians or philosophers. He went straight to God and asked two questions: "Why?" and "Why me?" He refused to take God's silence for an answer or to let God off the hook (Peterson, *Led by Suffering*, 5).

We may summarize Job's macrostructure with the following précis: Job, a man of virtue and piety, lives on the borderlands of the Arabian desert probably during the patriarchal period. His fortune and reputation are superior to all in the region. Through the instigation and agency of Satan, who doubts the genuineness of Job's virtue, God permits Job to

3

experience a succession of calamities involving his property, family, and physical body. His wife counsels him to curse God and die. Job refuses and maintains his trust in God in the midst of horrific suffering.

Hearing of his suffering, three friends come to console and counsel him. Job curses the day of his birth because of his suffering. His three friends, believing they understand God's providence and justice better than Job, rebuke him and call on him to repent of whatever sin he has committed to earn God's wrath. Job continues to maintain his innocence and expresses exasperation at God that he cannot understand why God has permitted his calamities.

Job and his friends engage in three rounds of arguments over these issues. Then a young man, Elihu, steps in. He finds fault with all parties, defends divine providence, and points out that reproof and changed behavior are the designed goals of suffering.

Finally, God intervenes, and through a series of questions he asks Job about how the universe and earth were created and are operated by God's power and providence, indicating that these things, along with Job's suffering, are beyond human understanding. God rebukes Job for his audacity of asking the "why" question of suffering. Job submits to God in humility. God expresses displeasure with Job's three friends and rebukes them for not speaking correctly about God and his ways.

Job's suffering ends, and God blesses Job with twice his former wealth, blesses Job with ten children, and gives him many more years of long and happy life.

George O'Neill well summarized the book's universal appeal:

> The eternal conflict between good and evil; the right
> interpretation of this conflict, of its bewildering vicissitudes
> and baffling consequences; the difficulty in a distracted and
> suffering world of maintaining faith in a Creator and Ruler
> who is wise, loving, and omnipotent, of equating rewards
> and punishments, either in this mortal life or in a dimly
> described future, with men's good or evil conduct—these are
> problems over which from the beginning of time the thinker
> has tormented his brain and the ordinary man has brooded in
> bewilderment or anguish. (*World's Classic*, 16)

Job is a book that grapples with the most agonizing riddle of human existence, the problem of evil and suffering. It is a book full of God and humanity. It is as universal as nature and as ubiquitous as air.

The two most important persons to heed in the book are God and, coming in at a distant second, Job. It is not only important to take note of what Job says and does in his suffering but perhaps even more important to note what he does not say and do. Though Satan said Job would curse God if he lost everything, and his wife counseled him to do just that when he did lose everything, nevertheless Job did not curse God. You don't get rid of the problem of suffering by getting rid of God. Let that sink in for a moment. Job is not like many who look at suffering and evil in the world and draw the conclusion that either there is no God or that God is impotent to stop all suffering and evil. Since God doesn't give an explanation for all human suffering, they merely decide God doesn't exist.

Job does not explain his suffering or give us direct counsel about how to respond when we ourselves suffer. He does not go on the circuit doing seminars on suffering. His response to God's response at the end of the book indicated it was enough for Job—and it must be enough for us as well. More than we need answers when we suffer, we need God.

Background and Recent Studies on Job

Job appears in the Hebrew Bible among the third grouping of books known as the "Writings." It is one of the poetic books of the Old Testament, along with Psalms, Proverbs, Ecclesiastes, and Song of Solomon, all of which are part of the ancient Near East (hereafter ANE) wisdom tradition. The key focus of wisdom literature is the art of living well. Two broad emphases of wisdom material occur in the Old Testament: *lower wisdom*, with an emphasis on practical things for everyday life. Proverbs fits this category. The second category, *higher wisdom*, emphasizes ultimate issues of life. Job, along with Ecclesiastes, fits this second category.[1]

Job's Suffering and the ANE

There are both similarities and distinctions between Ancient Near Eastern wisdom literature and Old Testament Wisdom literature

---

[1] Helpful works on these and many other issues in Job include Beuken, *Book of Job*; Perdue and Gilpin, *Voice from the Whirlwind*; and Zuck, *Sitting with Job*. This last volume is especially helpful to the preacher.

(House, *OT Theology*, 425). There are a number of ANE parallels in Job.[2] Many scholars accept that the book has ANE origins, but they . . .

> debate whether the tale is a straightforward rendering of an old oral tale (probably originating in Edom or North Arabia, the likely site of Job's homeland, Uz; Job 1:1) or a sophisticated literary imitation of such a tale. (Newsom, "Job, Book of," 814)

However, the description of suffering in Job differs from the descriptions of suffering in literature in the ANE. The following chart illustrates the differences.[3]

ANE	JOB
Health was the primary issue.	Job lost wealth and family before health.
The goal was appeasement of angry gods due to ritual offense.	No appeasement of God—he is not angry.
Gods reaped benefits from labor of humans. Humans reaped benefits from favor of the gods.	Job did not operate according to that Great Symbiosis.
Sufferers acknowledge offenses when they know what they are. They claim ignorance.	Job claims innocence.
No theme of the gods' justice or man's righteousness.	God is presumed to be just; Job claims righteousness.
The piety/prosperity matrix is affirmed by the sufferers.	Job's friends voice this, but not Job.

[2] For summary studies of the relationship of Job to the ANE, consult Hartley, "Job 2," 346–61; Curtis, *Interpreting*, 88–100; and Newsom, "Job, Book of," 813–14.
[3] Keener and Walton, *NIV Cultural Backgrounds Study Bible*, 824.

Sufferers not declared innocent.	Job is declared innocent by God.
The gods are inscrutable because they are capricious and have not communicated proper ritual practice.	God's inscrutability results from his infinite wisdom and human limitations.

How can we best understand the notion of suffering in Job? Goldingay is helpful at this point:

> On any understanding, the chapters introduce the way suffering tests, whether this is divinely determined or satanically instigated or "just one of those things." It brings out whether we will maintain our integrity or revile God and die (Job 2:9); in the context of suffering, a central issue in Job is "a struggle to maintain integrity and faith." Suffering brings out whether we will try to maintain silence or turn our back on God rather than batter on God's chest (Job 3–27). It brings out whether we can live with ignorance or insist on being the center of the universe, and whether we think we could run it better than God (Job 38–41). It brings out whether we will make our home on the ash heap forever or eventually determine that enough is enough (Job 42:6). It brings out whether we will agree to the dubious theology of our advisers or insist on telling the truth about God (Job 42:8). (*Israel's Life*, 684)

Job: Fact or Fiction?

It is difficult to interpret Job in any other way than as a factual, historical account. This is the way Job has been viewed traditionally. There are several strands of evidence confirming the historicity of the book.

- Job 1:1 begins with a historical statement similar to what we find in Judges 17:1 and 1 Samuel 1:1.
- Ezekiel mentions Job twice in conjunction with Noah and Daniel (Ezek 14:14,20).
- James refers to Job in James 5:11 as a historical person.

Contrary to the opinion of some, Job is more than a nonhistorical work of imaginative literature (Estes, *Handbook*, 19).[4]

Job: Prose or Poetry?

From a discourse perspective, Job is both prose and poetry. As Seow noted,

> Neither the prose tale nor the poetic middle can stand alone. Without the prose tale, the poetry lacks context; without the poetic middle, the story lacks theological depth and vibrancy. The prose narrative by itself is not a complete story, and neither is the poetic middle. (*Job 1–21*, 29)

Why Study the Book of Job?

In and of itself, Job seems to be the record of an unanswered agony, as G. Campbell Morgan put it (*Answer of Jesus*, 9). Job is a book that speaks to the heart of human existence and experience. Yet the book has proved to be elusive in many ways. "Try to pin this book down and it slips like sand through your fingers" (Gibson, *Job*, 1).

It is imperative that Job be read with New Testament glasses. In fact, Job simply can't be interpreted correctly apart from the cross. In the book of Job itself, there is no answer given as to why he suffers. The reasons become clearer in the light of the cross. I have concluded that Job is not so much a book about suffering as a book about God.

Some people are prone to offer armchair answers for wheelchair questions (Ash, *Job*, 18). Job asks wheelchair questions, but he deserves something more than armchair answers like he received from his three friends.

At the end of the book, God has not answered Job's questions or explained the reason for the situation (which the reader knows because the narrator explained it). However, Job learned that God's perspective is bigger than answering his questions. So it's the places in the book that lack responses, places that leave us pondering the mysteries of God, that may give us clues (from a thirty-thousand-foot perspective) to the understanding of the book.

---

[4] Though the dialogue is couched in poetic style, there is no reason to doubt the historicity of the book or the dialogue. Scripture often reports dialogue in other than verbatim form.

In his excellent sermons on the book of Job, Christopher Ash suggests seven reasons the book should be studied with seriousness: to (1) understand God for who he is; (2) grapple with God's sovereignty; (3) reject false gospels (the prosperity gospel and the therapeutic gospel); (4) identify with those who suffer; (5) find hope in the midst of pain; (6) develop your emotional palate (learn to feel, desire, and grow more sensitive to all life experiences); (7) encounter the living God (*Job*, 17–23).

Several cautions are worth noting in reading and preaching Job:

- Care should be exercised in how we interpret individual verses from Job. It is unwise to pull isolated verses from Job out of context and use them to try to understand God or make theological assertions.
- Care should be exercised in interpreting the poetic and metaphorical language often found in Job. Edward Curtis speaks an important word on this subject:

  Poetry has the power to capture the emotion and the intensity
  of his experience. Job's descriptions of his ailments were
  not meant to enable the astute exegetes to diagnose his
  malady, but to reveal the depths of his pain and struggle.
  His frustration, confusion and even anger can be felt in the
  poetry of the book, and exegesis of this material should
  be as concerned to capture its emotional aspect as it is to
  identify literary structure and explain unusual words and
  grammar. The goal is not to analyze the poetry and recast it
  into propositions that constitute the teaching of the passage.
  Neither is the goal to eliminate all **ambiguity** or to answer
  every theological or philosophical question posed by this
  poetic text. (Curtis, *Interpreting*, 121; emphasis in original)

- Care should be exercised in interpreting Behemoth and Leviathan in Job.
- Care should be exercised in applying Job in our preaching and teaching. Job does not offer application in a straightforward manner since it is narrative and poetic in terms of genre.
- Care should be exercised in interpreting the dialogue section of Job. As Parsons cautioned, "Preachers who ignore the dialogue or try to pull some principle without an awareness of the

immediate and overall context are in danger of not only distorting the story of Job but also misrepresenting (however unwittingly) the message for today" ("Guidelines," 395).

• Care should be exercised in reading Job first in its Old Testament narrative and poetic setting, then reading it in light of the New Testament.

Authorship[5]

Job the man and Job the book are shrouded in obscurity. The book of Job is littered with the potholes of our ignorance. We don't know who wrote Job. We don't know when Job was written. We don't know anything about Job other than what is recorded in the book. Traditional wisdom assigns the book to Job himself, though there is no internal or external evidence to confirm this. Though some have suggested Moses as the author, this is unlikely. Linguistic clues point to an early provenance of the book, most likely sometime during the early patriarchal period. Since the author uses *Yahweh* throughout, the covenant name for God, it is likely the author was an Israelite.

Other suggestions have included Ezra, Solomon, and Elihu. Those who suggest Elihu rely on Job 32:16-17: "When I had waited, (for they spake not, but stood still, and answered no more;) I said, I will answer also my part, I also will shew mine opinion" (KJV). This statement does not occur in the context of conversation, but the author is expressing his own thoughts in first person, after which the conversation resumes, and Elihu is speaking (McGee, *Poetry*, vii). Some have concluded from this that Elihu may have been the author.

The suggestion of multiple authorship based on linguistic factors falters on two grounds: (1) There is no evidence of different configurations of the book. If such existed, they have not been preserved. (2) The orthographic archaisms (old spelling of words) evident in the poetic middle are found also in the prose sections, "corroborating the view that a single composer was at work" (Seow, *Job 1–21*, 27). Seow concluded that different genres and styles in Job "may not be indicative of multiple authorship but may point to a single author" (*Job 1–21*, 28).[6]

---

[5] For summaries of the authorship question, see Walton, "Job 1: Book of," 333–46.
[6] On the Jewish orientation of the book of Job, see Dunham, *Pious Sage in Job*, 159–60.

Date of Job

Whatever the date for the composition of Job, the time period of events need not be considered the time period of composition. We should distinguish the setting of Job from the date of composition. Several views have been suggested, ranging from the patriarchal age to as late as the second century BC. The evidence points to an early date for Job, probably in the patriarchal era:

1. Most common uses of names for God are *'Eloah* or *Shaddai*; the latter means "Almighty." These are names familiar to the patriarchs.
2. The lifestyle of Job is parallel to patriarchs.
3. The concept of priesthood was not unknown, but a separate priesthood had not totally developed (1:5; 42:8).
4. Coinage is referred to as "qesitah" (42:11), which likely places the book in a patriarchal time frame. (This term is used also in Gen 33:19 and Josh 24:32.)
5. The musical instruments named in Job 21–30 indicate ancient instruments.
6. The linguistic nature of the book reflects an ancient context. Approximately two-thirds of the vocabulary used in Job comprises loan words.

These are the arguments for placing the setting of Job in the time of the patriarchs:

1. The length of Job's life span. "Job lived 140 years after this and saw his children and their children to the fourth generation. Then Job died, old and full of days" (42:16-17). People experienced much longer life spans in the time of the patriarchs.
2. Job acted as the high priest in his family. There is no mention in Job of any formal priesthood being in place. Though an argument from silence, it may indicate an early setting for Job.
3. Eliphaz the Temanite was descended from Eliphaz the son or Esau. "These are the names of Esau's sons: Eliphaz son of Esau's wife Adah, and Reuel son of Esau's wife Basemath" (Gen 36:10). Though not conclusive, this indicates that the name *Eliphaz* was a patriarchal name (McGee, *Poetry*, viii).

Name of the Book, Integrity, and Canonicity

The name *Job* has been thought to mean different things, including "hated or persecuted one," "the penitent one," or "to spring forth." The book reads like a unified whole, not a compilation of redacted parts by different authors. Job was accepted among the canonical books by the Qumran community by at least 100 BC.

In various translations, the order in which Job appears varies. In the Masoretic Text the order is Psalms, Proverbs, Job. In the Talmud the order is Psalms, Job, Proverbs (200–150 BC). In the Latin Vulgate Job precedes Psalms and Proverbs (AD 400; this was ultimately followed by the Council of Trent, which established the modern Christian canonical order).

I have not endeavored to cover the ground of debates over textual authenticity and proposed interpolations. This information can be studied in the various technical commentaries and introductions to the Old Testament. I am treating the text we have in hand.

Unity of Job

Scholars have also argued over the issue of whether the book of Job is a unified whole written by a single author or was compiled over time by various authors. Much has been made over the seeming inconsistency in how Job's reaction to God is portrayed. However, a careful study demonstrates consistency and coherence. Each section is integral to the message of the entire book.

Background of Job

What is the setting of Job? Job is introduced as living in the land of Uz, an unknown location somewhere outside of Israel. The most likely location is somewhere in Edom (see Lam 4:21). The time period is generally viewed as the patriarchal age somewhere in the second millennium BC.

Uz is mentioned three times in the Hebrew Bible but nowhere else in Middle Eastern literature or the ANE.

> Maimonides did not hesitate to treat the word [*'uz*] as a common noun, pointing out that it is the imperative of 'to take advice or counsel': The name *Uz* therefore expresses an exhortation to consider well this lesson, grasp its ideas and comprehend them, in order to see which is the right view. (Wolfers, *Deep Things*, 84)

When all the evidence is considered, there is simply not a good extrabiblical parallel to Job. "The Babylonian Theodicy" probably comes closest to Job of all the background suggestions, but still the connection is too tenuous. The background of the book is most likely early second millennium BC.

Theme

There is no unanimity on the question of the main theme of Job. In times past the theme was generalized as an attempt to answer the question of why the righteous suffer. However, as everyone discovers upon even a cursory reading of Job, that question is never answered—by God or anyone else.

Perhaps a productive trail is to consider the book something of a theodicy—a justification of God explaining how a good and just God can permit human suffering, especially by the righteous. But the book never answers that question either.

Probably the best thematic statement for Job is that it refutes the idea, popular in every age, that all suffering is a sign of God's displeasure or a result of unrighteous conduct on the part of the sufferer. One thing is clear: the book of Job clearly refutes both concepts.

Estes identifies three key purposes for the book of Job: (1) "to challenge the mistaken assumption that personal sin is always the cause of suffering," (2) "to explore human limitations in probing the issue of divine justice," and (3) to reveal that "as the sovereign ruler of the universe, Yahweh is free and beyond human comprehension." Job seems to be focused more on the purpose of God in suffering (future) rather than the cause of suffering (past). In a real sense, the key question in the book of Job is not the question of suffering, but "What is the nature of God?" (Estes, *Job*, 4–5).

Suffering in Job

The question of suffering is theoretical for some, theological for others, but for those in its throes, it is an intensely personal and existential question. Everything in Job ricochets off the reality of pain.

Job begins as something of a disputation between God and Satan, continues as a disputation between Job and his friends, and culminates in something of a disputation between Job and God, where God disputes and Job listens. Many have noted the feel of a courtroom scene, as arguments and counterarguments abound.

In essence, Job's three friends refuse to hear his case. As a result, Job has to appeal to a higher court—God's. This appeal is explicit at the end of Job 31, which employs the language of a legal proceeding. As Westermann noted, Job's three friends advance arguments in their speeches. Job, however, doesn't engage in arguments; with only one exception, Job expresses himself in laments. "This incongruity between the speeches of the friends and the speeches of Job is the most noticeable and also the most important structural clue in the book" (*Structure*, 4–5).

Westermann continued:

> However, Job had already turned to this higher court—
> cryptically, to be sure—*before* the onset of the disputation. A
> straight line leads from this opening accusation against God
> in chap. 3 to Job's summoning of God at the end of chap.
> 31. The bracketing of the dialogue section (chaps. 4–27) by
> the element of lament, in which Job turns directly to God,
> corresponds substantively to the incongruity noted within the
> dialogue section. There is then only one way to see the whole
> of the Book of Job: the encompassing confrontation is that
> between Job and God, while within this confrontation stands
> the one between the friends and Job. What happens between
> the friends and Job begins with the first speech of Eliphaz
> (chap. 4) and ends with Job's answer to the third speech of
> Eliphaz (chap. 23; on chaps. 24–27 see below). What happens
> between Job and God begins with the lament in chap. 3 and
> ends with God's answer to Job's final, summarizing lament
> in chaps. 29–31, which climaxes in Job's summoning of God
> (31:35-37). (*Structure*, 5–6; emphasis in original)

Structurally speaking, the back-and-forth between Job and his three friends (Job 4–28) is bookended by Job's lament (Job 3; 29–31). Job addresses God in his lament and summons him to respond (31:35-37). After Elihu has his say, to which Job does not respond, God steps in and responds (Job 38–42). In the midst of Job's suffering, he cries out to God, God answers, and Job submits to God. This is the gist of the book of Job (*Structure*, 6).

Retribution Principle

Scholars are generally agreed that some form of the retribution principle plays a part in Job.[7] The age-old questions—Why is there suffering in the universe? Why do the innocent suffer?—are brought to a head in Job. What are the possible reasons for suffering? We might posit two broad categories: suffering that God causes directly, and suffering that God permits but is caused by others. In this latter category we might posit five possibilities for the cause of suffering: (1) nature; (2) personal negligence, accident, or sin on the part of the sufferer; (3) personal negligence, accident, or sin on the part of others; (4) no known cause; (5) Satan.

In Job's case Scripture is clear: his suffering is allowed by God but caused by Satan. But we should be cautious of relegating the retribution principle to the ash heap. Some have concluded from their reading of Job "that the universe lacks a moral economy in which deeds are met by appropriate and commensurate reward and punishment" (Fox, "God's Answer," 1). Michael Fox rejects this thesis. God does not deny the existence of divine justice in Job. Rather, Job teaches that we should be like Job—maintaining our faith in God even when it appears we are the victims of divine injustice. Job's suffering is indeed a high price to pay, but the payoff is immense. Human love and loyalty to God can be rendered truly and sincerely without being bought by favors from heaven.

Literary Characteristics

The fact that Job is likely a work to be dated in the patriarchal period may explain the frequent difficulty in style and the resultant differing translations of words and phrases among modern translators.

How should we categorize the genre of Job? The book is often viewed as one long poem bounded with a narrative prologue and epilogue. The bulk of the book contains speech cycles between Job and his three friends, followed by the speech of Elihu, and culminating in Yahweh's speech and Job's response.

---

[7] For a helpful description and summary of the retribution principle, see the article in Keener and Walton, *NIV Cultural Backgrounds Study Bible*, 823.

Some have described Job's genre as a legal disputation. Though legal metaphors occur, it seems unlikely that this is the dominant characteristic of Job. The author of Job possesses an "extraordinary metaphoric inventiveness." Job employs a wide range of unexpected semantic fields for the sources of his similes and metaphors: weaving, agronomy, labor practices, meteorology, varying crafts, and food preparation (Alter, *Wisdom Books*, 8–9).

Preaching the Biblical Imagery in Job[8]

Job is one of the most image-laden books in Scripture. In addition to the obvious suffering motif, one finds prosperity imagery in the opening prologue and concluding dialogue. Imagery of a quest motif is clear from Job's undertaking a search for the meaning of innocent suffering. The book is replete with irony. There is the irony of orthodoxy represented by Job's three friends, though their orthodox traditional explanation simply does not apply to Job. Job's accusations against God have a certain irony about them as well, as the final chapters reveal.

Nature imagery in Job is frequent. Of interest is that the majority of this type of imagery seems to be negative (darkness, thirst, drought, famine). God's creative power is prominent, culminating in God's voice from the whirlwind with rapid-fire questions to Job about God's power and wisdom in the created order. These questions are rhetorical in nature, designed to reverse what occurs earlier in the book when Job questions God. Now God peppers Job with questions impossible for him to answer. The barrage of questions from God serves to put Job on notice that God providentially manages his world with divine wisdom and with no help from Job. God's reply to Job via nature imagery dramatizes God's superior knowledge and power beyond anything Job can begin to fathom (Ryken, "Job, Book of," 452–54).

Imagery concerning the human body is also prevalent in Job, especially disease imagery. Warfare imagery also abounds. God is an archer who shoots poisoned arrows; the terrors of God are "arrayed" in battle against Job (6:4). Such combative imagery is found several times in the book.

Legal imagery also occurs, as Job desires to bring a lawsuit against God as in a courtroom trial (10:32; 13:3,15,18; 23:4,7). Often missed is

---

[8] For a succinct and helpful summary, consult Ryken, "Job, Book of," 452–54.

the imagery of speaking and words, with nearly eighty references. The debate format is evinced by many uses of the verb *answered*.

Characters in Job

The following main characters appear in Job.

Job.[9] Job desperately pleads for justice and believes only God can resolve his crisis (7:20-21; 10:1-2; 13:3,15-19,22-24; 19:25-27; 23:10-16). Job oscillates between despair and faith. He argues with God, and even when he cannot find God, he never stops yearning for a confrontation (9:32-35; 13:3,16,22; 16:18-22; 31:35-37) (Murphy, *Tree of Life*, 38). Don't miss Job, the man of prayer, in the book. Job prays to God consistently throughout the dialogues. In every single speech to the friends, Job begins by talking *about* God and then shifts to talking *to* God. The book begins with Job's prayers for his children in 1:5 and ends with his prayer for his three friends in 42:8.

Satan. In Job, the character who appears accusing Job is referred to in Hebrew as "the Satan," always with a definite article. The word, which in Hebrew means "accuser," can be used to describe other people, either by function or office: 1 Samuel 29:4; 1 Kings 5:4; 11:14,23-25; Psalm 109:6; Numbers 22:22 (in reference to the angel of the Lord).

Some have noted there is nothing intrinsically evil emerging from the profile of "the Satan" in Job. This raises the question of whether this character should be identified with "Satan" in the New Testament. There would appear to be good reasons for making this identification. Satan is the great accuser. He accuses three times in the Bible: in the garden of Eden—accusing God to man; in Job—accusing Job to God; and in the Gospels—accusing the God-man during the wilderness temptation.

In Job's prologue Satan appears something like the elementary school tattletale. He's the guy "responsible for making sure that no one gets away with anything they should not be getting away with" (Westermann, *Structure*, 6).

Eliphaz, Bildad, Zophar. The identities of Job's three friends—Eliphaz the Temanite, Bildad the Shuhite, and Zophar the Naamathite—are also shrouded in obscurity. The usual view is that all three were Edomites.[10]

---

[9] See the excellent discussion in Longman, "Job 4: Person," 371–74.

[10] "Teman was an Edomite town on the border of the Judean Negev. Shuah is unknown, and Naamah (Jos 15:41) was a Judean town on the border of Philistia, to the Northwest of the Negev" (Wolfers, *Deep Things*, 89–90).

Eliphaz was from Teman (meaning "right hand" or "south"; Job 2:11), a district and town that may have been named after the grandson of Esau (Gen 36:11,15), who bears the same name. This links Eliphaz to an Edomite ancestry and provenance. The name *Eliphaz* appears fifteen times in the Hebrew Bible. Eliphaz was probably the oldest of the three friends.[11]

Dunham thinks Eliphaz is a representative of the ANE's theology of retributive justice with its concomitant divine appeasement of God in order to obtain righteousness before God by humanly prescribed means rather than by divine means.[12] Current opinions on Eliphaz are wide-ranging:

> Eliphaz becomes a strident fundamentalist so dogmatic in his assertions that he undermines their potency and vitiates his own theological reference point. Or, he remains a sophisticated sage whose biggest mistake is, understandably, that he lost his temper. Others view Eliphaz as a narcissistic, implausible disputant who has fabricated a visionary experience to leverage himself against the hapless victim. A few claim him a naïve, effectual counselor whom Satan dupes and exploits to harass Job. Others understand him as an unwitting farce, the caricature of the wise counselor and the ideological buffoon who serves as welcome comic relief to the anguish of Job. A handful see him an admirable sage who utilizes the gamut of cultural and traditional resources to shepherd Job toward reconciliation with God. (Dunham, *Pious Sage*, 111–12)

Bildad the Shuhite probably hailed from Aramean territory on the west bank of the Euphrates River. The term *Shuhite* could refer to ancestry rather than city of origin, as noted by Beck ("Shuhite," 341). Shuhach was a son of Abraham and Keturah (Gen 38:2), and his descendants would likely be known as Shuhites.

Bildad approaches Job more from the avenue of tradition (8:8-10; 18:17). Tradition becomes the infallible interpreter of the situation. Today's questions need yesterday's answers. He has something of the personality of a retired army colonel. Like Eliphaz, he implicates Job's

---

[11] See Kyle Dunham, *The Pious Sage in Job*.

[12] Dunham, *Pious Sage*, 14. On how Eliphaz has been viewed in the history of interpretation, consult pp. 15–89.

children as the reason for Job's suffering (8:4,8). Your kids deserved it, Job! Bildad's motto is, "God always punishes evil and always rewards good." Bildad informs Job that the wicked face loss of property (18:14) and loss of their children (18:19).

Zophar probably came from Na'ameh, a mountainous area in northwestern Arabia. He may have been the youngest of the three by virtue of being mentioned last, but he was the most impetuous of the three friends in his debating style marked by intolerance and dogmatism. Zophar operates on the premise that wisdom comes via reason (11:5-19; 20:4-29). He is the most sarcastic of the three friends, and unlike Eliphaz and Bildad, Zophar refuses to admit the possibility Job might be innocent. God has punished Job less than what he deserves (11:5-6). Zophar accuses Job of oppressing the poor and seizing their houses in his second speech (20:19). Zophar does not speak at all in the third round of speeches.

Each participant follows a particular style. Seven of the eight speeches begin with a rhetorical question. The important thing to note about Job's three friends is not so much their view of suffering as their view of authority. It has often been said that Eliphaz bases his comments more on experience (4:8,12-21; 5:3,27; 15:27). In essence, Eliphaz says to Job: "Let my experience interpret yours." Eliphaz concludes that Job is being punished for what he did not do as much as for what he did.

With respect to suffering, all three friends assume the retribution principle is always true. Sin results in punishment (retribution), and therefore Job must be suffering due to his own sin or at least the sins of his children. The fate of the wicked can be explained as a cause-effect continuum between our actions and God's response. Eliphaz informs Job that if he had returned to the Lord, his children would not have been punished (5:25). In his second speech Eliphaz accuses Job of turning against God.

Though two of the three friends entertain the possibility of Job's innocence, all three call on him to repent and pray to God for healing and forgiveness. The irony here is that at the end of Job, God will instruct the three friends to seek Job to pray for them since they did not speak rightly concerning God.

Job's frustration with his three friends is evident. He likely would have unfriended them on Facebook. They started out well from a pastoral care perspective. They gathered around Job in silence for seven days. But problems began when they started to speak. In each of their

speeches there is an evident increase in the severity of their condemnation of Job. They offer no positive spin on Job's predicament. They
lecture Job directly but never speak directly to God, as Job sometimes
does in his response to their speeches. They force their errant theological remedies on Job's intense suffering. Job's friends evidenced better
theology when they were quiet!

Elihu. Elihu is the mysterious figure who appears out of thin air in
the narrative. Of note is his Hebrew name. There is no statement of his
having journeyed to see Job as with the other three friends. He may have
been a resident in the same general vicinity as Job.[13]

Elihu is something of a mediator in the narrative. He is critical of
Job because Job insists he is right before God, but he is also critical of
Job's friends because they have offered nothing helpful to Job (32:1-5).

The enigmatic figure Elihu has engendered considerable scholarly
discussion and debate. First, the authenticity of the Elihu discourse is
debated, with many suggesting the Elihu speeches are not part of the
original poem of Job. Linguistic and stylistic variations in the Elihu discourse persuade many against its authenticity. Second, why do both Job
and God ignore Elihu in the narrative? Third, though Elihu is credited
with wise insights, the severity of his tone occasionally exceeds that of
the three friends.

Cosmogony (Origin of Universe) and Cosmology (Structure of Universe)

Job contains many references to issues of cosmology and cosmogony.[14]

- Job 9:6—world rests on pillars
- Job 38:4-6—world rests on foundations
- Job 26:11—pillars of the heavens quake
- Job 9:6-9—God controls the sun, makes the stars, controls the sea
- Job 26:7—God stretches out the heavens

Job contains a theology of creation mentioned in 9:5-10; 26:5-14;
and 10:3,8-12,18; 28; as well as 38–41. Genesis 1 expresses God's delight
in his creation, and in God's response to Job (38–41), God takes him on

---

[13] Wolfers posits that Elihu's nationality and Job's "may fairly be assumed to be the
same" (*Deep Things*, 90).

[14] For a good discussion, consult Fyall, *Now My Eyes Have Seen You.*

something of a guided tour of creation, including animal life, to demonstrate Job's lack of knowledge and wisdom.

History of Interpretation[15]

Little is said about the book of Job from the church fathers of the first two centuries. Clement uses Job 28:22 to support the descent of Christ to hell (*Stromateis*, 6.45.1–2). Cyprian presents Job above all as an example of humility, patience, generosity, and endurance of sufferings understood as tests for the just (*Ad Quirinum testimonia contra Iudaeos*, 3.1.6,14,54; *De opera et eleemosynis*, 18). Job 14:4-5 occupies a key place in Origen in his distinction between Christ and others concerning sin. Augustine used Job 14:4-5 to support his anti-Pelagian doctrine on the universality of sin in humanity.

Among the early church fathers, there were two trends in interpretation. Chrysostom found in Job a model of self-denial for those struggling with the devil. Job's trust in his Redeemer (Christ) is the book's clear and distinctive meaning according to Chrysostom (Wilson, "Job, Book of," 384).

A second approach is the allegorical and moral interpretation of Gregory the Great, who saw in Job a type of Christ (*Morals on the Book of Job*).[16] Gregory's lectures on Job were highly influential throughout the medieval period. His *Moralia* exceeds one million words. The gist of his approach to Job is that suffering creates the opportunity for spiritual growth.

During the medieval period, Maimonides viewed Job as a book centered on the issue of God's providence. He considered Job a parable about a nonhistorical person. Aquinas, though influenced by Maimonides, viewed Job as a historical figure and argued against allegorical and moral interpretations of the book. Aquinas's commentary on Job remains one of the finest works on Job during this period (*The Literal Exposition on Job*).

With the advent of the Reformation, Luther and Calvin continued in the vein of Aquinas by viewing Job as a historical figure and interpreting the book literally. Luther offers little in the way of a Christological reading of Job. Calvin produced 159 sermons on Job from 1554 to 1555

---

[15] On the history of interpretation of Job, see Wilson, "Job, Book of," 384–89; Mara, "Job," 414–15; and for a more detailed summary, Allen, "Job 3: History," 361–71.

[16] The *Moralia*, a series of lectures given by Gregory in the late sixth century, is a manual of ascetic theology where Job is a type of Christ and the church.

but wrote no commentary. Calvin stands in the Thomistic tradition, viewing Job as a treatise on divine providence (*Sermons from Job*).[17]

In the modern era, the historical-critical approach has dominated Joban studies with the focus on innocent suffering as a central theme. Mid-twentieth-century interpretation shifted away from diachronic issues to a focus on the present state of the text. This in turn has led to a focus more on the rhetorical and poetic features, literary genre, irony, satire, and parody, with greater attention to the dialogue and its discussion of the doctrine of retribution and theodicy. Many scholars viewed the dialogue portion of Job to be in tension with the prologue and epilogue. More common in recent years is the view that the prose and poetic sections of Job evince a coherent whole. Recent interpretation has also focused on the latter part of the book where God speaks and Job replies. A key issue here is the nature of God and human response.[18]

More recently, the book has been read as a literary and theological whole, which is how it should be read, especially for preaching.

> Other contemporary interpretations include the liberationist
> approach of Gutierrez, deconstructionist readings by Clines,
> a historicized reading by Wolfers (Job is the nation of Israel),
> and a variety of feminist, psychoanalytical, and philosophical
> perspectives. (Wilson, "Job, Book of," 385)

Wolfers reads Job as a historical allegory in which Job represents Judah in the late eighth or early seventh century BC after Sennacherib's Assyrian invasion devastated Judah (*Deep Things*).

In addition to the key question of suffering, interpreters of Job perennially struggle with three key issues raised by the plotline of Job. First, how is it that Job can demonstrate such endurance, faith, and fortitude in Job 1–2 yet in the twenty-nine chapters that follow frequently challenge God and occasionally seemingly charge God with injustice? Second, how is it that God can upbraid Job for his insolence in questioning God's works and ways yet declare that Job has spoken more wisely than his three friends, accept him as an intercessor for the three friends, and reward him as a saint following his suffering? Third, how is it that Job, in spite of his railings in Job 3–31, is considered by Scripture a model man of righteousness and patience amid suffering (Ezek 14:14; Jas 5:11)?

---

[17] For the tortured way Calvin struggled with the problematic theology of Job, see Schreiner, *Where Shall Wisdom Be Found?*

[18] See Clines, *Job 1–20*; Course, *Speech and Response*; Cheney, *Dust, Wind, and Agony*; and van der Lugt, *Rhetorical Criticism*.

Before attempting to respond to these questions, we should make certain we do not shortchange Job's genuine godly character as affirmed by God himself in the first two chapters, coupled with the severity of Job's suffering. He endured the loss of ten grown children simultaneously. He endured the loss of all his wealth-producing property save the land itself. He endured not only the loss of health but also the scourge of a hideous disease, a head-to-toe skin malady somewhat akin to leprosy, that relegated him to spending his days and nights at the city landfill as an outcast from society in unrelieved agony. The cumulative mental and physical anguish for months on end must have been maddening. That Job should actually challenge God and occasionally question God's justice concerning his suffering should not surprise us.

The miseries of the world never brought Job to the nonsolution of the problem—atheism, a course chosen by many today. Whatever God's present mood of silence toward Job in his suffering, Job cannot bring himself to believe that such is God's permanent character. On his darkest days, he still hints at God's just character (13:16) and believes that, in the end, both he and God will be vindicated.

Structure and Outline of Job

Job is predominately poetry bounded by an introductory prose prologue and a concluding prose epilogue. Chapter 28 is something of an editorial interlude. Broadly speaking, Job may be outlined in the following manner:

I.   Prologue (1–2)
II. Speech Cycles by Job and Friends (3–31)
    A. First Cycle of Speeches (4–14)
    B. Second Cycle of Speeches (15–21)
    C. Third Cycle of Speeches (22–26)
    D. Conclusion of the Dialogue (27)
    E. Interlude (28)
    F. Job's Final Assertion of Innocence (29–31)
III. Speeches by Elihu (32–37)
IV. Yahweh's Speeches (38:1–42:6)
V.   Epilogue (42:7-17)

Another way to express the structure of Job is to highlight the key speakers: the narrator speaking in the prologue and epilogue and the characters, including God, in the dialogue section (Clines, "Shape and Argument," 127–28).

I. Prologue (1:1–2:13)
   Narrator
II. Dialogue (3:1–42:6)
   1. Job and Three Friends, First Cycle
      Job (3:1-26)
         Eliphaz (4:1–5:27)
      Job (6:1–7:21)
         Bildad (8:1-22)
      Job (9:1–10:22)
         Zophar (11:1-20)
   2. Job and Three Friends, Second Cycle
      Job (12:1–14:22)
         Eliphaz (15:1-35)
      Job (16:1–17:16)
         Bildad (18:1-21)
      Job (19:1-29)
         Zophar (20:1-29)
   3. Job and Three Friends, Third Cycle
      Job (21:1-34)
         Eliphaz (22:1-30)
      Job (23:1–24:25)
         Bildad (25:1-6)
      Job (26:1-14)
      Job (27:1–28:28)
      Job (29:1–31:40)
   4. Elihu
      Elihu (32:1–33:33)
      Elihu (34:1-37)
      Elihu (35:1-16)
      Elihu (36:1–37:24)
   5. Yahweh and Job
      Yahweh (38:1–40:2)
         Job (40:3-5)
      Yahweh (40:6–41:34)
         Job (42:1-6)
III. Epilogue (42:7-17)
   Narrator

The narrator includes scenes with dialogue in the prologue and epilogue. In the dialogue section, Job initiates conversation for the most part. He speaks first and the friends reply to him. After Bildad's third speech the friends do not speak again. However, Job speaks again three times without any response from the three friends. Elihu speaks four times, but Job does not reply. Interestingly, when God speaks, he—not Job—takes the initiative. God initiates dialogue and Job responds. Also, the continual trajectory of the speeches tends toward silence. Bildad's third speech is the last word heard from the three friends. Elihu speaks but no one responds. Job speaks but in the end silences himself when he lays his hand over his mouth (40:4-5). God speaks to Job, then to Eliphaz (representing the three friends), and then concludes his speech with actions: he restores Job's health, position, fortune, and family (Clines, "Shape and Argument," 127–29).

Paul House collates his treatment of the structure of Job under four broad headings (*OT Theology*, 428–38):

1. The God Who Lets the Faithful Be Tested (1–2)
2. The God Whose Reputation Is at Stake (3–37)
3. The God Who Answers the Faithful (38:1–42:6)
4. The God Who Vindicates the Faithful (42:7-17)

Lewis suggested that the macrostructure of Job may be viewed as a chiastic structure (*Approaching Job*, 49):

A: Job Described as Blameless and Upright (1:1)
   B: Has Much (1:2-3); Loses Everything (1:13-22; 2:7)
      C: Described as a Priest (1:5)
         D: On Dust and Ashes (2:8,12)
            E: De-creation Monologue (3:1-26)
               F: Dialogues (4–27)
                  G: Poem on Wisdom and Final Defense
                    (28–31)
               F': Additional Dialogue/Elihu Speeches (32–37)
            E': God's Speeches/Re-creation (38–41)
         D': Off Dust and Ashes (42:1-6)
      C': Described as a Priest (42:7-9)
   B': Restoration of Belongings (42:10-15)
A': Job Dies Old and Content (42:16-17)

Within the three speech cycles, Job 4–26, much of the material is redundant, as the arguments of the friends all sound much alike. The dialogue section, Job 4–28, is framed by the laments of Job (chaps. 3 and 29–31), which stand outside the disputation and are strictly laments, lacking any sort of address to the friends. Job's final soliloquy (Job 31) contains both his oath of innocence and a self-curse, reminiscent of his first soliloquy in Job 3. The two soliloquies bookend three cycles of speeches (disputations) between Job and his friends.

Each of the speeches of the three friends is progressively shorter in each cycle, and Job's response is progressively shorter, yet longer than the speech of the friends. Everything moves toward the final dialogue between Job and God.

In the third cycle of speeches, the symmetry is broken as there is no address by Zophar. Job makes another speech introduced by a different formula than before: "Then Job continued to take up his taunt and said" (27:1, author's translation).

Asymmetry may be as much a part of a narrator's art as is symmetry. The discussion between Job and his friends is deteriorating, which may be reflected in this asymmetry. The poem concludes by redefining wisdom according to Job's character—wisdom is the fear of God and avoidance of evil (28:28). See 1:1,8; 2:3 (Seow, *Job 1–21*, 29–30).

One of the great ironies of Job is that his friends spend all their time trying to help Job find wisdom in his suffering, whereas it is precisely in Job, a man who fears God and turns away from evil, that wisdom is found (Seow, *Job 1–21*, 31).

One of the great mysteries of Job is the Elihu speeches. They all occur without a response from Job (32:6–33:33; 34:2-37; 35:2-16; 36:2–37:24). Nor does God ever mention Elihu. Some view the Elihu speeches as secondary for the following reasons:

- Elihu is not mentioned in the prologue.
- Elihu is thought to be repeating arguments the others have given.
- His speeches unnecessarily interrupt the transition between Job's final words in 31 to the beginning of God's response in 38.

But the larger literary context may explain the Elihu speeches and their importance. Elihu's intervention is precisely in the correct position in Job's structure—between the wisdom dialogue (3–31) and the divine speeches (38–41) (Seow, *Job 1–21*, 34).

Other interesting literary characteristics are found in Job. Fokkelman's poetic analysis based on meter (counting syllables) reveals Job's words make up exactly half of all the poetry in the dialogues (*Job in Form*, 8). Job's speeches come in two parts: response directly to the friends and address to God. Furthermore, God's questions in Job are an interesting literary study. He questions Satan via direct questions but questions Job via rhetorical questions.

Outlining Job for Preaching

Option 1: *Twenty-Three Sermons*

Prologue = Job 1–2		(Narrative)
Job 1	– Sermon 1	
Job 2	– Sermon 2	
First Cycle of Speeches = Job 3–14		
Job 3	– Sermon 3	(Job's Speech)
Job 4–5	– Sermon 4	(Eliphaz)
Job 6–7	– Sermon 5	(Job's Response)
Job 8	– Sermon 6	(Bildad)
Job 9–10	– Sermon 7	(Job's Response)
Job 11	– Sermon 8	(Zophar)
Job 12–14	– Sermon 9	(Job's Response)
Second Cycle of Speeches = Job 15–21		
Job 15	– Sermon 10	(Eliphaz)
Job 16–17	– Sermon 11	(Job's Response)
Job 18	– Sermon 12	(Bildad)
Job 19	– Sermon 13	(Job's Response)
Job 20	– Sermon 14	(Zophar)
Job 21	– Sermon 15	(Job's Response)
Third Cycle of Speeches = Job 22–26		
Job 22	– Sermon 16	(Eliphaz)
Job 23–24	– Sermon 17	(Job's Response)
Job 25	– Sermon 18	(Bildad)
Job 26–27	– Sermon 19	(Job's Response)
Job's Monologue = Job 28–31		
Job 28–31	– Sermon 20	(Job's Summary Defense)
Elihu's Speech = Job 32–37		
Job 32–37	– Sermon 21	(Elihu)

God Speaks = Job 38:1–42:6
    Job 38:1–42:6 – Sermon 22 (God Speaks)
Epilogue = Job 42:7-17
    Job 42:7-17 – Sermon 23 (Epilogue)

Option 2: Fifteen Sermons
Prologue = Job 1–2
    Job 1–2 – Sermon 1 (Narrative)
First Cycle of Speeches = Job 3–14
    Job 3 – Sermon 2 (Job's Speech)
    Job 4–7 – Sermon 3 (Eliphaz's Speech and Job's Response)
    Job 8–10 – Sermon 4 (Bildad's Speech and Job's Response)
    Job 11–14 – Sermon 5 (Zophar's Speech and Job's Response)
Second Cycle of Speeches = Job 15–21
    Job 15–17 – Sermon 6 (Eliphaz's Speech and Job's Response)
    Job 18–19 – Sermon 7 (Bildad's Speech and Job's Response)
    Job 20–21 – Sermon 8 (Zophar's Speech and Job's Response)
Third Cycle of Speeches = Job 22–27
    Job 22–24 – Sermon 9 (Eliphaz's Speech and Job's Response)
    Job 25–27 – Sermon 10 (Bildad's Speech and Job's Response)
Job's Monologue = Job 28
    Job 28 – Sermon 11
Job's Summary Defense = Job 29–31
    Job 29–31 – Sermon 12
Elihu's Speech = Job 32–37
    Job 32–37 – Sermon 13 (Elihu's Speech)
God Speaks = Job 38:1–42:6
    Job 38:1–42:6 – Sermon 14 (God Speaks)
Epilogue = Job 42:7-17
    Job 42:7-17 – Sermon 15 (Epilogue)

Option 3: *Eight Sermons*

Prologue = Job 1–2

    Job 1–2   – Sermon 1   (Narrative)

First Cycle of Speeches = Job 3–14

    Job 3–14   – Sermon 2   (Job's Speech; Speeches by Eliphaz, Bildad, Zophar, and Job's Response)

Second Cycle of Speeches = Job 15–21

    Job 15–21   – Sermon 3   (Eliphaz, Bildad, Zophar Speak, and Job's Response)

Third Cycle of Speeches = Job 22–27

    Job 22–27   – Sermon 4   (Eliphaz and Bildad Speak, and Job's Response)

Job's Monologue = Job 28–31

    Job 28–31   – Sermon 5   (Job's Summary Defense)

Elihu's Speech = Job 32–37

    Job 32–37   – Sermon 6   (Elihu's Speech)

God Speaks = Job 38:1–42:6

    Job 38:1–42:6 – Sermon 7   (God Speaks)

Epilogue = Job 42:7-17

    Job 42:7-17   – Sermon 8   (Epilogue)

God, Satan, and Job—the Test of Suffering

JOB 1–2

Main Idea: Job's test of faith in the midst of suffering demonstrates his true character and love for God.

I.   Job: His Character, Wealth, and Family (1:1-5)
II. The Heavenly Scene: Satan Challenges God concerning Job (1:6-12).
III. Job Responds to His Sudden Disasters with Total Trust in God (1:13-22).
IV. Satan Afflicts Job with Physical Suffering (2:1-6).
V.   Job's Wife Advises Him to Renounce God (2:7-10).
VI. Job's Three Friends Arrive and Mourn with Him (2:11-13).

Although not a commentary on the book of Job, Philip Yancey's *Disappointment with God: Three Questions No One Asks Aloud,* grew out of a theology graduate student's paper on Job. The student, Richard, asked Yancey to evaluate his paper in hopes it would be good enough to develop into a book on Job. It was, and the book materialized over time. But Richard himself, after experiencing several crises in his life, eventually lost faith in God and turned away from him. Yancey's engagement with Richard during this time led him to ponder three questions: Is God unfair? Is God silent? Is God hidden?

If God loves us and desires our love, why does he permit us to suffer? Why does God seem so distant? Yancey concludes that the book of Job is not directly about pain and suffering as much as it is about faith in its starkest form. Job gained a faith that can never be shaken because it came out of having been shaken. "Faith means believing in advance what will only make sense in reverse" (Yancey, *Disappointment,* 201).

The book of Job teaches us that Suffering 101 is a required course in the school of life. Professor Pain is the teacher, and he is a tenured professor. There are no course substitutions. You cannot cut class. No one is exempt from Suffering 101. Put your finger in a bucket of water. If, when you remove it, you leave a hole in the water, then you are special.

If not, you are just like everyone else. There is no way to upgrade from suffering to first class in your Christian life.

Take a look at Job. He worked harder than anyone else. He was a pious man who worshiped God. He was also a blessed man. He began life's journey in first class. But even he could not escape suffering. Job learned lessons of humility before God and dependence on God. These are lessons God teaches all of his children. In some ways the book of Job is our textbook for Suffering 101.

Self-sufficiency is an American hallmark. I suppose we come by it from the pioneer spirit of our early heroes: Daniel Boone, Lewis and Clark, Davy Crockett, and the like. Our motto is often the line from William Henley's poem "Invictus": "I am the master of my fate; I am the captain of my soul." The essence of sin, though, is self-sufficiency. The essence of Christianity is God-sufficiency. In order to diminish our self-sufficiency and develop God-sufficiency, God allows suffering in our lives.

Like temptation, suffering is universal; and like temptation, suffering is infinitely varied. Job suffered not only physically but mentally, emotionally, and spiritually. Studying Job is like an inoculation—it doesn't keep you from suffering, but it teaches you how to endure suffering.

We Christians learn that Jesus, the Suffering Servant of Isaiah 53, is our companion on the road of suffering. He is our example for how to respond to suffering and win the victory through it.

Job 1–2 constitutes the prologue to the book. It is absolutely crucial not only to the plot of the narrative but also to the theological point of the book. The prologue functions in at least two important ways for the discourse: literarily and theologically. Literarily, the prologue introduces the setting and characters. It announces the reason for the conflict in the book. From a narrative standpoint, the stakes couldn't be higher.

Theologically, the prologue demonstrates that God is not uninvolved in human suffering, that evil often plays a role in suffering, and that sometimes suffering is not the result of individual human sin. "The book of Job is . . . a theological argument conducted in poetry" (Alter, *Wisdom Books*, 6). As Greenberg noted, "The author of Job had a dedication to theological honesty" (*Job*, xx–xxi). Again, the stakes could not be higher.

The prologue consists of five paragraphs: 1:1-5, 6-12, 13-22; 2:1-8, 9-13. One could preach a sermon per paragraph or a sermon per chapter.

Job: His Character, Wealth, and Family
JOB 1:1-5

Job begins much like the opening line that scrolls across the screen of *Star Wars*: "A long time ago in a galaxy far, far away." The curtain opens and we are introduced to Job, his location, position in life, and relationship to his children. Verse 1 identifies Job as being from "Uz," a term that probably designates a location somewhere in Edom, a large territory east of the Jordan River, southeast of the Dead Sea, near modern-day Jordan. In Lamentations 4:21 and Jeremiah 25:20, Uz is mentioned separate from Edom. The name appears three times in Genesis: 10:23; 22:21 (where Nahor's son is named "Uz"); and 36:21.[19]

Four key statements express Job's virtue and piety in verses 1-2. The four are paired in two groups such that the former expresses primarily personal integrity and the latter devout faith.

Job's integrity was described as "complete." The Hebrew word does not mean sinless perfection but rather connotes wholeness of character, innocence, truthful living. Job was a man who took sin seriously. He walked in close fellowship with God and delighted in obeying God's law (Ps 119:1). Second, he had "integrity," a Hebrew word describing Job's morality in terms of conduct. The Hebrew term connotes that which is "level" or "straight," and hence just. The word is often used in the Old Testament of people who are pleasing in the eyes of God (e.g., 1 Kgs 15:5). Job's motivations were pure, and his personal dealings were fair and honest. Ezekiel's Mount Rushmore lists Job along with Noah and Daniel as the most righteous men of all times (Ezek 14:14,20).

Third, he "feared God," meaning Job reverenced and worshiped God. Job desired more than anything to obey God's will. He was utterly devoted to God in worship and service. Scripture says, "The fear of the LORD is the beginning of wisdom" (Ps 111:10; Prov 9:10), and Job's lifestyle included wisdom, right worship, right thinking, and right conduct. Fourth, Job "turned away from evil." This phrase occurs frequently in Psalms and Proverbs (Pss 34:14; 37:27; Prov 3:7; 13:19; 16:6). His lifestyle demonstrated right living as morally evaluated. These last two characteristics, fearing God and turning away from evil, are Hebrew participles and express activity begun and continued. The two terms appear

---

[19] On the meaning and location of Uz, see Owen, "Land of Uz," 245–47.

together in Job 28:28. These four characteristics play a crucial role in the developing tragedy about to unfold.

Job was not only godly; he was also wealthy. His seven thousand sheep, three thousand camels, and five hundred yoke of oxen are the narrator's way of informing the reader of Job's vast wealth. Camels were expensive animals and reflect great prosperity.

In the Old Testament, children are a blessing from God. Job has seven sons and three daughters. There is no reason to interpret these numbers other than literally. Job is presented as one who is a good father and spiritual leader to his seven sons and three daughters, as evidenced by the fact that his children spend time together and Job regularly offers sacrifices for them in case any of them may have sinned against God. After his children complete their times of feasting, which probably occurred on their respective birthdays, Job performed the role of a family priest. He was the first one to show up at the altar at the crack of dawn, ready to offer sacrifices for each of his children in case any of them had "cursed God in their hearts."[20] Richard Halverson, former chaplain of the US Senate, once prayed, "Forgive those of us who give family such a low priority. . . . Help the Senators not to be so busy trying to save the nation that they let their children go to hell" (Gariepy, *Portraits*, 17–18).

Job is described as the greatest of all the "sons of the East." The phrase in Hebrew is often applied to those Arab races that dwelt between the Nile and the Euphrates (e.g., Judg 6:3). Job was the wealthiest of all in this region. He was the largest stockholder on the Wall Street of the East.

Job begins with something of that Disneyesque feel, like the old 1960s Sunday night television show *Wonderful World of Disney* used to begin—with a beautiful castle, lights, happy music, and rainbow colors spangled everywhere. It's a feel-good scene, but it won't last. If Job 1:1-5 says anything to us, it seems Job sunned himself in the unclouded favor of God.

---

[20] Gleason Archer's skepticism concerning the piety of Job's children is unwarranted since nothing in the text speaks to the issue either way (*Book of Job*, 29). John Hartley is closer to the mark: "The details witness to the closeness and the affluence of Job's family, not to the fact that Job's children were given to frivolous living" (*Job*, 69).

The Heavenly Scene: Satan Challenges God concerning Job
JOB 1:6-12

Now the scene suddenly shifts from earth to heaven. The "sons of God," angelic beings, came to "present themselves" before the Lord. Among them was Satan. The scene of God sitting in counsel with his holy angels occurs several times in Scripture (1 Kgs 22:19; Isa 6:1-3; Dan 7:9-10; Rev 5:6-14), though in none of these cases is God recorded as speaking to any of the angelic creatures as in this situation. Since the text does not say, we can only surmise that Satan's presence was required by God.

In the Hebrew text "Satan" is "the Satan," the article indicating a title rather than a name. Satan is a personal and powerful supernatural being. While some disagree, there seems to be no reason to identify this character as anyone other than the Satan who appears regularly on the pages of the New Testament.[21] Old Testament references to Satan include Genesis 3; Isaiah 14; and Ezekiel 28. The Old Testament does not explicitly mention the origin of Satan, nor does it explicitly relate Lucifer, the serpent, and Satan. Yet given the full scope of what Scripture says about Satan, it would seem all these references are to the same individual. As with the other angels, Satan is referred to as a "son of God." Job 1–2 clearly teaches Satan is under the control of God. Satan attempts to harm humanity and delights in humanity's misery.

The Lord asks Satan whence he has come. "What have you been up to?" Satan responds he has been roaming the earth. First Peter 5:8 speaks of Satan in similar terms. Satan is a world traveler. He could sing the Johnny Cash song, "I've Been Everywhere." You can almost picture Satan as he saunters into the heavenly council from his recent random world tour, one hand in his pocket, the other picking his teeth, disdainful of all the other angels, waiting for an opportunity to stir up trouble. Satan's job description includes inspection and examination. He's an unspiritual detective we might say, who hurries up and down the earth

---

[21] "Never idle, Satan always on the prowl as 'the prince of this world' (John 12:31), blinding minds (2 Cor. 4:4), stealing God's Word (Matt. 13:19). Opposing God's work (1 Thess. 2:18), sowing tares (Matt. 13:37-40), tempting God's people (1 Cor. 7:5), attacking God's Word (Gen. 3:1), spreading false doctrine (1 Tim. 1:3), persecuting God's church (Rev. 2:10), and deceiving the nations (Rev. 16:14)" (Lawson, *Job*, 16). D. L. Moody once said, "I believe Satan to exist for two reasons: first, the Bible says so; and second, I've done business with him."

with clipboard in hand. Like an emperor's spy, Satan has been looking for any secret disloyalty to the crown. The unfolding plot in this paragraph incorporates several surprising twists. One usually finds in Scripture that it is Satan who challenges God. The striking thing about this account is that God challenges Satan. "Have you considered my servant Job? No one else on earth is like him, a man of perfect integrity, who fears God and turns away from evil" (v. 8). This is the Lord's assessment of Job's character and conduct, and it is identical to what was said about Job in 1:1-5. Imagine being endorsed by God himself in such a fashion! What a blurb on your biography! What a recommendation on Job's LinkedIn! Yet in the question itself the divine fisherman goes fishing with the bait: "Have you noticed my servant Job?" Satan takes the bait.

Satan's response to God's statement about Job's righteousness in verses 9-11 is cynicism at its finest. Satan queries God: Does Job fear God for no reason? You have protected him, God, like a farmer who piles rocks along the edge of a field and then places a hedge of long thorns to keep animals from getting in. Furthermore, you have blessed him immeasurably. You think Job serves you out of the goodness of his heart? No one ever had it so good as Job! You pamper him like a pet; you make sure nothing bad ever happens to him, his family, or his possessions. You bless everything he does; he can't lose! Satan is not able to point to any sinful action by Job, so he raises the question of motivation.

The great Methodist preacher of days gone by, Clovis Chappell, notes just how shrewd Satan is with his question about Job.

It is shrewd because it attains all the weight of an assertion without incurring any of its risks. . . . A slanderer who makes a positive assertion runs at least a twofold risk: First, he is in danger of being detected. He runs the risk of embarrassment by being caught in a lie. "Therefore," advises Satan, "if you are out to slander somebody, put your lie in the form of a question. Then you will be safe. Nobody can prove you are lying if you merely ask a question." (*Sermons*, 21)

Satan's question is shrewd for another reason. Chappell continues, "It . . . puts its finger on the acid test of the worth of any deed. No deed is either good or bad in and of itself. Its goodness or its badness depends on the motive that is back of it" (*Sermons*, 22). To put this in modern context, it's like Satan is saying, "Yeah, I know Job belongs to the church.

He is a faithful giver, and he helps the poor. He is always on the right side of every question that arises. But if you stop paying him a big salary and put him on skid row—stop furnishing him with luxuries and a Lexus and instead give him leprosy—he will curse you to your face."

Satan's theory is that people worship God for some reward, either material, personal, or spiritual. Like every other godly person in Satan's estimation, Job was a phony. Satan insinuates that Job acts well because he is rich and comfortable. "Change that and you will see Job's true colors" is Satan's ploy. "People worship God for self-profit. You think Job loves you for your own sake? Ha! He never has and he never will." Satan undertakes to prove that Job's goodness, and by implication that of any person, is but a veiled selfishness—an insurance policy against loss of God's blessings. Even worse, Satan's criticism is aimed at God as much as it is at Job. Satan is the vulture who claims to be a mockingbird.

Then Satan offered a challenge to God: take all of Job's temporal blessings away from him, and you will soon discover the hypocritical basis of Job's piety. What is amazing here is that the non-omniscient accuser couldn't know for sure Job's motives, but the omniscient God already knew the answer to Satan's challenge about Job's piety. God did not need to test Job to find out the sincerity of his loyalty.

Given God's omniscience, the reader might be shocked to learn that God accepts Satan's challenge and grants him the freedom to destroy all of Job's possessions, including his own children. Why, then, did God agree to Satan's challenge?

Neither this text nor any other in the book of Job answers that question. We might presume that so fundamental an issue as the motivation for worship and obedience needed to be settled once and for all—for the angelic community as well as for humanity. Perhaps that is a major reason for the book of Job being in the canon of Scripture. One can only wonder what must have been the reaction of the other angels in the council since the text does not say. Did they turn to one another and murmur under their breath, "Maybe old slew foot has a good point? What if Job is serving God because of God's blessings? No doubt, many humans do worship God behind a cloak of self-interest."

So God accepts Satan's challenge: "Very well, everything he owns is in your power. However, do not lay a hand on Job himself." Strange prewar circumstances when the enemy has to seek permission and tactics from the commanding officer of the other army before battle begins! God gives Satan the green light to inflict suffering on Job. But with that permission (to destroy Job's property) comes a prohibition (not to touch Job's physical body or life).

Some try to see some kind of wager here between God and Satan. This is not a bet; it is a test. Two things are crucial to notice here. The key issue is Job's motivation for his fear of God. Crucial to the story from an audience standpoint is that we must know God's attitude toward Job and the fact that he has permitted Satan to interfere in Job's life in such a drastic fashion. God is permitting Satan to bring suffering on Job, even though Job did nothing to merit this suffering. God put limitations on what Satan could do to Job. Even Satan is under God's control. Or, as Martin Luther put it, "Even the devil is God's devil." No borders can keep Satan out when God grants him the passport to enter your realm. No amount of piety or performance of religious rites can build such a hedge of thorns around our lives that we are forever safe from Satan's evil. God allows Job to be tested—he does not endow him with preferential treatment for his piety. But at the same time, Satan "cannot touch a hair upon the back of a single camel that belongs to Job, until he has Divine permission" (Ash, *Job*, 45).[22]

"So Satan left the LORD's presence" (v. 12). With license to wreak havoc in hand, like a teenager who just got his driver's license, Satan darts out of the heavenly council to launch his fiendish plan into action.

Job Responds to His Sudden Disasters with Total Trust in God
JOB 1:13-22

Suddenly, an avalanche of woes cascaded over Job in a single day. The third paragraph of Job 1 begins with a statement about setting: "One day when Job's sons and daughters were eating and drinking wine in their oldest brother's house, . . ." This statement refers to information given about Job's children in 1:1-5, and this identical statement is repeated in verse 18. On this single fateful day, four disasters befell Job: (1) all his oxen and donkeys were destroyed; (2) all his sheep were destroyed; (3) all his camels were destroyed; (4) all his children were killed (it may be no coincidence that four characteristics of Job's piety were listed in

---

[22] Or, as the seventeenth-century Scottish Presbyterian preacher, James Durham, put it, "[Satan] nor none of his instruments can stir a tail of any of their beasts without God's permission" (*Lectures*, 18).

1:1-2). The agent of these disasters is Satan himself, who uses human, natural, and supernatural means to bring them about.

Sabeans, from the region of southeast Arabia known today as the country of Yemen, suddenly attacked Job's oxen and servants, taking all and leaving only one servant alive to return and inform Job. Then "God's fire" fell and destroyed all Job's sheep and his servants, save one who returned to Job to report the disaster. This is most likely a reference to lightning sparking a desert fire, which would have spread quickly.

Next the Chaldeans, from the lower part of the Mesopotamian valley near modern Kuwait, stole all Job's camels and killed all but one servant, who arrived immediately on the heels of the previous two servants to report to Job. Finally, a "powerful wind" like a tornado struck the house where Job's ten children were celebrating, snuffing out their lives like an extinguished candle. As previously, only one servant escaped to inform Job.[23]

The shock and horror of this news is impossible to fathom, as none of us has ever experienced such a devastating disaster in a single day of life. Job's faith was T-boned! In one fell swoop Job was stripped of fortune and family and left emotionally reeling. Job was the richest man around, but in a single day he was wiped out—left with nothing but bankruptcy and ten fresh graves.

Perhaps even more shocking is how Job responds. Stunned by it all, he remained silent until he was told of the death of his children. At this point,

> Job stood up, tore his robe, and shaved his head. He fell to the ground and worshiped, saying: Naked I came from my mother's womb, and naked I will leave this life. The Lord gives, and the Lord takes away. Blessed be the name of the Lord. (1:20-21)

---

[23] Hartley noted that "the cause of destruction alternates between earthly and heavenly forces coming from all four points of the compass: the Sabeans from the south, lightning from a storm out of the west, the Chaldeans from the north, and the treacherous sirocco blowing off the desert to the east. The number four also symbolizes full measure, totality" (*Job*, 77).

This thrice-repeated refrain, "And I alone have escaped to tell you," is aptly picked up and used by Melville as the heading to his haunting epilogue of *Moby-Dick*, when everything and everyone on the *Pequod* is wiped out, leaving only Ishmael surviving. Dostoevsky, in his *The Brothers Karamazov*, has Ivan Karamazov proclaim, "If the suffering of children serves to complete the sum of suffering necessary for the acquisition of truth, I affirm from now onward that truth is not worth such a price. What kind of a God would require the death of Job's children to teach him a lesson in truth?" This is the question often raised today by many when confronted with the prologue of Job.

In this short statement Job ranges from the womb to the tomb. In the midst of his tragedy, he was still able to distinguish between the truly spiritual essentials and the superfluous. Alexander Maclaren titles his sermon on Job 1:21, "Sorrow that Worships" (*Esther, Job*, 29). Job's words here are not an expression of stoic indifference. Rather they are

> the unpremeditated interpretation of what seemed like a terrible calamity. Immediately upon receipt of staggering news he instantly found a satisfying explanation of the unkindly Providence which had wrecked his life. . . . It is a great thing for a man to realize when he seems to be overwhelmed that he is really overshadowed. (Holden, *Chapter by Chapter*, 145)

Job's piety was not dependent on his prosperity. The modern so-called prosperity gospel, which is no gospel at all, did not have its tentacles around Job. Propogandists of the health and wealth gospel, the name-it-and-claim-it crowd, promise us health and wealth if we believe in the vending-machine God who dispenses blessings, monetary and otherwise, in accordance with our willingness to give our money to God (through their ministries of course). Avoid such people. Though some may be sincere, most of them are false prophets.

"We have developed such a mastery of the worship of self rather than the worship of God that we often fail to know the difference between the two" (Ciholos, *Consider My Servant*, 44). True worship can occur even when we do not understand God or find him in our suffering. Job does not claim his rights and privileges. He rightly recognizes God *owns* us; he does not *owe* us. Life begins without privilege—a gift of God. Life ends without advantage; we can take nothing with us into eternity.

Job's response of tearing his robe and shaving his head was one of traditional mourning (see Keener, *NIV Cultural Backgrounds Study Bible*, 828). Yet, in spite of the tragedy and in the midst of his emotional extremity, Job fell to the ground to worship God. Job acknowledged, first, that he entered this world with nothing and would one day depart in the same condition. Second, Job acknowledged God's ownership of all his possessions, and therefore God has the right to do with them whatever he pleases. Finally, in all things—good or bad, happy or sad—the name of the Lord is to be praised. More important to Job than all his possessions, even his relationship to his own children, was his relationship to

God. Job knew how to distinguish between the gift and the giver, and it is the giver who is to be praised—always.

When Job spoke of blessing the name of the Lord, he employed the same Hebrew word rendered "curse" in verse 11. Satan bragged that he could extract the hostile sense of this word from Job's lips against God. But instead of cursing, Job blessed the name of the Lord and in the action once again made a liar out of Satan. In Dr. Seuss's *How the Grinch Stole Christmas*, the Grinch was wrong about the Whos down in Whoville. He thought if he stole their toys and all their Christmas decorations, they would not celebrate Christmas. But every Who down in Whoville, the tall and the small, joined hands in the town square on Christmas morning and celebrated—without toys, food, or decorations. As the Grinch was about the Whos, Satan was wrong about Job.

Significant in Job's response is his use of God's personal name in Hebrew, *Yahweh*, no less than three times. While Job lived away from the land and people of Israel, he knew and worshiped the one true God.

The final narrator comment in verse 22 is crucial to the plot of the book: "Throughout all this Job did not sin or blame God for anything." Unlike so many would have done and still do in similar circumstances, Job did not blame God. In the face of what appears to be a cold-blooded toying with the life and fortune of Job, lesser men would no doubt have cursed God. Verse 22 articulates two crucial propositions that set the stage for the remainder of Job: (1) Job did not charge God with any wrongdoing. (2) To do so would have been sinful.[24]

It is easy for us to get touchy with God when he doesn't act according to our theology. Job never knew the preface to his suffering as we do. It's easy to imagine how he might have felt. "Lord, I have served you faithfully, and what do I get? Empty fields, empty barns—and dead children." Satan may have received God's permission to afflict Job, but Job never gave *his* permission for God, Satan, or anyone else to turn his life into total havoc by this onslaught of tragedy and suffering. The surest

---

[24] "One possible reason that the narrator has claimed that Job did not charge God with empty and worthless actions is that we, the readers, are in fact quite ready to believe that is precisely what God in fact *has* done. The terrible test of Job, on the face of it, appears to be quite worthless, and the fact that Job does not call it so merely serves to emphasize its worthlessness" (Holbert, *Preaching Job*, 9; emphasis in original).

way to discover that the principles on which we base our lives are valid is when they—and we—are tested. Job's response to his suffering is an example to all Christians. No matter how much we suffer in this life, it is unlikely any one of us will suffer to the extent that Job suffered. Acknowledging God's sovereignty to do what he wills with our lives and worshiping him no matter what are the appropriate responses to all suffering.

Thomas Brooks, a Puritan, wrote in his *The Mute Christian under the Smarting Rod,*

> God, who is infinite in wisdom and matchless in goodness, hath ordered our troubles, yea, many troubles to come trooping in upon us on every side. As our mercies, so our crosses seldom come single; they usually come treading one upon the heels of another; they are like April showers, no sooner is one over but another comes. It's mercy that every affliction is not an execution. . . . The more the afflictions, the more the heart is raised heavenward.

The prologue makes clear that Job did not face his trials because of his sin but because of his righteousness! God bragged about Job! It was like God was saying, "Good job, Job!" The lesson is clear: righteousness does not guarantee exemption from suffering.

Satan Afflicts Job with Physical Suffering
JOB 2:1-6

The scene shifts from earth back to heaven. A second time God and Satan engage in dialogue. In the first encounter Satan is "with" his fellow angelic beings, but now he explicitly comes among them "to present himself before the LORD," further emphasizing Satan's necessary obedience to God.

In 2:3 God announces rather triumphantly that Job's response to Satan's inflicted suffering has proven Satan wrong. Furthermore, God charges Satan with "inciting" him to "destroy" Job "for no good reason." The Hebrew verb translated "destroy" means "swallow up" and is in the intensive (*piel*) form. The translation "for no good reason" indicates "without cause." Job is suffering for no cause or failure on his part. Satan had used this same word of Job back in 1:9. Recall Satan's argument: he said that Job did not serve God "for nothing." If Job were to lose all of his material wealth, he would curse God. God's use of this term is a rebuke to Satan and his previous charge against Job. "You tried to trick me into destroying him, but it didn't work."

The word translated "incited" in Hebrew means "allure or stir someone to a course of action he would not normally take" (cf. 1 Chr 21:1). God conceded that Satan had persuaded him to act toward Job contrary to what Job deserved, but this should not be interpreted to mean that God acted in a way contrary to his will in the situation, such that Satan twisted God's arm to act against his will.

Both the narrator and God himself described Job as a man of "integrity" (1:1,8). Despite Job's suffering, his integrity remains intact. Satan responds by accusing Job of really only caring about himself. If God would permit Job to lose his health, Job would then curse God. Whereas Job continually feared that one of his children might have cursed God in his heart in Job 1:4-5, Satan now suggests that Job would curse God in open defiance if he were deprived of his health. Here, as in 1:11, Satan wants Job to commit a sin of speech.

The "skin for skin" saying refers to the concept of bartering in the ANE and essentially means God's attack on Job's life will be answered by Job's curse. Why? Because, insists Satan, everything a man possesses he will give for his life. The score is God = 1, Satan = 0. But Satan is a sore loser and asks for a change in the rules.

Job's Wife Advises Him to Renounce God
JOB 2:7-10

Satan launches his attack on Job's body, smiting him with one of the most loathsome diseases of the day by covering him with painful sores, or boils, "from the soles of his feet to the top of his head." A single boil on the skin is painful enough, but to be covered in them would be nearly unbearable. It is difficult to imagine his agonizing pain and abject misery.

Many theories have been proposed for the skin disease that struck Job based on the descriptions found in the book. Leprosy and elephantiasis are common suggestions. Whatever the disease, the symptoms included the following: bodily disfigurement (2:12), sleeplessness (7:4), worm-infected sores (7:5), sores that scab over, crack, and ooze (7:5), nightmares (7:14), choking (7:15), depression (7:16), putrid breath (19:17), emaciation (19:20), loss of teeth (19:20), pain throughout the body (30:17), darkening, shriveling, and peeling skin (30:30), and fever with chills (30:30). In the culture of Job's day, such a malady was almost universally regarded as punishment inflicted by the gods for heinous sin. Job consigns himself to the "ash heap," the dump or landfill outside the city. Trash and dung would be deposited regularly and be burned once a month, leaving lots of ashes. His posture of sitting on the ground was an ancient sign of suffering (2 Sam 12:16; Jer 3:25; Lam 2:10). The intense itching, coupled with oozing pus that would become encrusted, could only be temporarily assuaged by scraping himself with pieces of broken pottery. Since Job did not know of the heavenly encounter and conditions of his suffering, he feared his illness was incurable and death was inevitable.

I find it interesting that in narrating Job's adversity, the author employs the opposite order to the narrative of his prosperity. In his prosperity the author proceeded from the greater to the lesser. In the adversity, the list is in the opposite order—the loss of wealth narrated first, then his offspring, then Job personally (see Aquinas, *Literal Exposition*, 84).

Job's wife speaks only here in the entire narrative. "Are you still holding on to your integrity? Curse God and die!" There are two ways to interpret her statement. She may have been responding out of anger at God by telling Job to curse God and commit suicide. A second option is she may have been responding out of deep sympathy for her husband by suggesting suicide. Whatever her motives, she becomes the mouthpiece of the devil by offering a terrible temptation to do exactly what Satan wants Job to do: curse God.

Commentators have not been kind to Mrs. Job. Augustine called her "the devil's assistant," and Calvin spoke of her as "Satan's tool."

She queries, perhaps sarcastically, "Are you still holding on to your integrity?" Interestingly, she employed the same expression God had used to describe Job in 2:3. "What's the point of being innocent after God has allowed or caused all this to happen to you, Job? Curse God and go hang yourself." This suicide counsel, if indeed it is such, was doubtless a great temptation for Job as he longed for the release of death in his first speech in Job 3. But the fact that Job never seriously contemplates suicide reminds us today that suicide is never the answer to suffering.[25]

---

[25] In Scripture, suicide is always framed in a negative light. See Ahithophel in 2 Sam 16–17 and Judas in Matt 27:3–5.

For Mrs. Job, it was all or nothing in this situation. If Job has been "cursed" by God seemingly without reason, then it should be fine for Job to curse God with good reason, she reasoned! Job rebukes his wife for speaking as a "foolish" woman. What she was saying amounted to self-contradictory nonsense since everything in our lives is ultimately derived from God. Job reminds his wife that God the giver has perfect prerogative also to be a withholder, or one who takes away. "Should we accept only good from God and not adversity?"[26] Mrs. Job wanted to apply her own standards of justice and fairness to God. Job's suffering, including the death of what were her children too, sharpened her sense of indignation. Job reminded her we cannot, indeed must not, judge God's actions according to our own expectations of the way things should be.

Missionary Jim Eliot died at the hands of the Auca Indians in the jungle of equatorial Ecuador. Later his wife, Elizabeth, and their small daughter, Valerie, returned to the village of the tribesmen who killed her husband. She brought with her the gospel, and many came to Christ. From this experience, she wrote about the difference between resignation and acceptance:

> Only in acceptance lies peace, not in resignation nor in
>   busyness.
> Resignation is surrender to fate.
> Acceptance is surrender to God.
> Resignation lies down quietly in an empty universe.
> Acceptance rises up to meet the God who fills that universe
>   with purpose and destiny.
> Resignation says, "I can't."
> Acceptance says, "God can!"
> Resignation says, "It's all over for me."
> Acceptance asks, "Now that I am here, what's next, Lord?"
> Resignation says, "What a waste."
> Acceptance asks, "In what redemptive way will You use this
>   mess, Lord?" (Davis, *Lord, if I Ever Needed You It's Now*)

---

[26] While the Hebrew term translated "adversity" often connotes moral evil or sinfulness (Deut 1:35), in this context it should be taken as referring to that which brings harm, pain, and destruction ("terrible" in Deut 7:15).

The narrator states, "Throughout all this Job did not sin in what he said." This is a strong statement in Hebrew that unequivocally states Job did not commit even the slightest error or sin in the situation. Job cursed the day of his birth in Job 3, but he did not curse God! In times of suffering, we need to guard our lips like Job. We should pray as did the psalmist in Psalm 19:14: "May the words of my mouth and the meditation of my heart be acceptable to you, LORD, my rock and my Redeemer." Whether by Satan's prompting or our own fleshly nature, rash speech often injures the cause of Christ.

Hartley's point about the motif of "cursing God" is key:

At this point it is important to note the sin of cursing God is pivotal to the prologue. Whereas Job feared that his children might speak lightly about God, the Satan will argue that Job would certainly curse God should he suffer loss (1:11; 2:5). Then Job's wife will urge him to curse God and die (2:9). With this motif the author focuses on the basis of an individual's relationship to God. Does a person worship God out of genuine love or primarily for God's blessing? This is the issue for everyone. (*Job*, 70)

Looking at Job 1–2 holistically, we see Job was tested in three ways. First, he was tested circumstantially with the loss of possessions and children (ch. 1). Second, he was tested physically with the loss of health (ch. 2). Third, he was tested theologically: "Does Job fear God for nothing?" (chs. 1–2).

Job never saw it coming and was left dazed and disoriented. Like Job,

Chippie the parakeet never saw it coming. One second he was peacefully perched in his cage. The next he was sucked in, washed up, and blown over.

The problems began when Chippie's owner decided to clean Chippie's cage with a vacuum cleaner. She removed the attachment from the end of the hose and stuck it in the cage. The phone rang, and she turned to pick it up. She'd barely said "hello" when "sssopp!" Chippie got sucked in.

The bird owner gasped, put down the phone, turned off the vacuum, and opened the bag. There was Chippie—still alive, but stunned.

Since the bird was covered with dust and soot, she
grabbed him and raced to the bathroom, turned on the
faucet, and held Chippie under the running water. Then,
realizing that Chippie was soaked and shivering, she did what
any compassionate bird owner would do . . . she reached for
the hair dryer and blasted the pet with hot air.
Poor Chippie never knew what hit him.
A few days after the trauma, the reporter who'd initially
written about the event contacted Chippie's owner to see how
the bird was recovering. "Well," she replied, "Chippie doesn't
sing much anymore—he just sits and stares."
It's not hard to see why. Sucked in, washed up, and blown
over . . . that's enough to steal the song from the stoutest
heart.
Can you relate to Chippie? Most of us can. One minute
you're seated in familiar territory with a song on your lips,
then . . . The pink slip comes. The rejection letter arrives.
The doctor calls. The divorce papers are delivered. The check
bounces. A policeman knocks on your door.
Sssopp! You're sucked into a black cavern of doubts,
doused with the cold water of reality, and stung with the hot
air of empty promises. (Lucado, *Eye of the Storm*, 11–12)

Job had no clue why he was suffering. The meaning of Job's calamity remained hidden from him. But as Spurgeon once said to the fellow
who asked him about suffering, "Young man, allow me to give you this
word of advice. You must expect to let God know some things which you
do not understand." Our limited view of reality leaves us in the place of
basic ignorance on many things, especially spiritual things. We forget
that we inhabit only a small corner of reality. Job learned this lesson,
and so must we.

Job's Three Friends Arrive and Mourn with Him
JOB 2:11-13

Bad news usually travels fast. The report of Job's suffering spread throughout the entire region of northern Arabia, Edom, and Transjordan. News
could not travel with celerity; it must have taken at least weeks for news
of Job's afflictions to reach others beyond the general vicinity. Job may

give some indication that his suffering had been more than just a few weeks when in 7:3 he speaks of "months of futility," and the lament in Job 30 likewise indicates a period of some time. Friends who had known him for many years heard the news and were deeply disturbed. They decided to pay Job a visit and console him in his sorrow. Eliphaz came from Teman, a principal site in the northern region of Edom. Bildad came from an area located on the Euphrates River, below the mouth of the Khabur River. Zophar came from Naamah, a location not easily identifiable. Naamah was a female descendant of Cain according to Genesis 4:22, and Solomon married an Ammonite princess by the same name (1 Kgs 14:21).

Arriving, they scarcely could conceive how low Job's suffering had brought him. They sat with him, wept with him, and for seven days kept silent in the face of such tragedy, a traditional time frame for grieving and mourning for the dead. The literal sense of the Hebrew translated "sympathize with him" is "nod the head" as a sign of sympathetic mourning. Their silence was truly a sign of sympathy and also a sign that there are times when words are inappropriate. They say nothing because, at this point, they have nothing to say.

The prologue ends with dark clouds that have chased away Job's sunshine. The clouds will not part nor the sun shine again until the final chapter.

Conclusion

Job 1–2 is like a movie director giving a press conference before the movie is released to explain the movie and give everyone a sneak peek (Yancey, "Fresh Reading," 142).

Many important principles and lessons can be gleaned from the prologue of Job. First on the list would be the evident providence, power, and sovereignty of God. He is in control. Second, suffering is inevitable. When we suffer, sometimes we understand and sometimes we don't, but either way we can always trust God. When I suffer due to my sin, I am blameworthy. When I suffer and I know I'm not to blame, my only recourse is to trust God and depend on him. When I suffer and members of my family think I or God is to blame, I must trust the Lord and obey him no matter what.

Job 1–2 teaches us that sometimes suffering happens to those who do not deserve it due to any personal sin. Sometimes our suffering is inexplicable and may remain so until we get to heaven. God does not end the book by saying, "Job, sorry about all this. Let me tell you what happened. It was like this: Satan came to me. . . ." Job teaches us that we must never mistake the silence of God for the indifference of God.

Job teaches us that though we may not understand the reason for our suffering, there is a reason in God's economy of things. C. S. Lewis was once asked, "Why should the righteous suffer?" He responded, "Why not?" They're the only ones who can handle it. Even when life loses its luster due to suffering, it is still worth living.

Most people don't have it as good as Job initially had it; most don't have it as bad as Job ended up either. In any case, Job's experience becomes an example to us as to how we should respond to our suffering: with humility and worship. Job did not know why. He will learn in the end an even greater truth than the answer to the question, Why? As long as God knows the answer, it doesn't matter whether we do or not.

We cannot always see or know the protection God has established around us, but you can bet your bottom dollar the devil can. Satan is always out to get us any way he can. But Job teaches us an even deeper truth: Satan is always out to get God any way he can. This is how he operated with his temptation of Eve in Genesis 3. Satan falsely implied to Eve that God did not mean the injunction regarding the tree of the knowledge of good and evil for *her good* but for the protection of *his privilege* (see Inch, *My Servant Job*, 16). Satan is after you not just to get you; he is after you to get to God. Don't ever think Satan will leave you alone permanently. Never trust Satan's cease-fires (Gariepy, *Portraits*, 22).

Another lesson learned is that material loss is no ground for blaming God or cursing God. Even under great stress, Job was careful with his lips. Neither is possession of wealth a sin. It becomes sin when you allow wealth to possess you. That is idolatry. Jesus warned in Luke 12:15, "Watch out and be on guard against all greed, because one's life is not in the abundance of his possessions."

Job's experience teaches us another important lesson. Suffering is a better barometer of our spiritual life than prosperity. There is nothing quite like adversity to bring out what we really are. Squeeze a sponge and what is inside will come out. In the storm we are tested, not in the sunshine.

> The hiding places of men are discovered by affliction.—As one has aptly said, "Our refuges are like the nests of birds; in

summer they are hidden away among the green leaves, but in winter they are seen among the naked branches." (Alexander, *Dictionary of Thoughts*, 10)

One ship drives east and another drives west
With the selfsame winds that blow.
'Tis the set of the sails
And not the gales
Which tells us the way to go.

Like the winds of the sea are the ways of fate,
As we voyage along through life:
'Tis the set of a soul
That decides the goal,
And not the calm or the strife.
(Ella Wheeler Wilcox, "The Winds of Fate")

Finally, we must put on New Testament glasses when reading and preaching Job 1–2. In one sense, Job's suffering cannot be paralleled with the suffering of Jesus on the cross for our sins. Job's suffering was not redemptive for himself or anyone else. But in another sense, Job becomes something of a type of our Lord Jesus in his suffering. In his humanity, Jesus too struggled with the suffering he was about to endure on the cross. This is evident by his great spiritual struggle in the garden of Gethsemane: "My Father, if it is possible, let this cup pass from me." Knowing full well all that awaited him at the cross, Jesus nevertheless chose to do the will of God: "Yet not as I will, but as you will" (Matt 26:39). Unlike Job, Jesus knew the purpose of his own suffering—the salvation of a lost world.

Suffering can darken your whole spiritual sky. When we suffer, we are convinced it is the most *restricting* thing that cramps and cripples our lives. Our first prayer is, "Lord, please take it away; I just can't live for you and serve you like this." Jesus walks with us in our suffering because he is the one who has been tempted in all things as we are, yet without sin, as the author of Hebrews tells us in Hebrews 4:14-16.

Paul Aurandt records the following story: February 15, 1921. New York City. The operating room of the Kane Summit Hospital. A doctor is performing an appendectomy. In many ways the events leading to the surgery are uneventful. The patient has complained of severe abdominal pain. The diagnosis is clear: an inflamed appendix. Dr. Evan O'Neill

Kane is performing the surgery. In his distinguished thirty-seven-year medical career, he has performed nearly four thousand appendectomies, so this surgery will be uneventful in all ways except two.

The first novelty of this operation? The use of local anesthesia in major surgery. Dr. Kane is a crusader against the hazards of general anesthesia. He contends that a local application is far safer. Many of his colleagues agree in principle, but to agree in practice they will have to see the theory applied.

Dr. Kane searches for a volunteer, a patient who is willing to undergo surgery while under local anesthesia. A volunteer is not easily found. Many are squeamish at the thought of being awake during their own surgery. Others fear that the anesthesia might wear off too soon.

Eventually, however, Dr. Kane finds a candidate. On Tuesday morning, February 15, the historic operation occurs. The patient is prepped and wheeled into the operating room. A local anesthetic is applied. As he has done thousands of times, Dr. Kane dissects the superficial tissues and locates the appendix. He skillfully excises it and concludes the surgery. During the procedure, the patient complains of only minor discomfort.

The volunteer is taken into post-op, then placed in a hospital ward. He recovers quickly and is dismissed two days later. Dr. Kane had proven his theory. Thanks to the willingness of a brave volunteer, Kane demonstrated that local anesthesia was a viable, and even preferable, alternative. Two facts made the surgery unique. I've told you the first: the use of local anesthesia. Second is the patient. The courageous candidate for Dr. Kane was Dr. Kane. To prove his point, Dr. Kane operated on himself (Aurandt, *More of Paul Harvey*, 79–80)!

Jesus is the doctor who became a patient in order to convince the patients to trust the doctor. Jesus the healer knows your hurts because he is Jesus the sufferer. Therefore, "hold fast" and "approach" or "draw near" (ESV), as the author of Hebrews exhorts us in Hebrews 4:14-16. Hold fast when everything nailed down comes loose in your life. Draw near to Christ when the howling storm of adversity and suffering pummels your life. He has been there. We may not know the reason for our suffering, but Christ does. Therefore, remain faithful no matter what. He will see you through!

Reflect and Discuss

1. Why are the four characteristics of Job listed in Job 1 important for him and for us?
2. Who is Satan, and why do you think he appears in the heavenly council?
3. How would you describe God's part and Satan's part in Job's suffering?
4. What should we learn from Job's response to his suffering in Job 1–2?
5. As a Christian, how should you respond to God when you suffer?

Wishing You Had Never Been Born

JOB 3[27]

Main Idea: Job's suffering drives him to curse the day of his birth, lament the day of his birth, and long for his death.

I. Job Curses the Day of His Birth (3:1-10).
II. Job Laments the Day of His Birth (3:11-19).
III. Job Longs to Die (3:20-26).

Job 3 begins the poetic section of the book, with speeches by Job, the three friends, Elihu, and finally God himself. Robert Alter suggests Job 3 "is a brilliantly apt prelude to all that follows" (*Wisdom Books*, 7). In a bitter outburst, Job regrets and curses his birth (3:1-10), laments and wishes he had been stillborn (3:11-19), and wonders why he should continue to live under such suffering (3:20-26). In essence, Job asks three questions: (1) Why was I even born? (2) Why didn't I die at birth? (3) Why can't I just die now? Job laments the day of his birth, the facts of his birth, and his life thereafter.

In this chapter we get to listen in on Job's soliloquy of intense loneliness in the midst of his suffering. Job is talking to himself—and to God in a sense. All he can do now is look back. He has no hope for the future. His pain and loneliness are so intense he has no rest. Job's lament extends beyond his suffering to encompass all undeserved suffering worldwide. Death puts all people on an equal basis. Only death brings rest and relief. Death brings silence. Death brings peace and security. These are the things for which Job longs.

Job Curses the Day of His Birth
JOB 3:1-10

Have you ever been so discouraged and depressed by your suffering that you despaired of life, even wishing you could die? Job was. His suffering was so extreme he preferred death over life.

---

[27] Preachers will find helpful Clines, "A Brief Explanation of Job 1–3," 249–52.

In Job 3:1-10 all is darkness for Job, as illustrated by his compounding of words like "darkness," "death's shadow," "cloud mass," "daygloom," "murk," and verbs describing the shutting down of the light (Alter, *Wisdom Books*, 7). Your birthday is always a special day. It used to be for Job but no longer. Job wishes he could adjust the calendar and delete the day of his birth. His mention of a "boy" ("male child") points to God's special favor and blessing from the perspective of the parents. Notice the intensifying Hebrew parallelism in verse 3. Not only does Job wish he had never been born, but he wishes he had never been conceived! The use of "darkness" in verse 4 is a synonym for gloom and depression. The same Hebrew word occurs in Psalm 23:4, "the darkest valley."

The Hebrew word for "curse" in verse 8 is often used in extrabiblical texts to mean a formalized curse by a witch doctor (cf. Num 22:6). Supposedly, such a curse was intractable once invoked. The word for "ready" connotes that which is trained or skilled, as in soldiers. The meaning of "Leviathan" is a key issue in the book of Job. In ancient mythology, Leviathan represents a sea monster, a dragon that seeks to destroy humanity and stands as an enemy to the gods.

Job pictures Leviathan as having keepers, professional curse-bringers, who can whistle for Leviathan and call him to come and destroy part of the created order. He wants them to stir up from the depths this chaotic, evil, supernatural sea monster whose design is always to bring disorder in place of order, depth in place of life, darkness swallowing life. (Ash, *Job*, 73)

Job's use of this named mythical creature in no way suggests his belief in the existence of such a creature. Likely Job is speaking poetically, using common mythology. As with Santa Claus, the mention of the name does not mean one believes he exists.

In verse 9 Job mentions twilight and breaking dawn. A new day began when the first three stars appeared in the sky, and morning came when last three stars disappeared with the rising of the sun. The morning stars are Sirius and the planets Mercury and Venus, whose size and brilliance make them easily visible at dawn. In verse 10 Job wishes the night he was conceived had never occurred. He wishes no "light" had been shed on the night his mother's womb was opened and he was conceived. Therefore, the night did not hide trouble from Job's eyes, though normally things are difficult to see at night. This part of Job is rich in metaphor.

Job Laments the Day of His Birth
JOB 3:11-19

Job turns from cursing to questioning. Notice the use of the word *why* several times. Job expresses his wish that he had died at birth. Job's wish for stillbirth would have eliminated his future suffering. Had Job been stillborn, he would have been able to rest in death. Earthly nonexistence would be better than what Job is experiencing now. Eugene Peterson expresses it well in *The Message*:

> *Obliterate the day I was born. Blank out the night I was conceived!*
> *Let it be a black hole in space. May God above forget it ever happened.*
> *Erase it from the books!* . . . *Rip the date off the calendar.* . . . *What's*
> *the point of life when it doesn't make sense, when God blocks all the*
> *roads to meaning?* (3:3-4,6b,23)

"Why did the knees receive me, and why were there breasts for me to nurse?" This reference to the "knees" either refers to his mother's taking him in her lap soon after birth or to the custom of placing a newborn on the knees of his father to symbolize the father's reception of the child (see Gen 48:12; Ruth 4:16). If Job's mother had not nourished him with breast milk, he would have died.

In verses 17-19 death is the great leveler of all people in society: kings and princes, oppressors and the oppressed. All die and go to "Sheol," a Hebrew term meaning the grave, the abode of the dead (7:9; 11:8; 14:13; 17:13,16; 21:13; 24:19; 26:6). Job frequently mentions departing from this life (3:21; 7:21; 10:21-22; 14:10-14; 21:21; 30:23; see 38:17).

Job Longs to Die
JOB 3:20-26

Job sees no end to his daily suffering. He lives in a constant state of fear with no interludes of peace. Job complains in verse 23 that God has "hedged" him in. This is the second time the metaphor has been used. Satan employed it in 1:10 to complain that God had hedged Job in to protect him from any trouble. Here Job used it to describe his feeling that God has hedged him in so he cannot escape his suffering.

All Job can see is his own suffering. His self-centeredness is showing. Like most of us, Job magnifies his suffering as if he were the center of the universe. His suffering is so intense, Job not only wants to undo his own life but to question the creation of the world. This is an interesting foreshadowing of what God himself will bring up to Job when he interrogates him in the final chapters. Pain has knocked on Job's door and seems to have become a permanent guest in his house.

Pain knocked upon my door and said
That she had come to stay,
And though I would not welcome her
But bade her go away,
She entered in. Like my own shade
She followed after me,
And from her stabbing, stinging sword
No moment was I free.

And then one day another knocked
Most gently at my door.
I cried, "No. Pain is living here,
There is not room for more."
And then I heard His tender voice,
"Tis I, be not afraid."
And from the day he entered in—
The difference it has made!

For though He did not bid her leave,
(My strange, unwelcome guest),
He taught me how to live with her.
Oh, I had never guessed
That we could dwell so sweetly here,
My Lord and Pain and I,
Within this fragile house of clay
While years slip slowly by!
(Martha Snell Nicholson, "Guests," in *Treasures*, 38)

In verse 24 Job's low sighs and groanings are the audible evidence of his pain. His cry is the cry of suffering but not the cry of defiance. Job wishes he had no past, and all he can see is a "no exit" sign to his future—a blank wall of hopelessness. Through it all, however, Job never seems to contemplate suicide as a way out of his suffering.

Job's suffering as he describes it in chapter 3 is comprehensive. He suffered in his circumstances. He suffered in his body. He suffered in his heart. He suffered in his mind. Job's pain blurred his perception of God. He views God as entrapping him. Job is looking at God through the wrong end of the binoculars (Estes, *Job*, 24). He is using his own experience to wrongly conclude that God is out to get him.

Phillip Yancey's book *Where Is God When It Hurts?* spoke to me many years ago when I read it. He describes our attitude concerning pain in our lives:

> I have never read a poem extolling the virtues of pain, nor seen a statue erected in its honor, nor heard a hymn dedicated to it. Pain is usually defined as "unpleasantness." Christians don't really know how to interpret pain. If you pinned them against the wall, in a dark, secret moment, many Christians would probably admit that pain was God's one mistake. He really should have worked a little harder and invented a better way of coping with the world's dangers. I am convinced that pain gets a bad press. Perhaps we should see statues, hymns, and poems to pain. Why do I think that? Because up close, under a microscope, the pain network is seen in an entirely different light. It is perhaps the paragon of creative genius. (*Where Is God*, 22)

There are many kinds of storms—snowstorms, hailstorms, rainstorms—but none is more difficult to endure than doubt storms. Such storms sweep upon us with a vengeance of gale-force winds of fear. Job was in a doubt storm where "the enemy is too big, the task too great, the future too bleak, and the answers too few" (Lucado, *Eye of the Storm*, 127).

August Tholuck was a nineteenth-century German evangelical. He preached a sermon in 1938 in Halle entitled "The Blessing of Dark Hours in the Christian Life" on Luke 22:31-32, where Peter's denial of the Lord is recorded. He describes the "dark hours" in our lives as Christians:

> Inasmuch as I am talking about dark hours in the Christian life, let me explain how I perceive them. There are two different kinds. First, there are dark hours in the Christian life when the sun has set, but the moon, or at least the

distant evening star, is still in the sky. These are the hours
when outward needs are pressing, and the comfort of the
gospel is far off; hours when, as the scripture expresses it,
the countenance of the Lord is veiled; hours like those when
David calls, "Lord, be merciful to me, for I am weak; heal
me, Lord, for my whole body trembles with fear, my soul
is very fearful; O Lord, why so long?" [Ps 6:2-3]. All of you
are certainly acquainted with this hour, are you not? And
you know well, do you not, that in such hours it sometimes
becomes difficult to believe in hope against hope, and you
have sometimes seen yourself standing in spirit at the edge of
the precipice at which Peter stood.

Yet these dark hours are by no means the most terrible.
These nights are not terrifying as long as the evening star
gleams from afar. However, there is another sort of dark
hour, when the night is total, when not only does the Lord
hide his countenance, but Satan reveals his. He steps before
the frightened soul and speaks to it of defiance, denial, and
betrayal, "Say farewell to God," he calls out, "and pray to me.
Then I will give you the riches of the world and its splendor"
[cf. Matt 4:8-9]. This was the hour when Job cursed the day he
was born [Job 3:1]. This was the hour in which Asaph called
out: "Is it to be in vain that my heart has lived uprightly and
I have always washed hands in innocence? I would almost
have said so, like the godless, but behold, by saying this I
would have condemned all your children who have ever lived"
[Ps 73:13,15]. That was the hour in which Judas rose from the
table and went out into the night [John 13:21-30].

Is it not true that one or the other of you has experienced
hours when Satan is desirous of you, when only a very, very
thin thread still connects you with your Lord, and Satan puts
his knife to it, intending to sever it? The Lord had prayed for
you, so Satan did not sever the connection. Then comes the
loud call: "Soul, I did this for you; what are you going to do for
me?" "Simon, Simon, when you have once turned back, then
strengthen the others." O, in one way or another you have all
become Peter's companions in his dark hour and his sifting.
(Crowner, *Spirituality*, 95–96)

We should never let our circumstances or our feelings become the measure by which we evaluate God. Our circumstances vacillate; God's character is unchanging. We need the reminder of Hebrews 13:8: "Jesus Christ is the same yesterday, today, and forever."

As with Job, the "why" question when it comes to suffering always surfaces. Like the character Tevye in the famous Broadway musical *Fiddler on the Roof*, we ask why God has brought so much adversity into our lives. Job will not receive an answer to his "why" question at this point. In fact, he will have to wait to the end of the book, and then the answering is surprising.

Reflect and Discuss

1. What exactly does Job curse and why?
2. Do you think anything Job says in this chapter is sinful? Why or why not?
3. How does Job feel God is treating him?
4. How do you think Job changed any of his views about God as a result of his suffering?
5. What do you say to God when you experience times of suffering?

Eliphaz's First Speech and Job's Response
JOB 4–7

Main Idea: Eliphaz explains Job's suffering as divine retribution, and Job affirms the reality of his suffering, pleads for death, accuses the three friends, and expresses his desire for their sympathy; then he expresses his frustrations to God.

I. **Eliphaz's First Speech (4–5)**
   A. Eliphaz consoles Job (4:1-6).
   B. Eliphaz affirms retribution (4:7-11).
   C. Eliphaz recounts his vision (4:12-21).
   D. Eliphaz finds no mediator (5:1-7).
   E. Eliphaz urges Job to seek God (5:8-27).
II. **Job's Affirmations (6)**
   A. Job affirms the reality of his suffering (6:1-7).
   B. Job pleads for death (6:8-13).
   C. Job accuses his friends (6:14-23).
   D. Job desires his friends' sympathy (6:24-30).
III. **Job's Frustrations (7)**
   A. Job's view: existence is servitude (7:1-6).
   B. Job's petition (7:7-10)
   C. Job's complaint against God (7:11-21)

Job 4–31 is a major section of the book that includes a series of speeches by Job's three friends followed by Job's responses. After Job's lament in chapter 3, the first cycle of speeches is found in Job 4–14, with Eliphaz speaking first (4–5) and Job responding (6–7). Eliphaz's first speech is usually divided into two sections: 4:2-21 and 5:1-27. In the first section many see the subdivisions as 4:2-11 and 4:12-21, with these further subdivided into four sub-stanzas: 2-6, 7-11, 12-16, and 17-21.

Eliphaz speaks first, possibly because he is the oldest and perhaps the wisest of the three friends, though this is not stated in the text. Eliphaz's theology is simple and clear: Job, you are suffering; therefore, you have sinned! This is the theology of retribution so common in the

ANE. Everyone has had the experience of a well-meaning friend giving ill-timed or ill-informed advice. For several chapters Job is about to endure three well-meaning friends who give him wrong counsel.

Eliphaz's First Speech
JOB 4–5

Eliphaz Consoles Job (4:1-6)

The comfort of friends in a time of distress is a welcome gift. But what do you do if those friends misdiagnose your problem and give you wrong counsel? The arrival of Job's three friends was a welcome tonic to Job's suffering, but it soon became apparent they overstayed their welcome. His three friends meant well, but their presence turned out to be more of a curse than a blessing. From the beginning their counsel and advice were wrong. By their words they compounded Job's suffering.

In 4:1-6 Eliphaz introduces his speech. Having heard Job's tirade in Job 3, Eliphaz is cautious: "Should anyone try to speak with you when you are exhausted?" In verses 3-4 he compliments Job on his past counsel to many, but then by way of mild rebuke he essentially says to Job that now he is panicked and perhaps needs to take his own medicine. Job the encourager could now not encourage himself. Eliphaz asserts that a clear conscience does not necessarily make one innocent (v. 6). It is the Lord who judges.

Eliphaz Affirms Retribution (4:7-11)

Eliphaz outlines his basic argument of retribution—righteous people do not suffer; only sinners do. In essence, he appeals to his experience in the world and concludes that suffering is a result of personal sin. Eliphaz cannot accept the fact that suffering may come to the innocent. What Job needs to do is clear: repent, clean up his life, and God will forgive him. Eliphaz says to Job, in essence, "The good guys always win, and the bad guys always lose. No truly innocent person ever ended up on the scrap heap."

Eliphaz Recounts His Vision (4:12-21)

Eliphaz describes a mysterious vision he experienced during the night. A ghostlike figure entered his room. It's almost as if Eliphaz tries to scare Job into listening to reason with a ghost story! From the vision, Eliphaz learned the utter holiness of God such that even the angels who stand in God's presence are defiled. If that is the case, then no mere human being has any chance of standing blamelessly before God. What Eliphaz concluded about God's holiness is certainly true. But his conclusion about the retribution principle is flawed.

Whether Eliphaz's dream is to be taken as a divine revelation from the Lord is debatable. The text does not say either way. The text does not employ the common phrase "the word of the LORD."

Several lessons may be gleaned from Job 4. Eliphaz starts off on the right foot as a comforter and counselor. He is polite, is tender, maintains his convictions, and expresses himself with candor. He is theologically correct on two major points: one supreme being exists; God is sovereign and superintends individual human lives.

However, Eliphaz errs on a major theological point that keeps him on an ever-widening trajectory away from his target—the retribution principle. This principle teaches that God always operates with retributive justice in this life. He preserves the innocent and destroys the wicked.

Though this is valid as a general principle, it is not invariable in human life, nor is it an adequate explanation of suffering. So prevalent was this error in the days of Jesus that he had to lay down with force the opposite principle in Luke 13:1-5. And in reference to a blind man, Jesus was asked, "Who sinned, this man or his parents?" Jesus responded, "Neither" (John 9:2-3). Eliphaz's fatal theological mistake is his judgment of character based on circumstances. He was wrong about Job.

Scripture makes clear that suffering is sometimes punitive and sometimes disciplinary. Yet suffering is not necessarily connected with personal sin. Scripture does indicate that in some sense suffering seems necessary to fallen humanity. It has a purifying and sanctifying effect on human character.

Eliphaz Finds No Mediator (5:1-7)

Eliphaz warns Job to be careful about what he says to and about God. In essence, "Don't question God." In Job 5 Eliphaz basically says to Job, "Look, if I were in your shoes, I would repent, and God would restore me. Humanity stands condemned before God and thus has no chance. Man is a nobody in God's sight." This is true enough in one sense, but Eliphaz misses the point. He thinks prosperity is the result of righteousness and adversity is the result of sin. But such a partial and inadequate explanation simply doesn't cover all human experience.

In 5:1-7 Eliphaz asserts, "Call out! Will anyone answer you? Which of the holy ones will you turn to?" (v. 1). The "holy ones" is a reference to angels. Eliphaz point-blank tells Job his children died because of his sin (v. 4)! When Eliphaz says, "For distress does not grow out of the soil, and trouble does not sprout from the ground" (v. 6), he is saying that Job's troubles are not the result of mere chance. Verse 7 states, "But humans are born for trouble as surely as sparks fly upward." This can be interpreted in two ways: either a person brings trouble on himself, or fate is at work.[28]

Eliphaz Urges Job to Seek God (5:8-27)

This is the third section of Eliphaz's speech. Here his supposed piety is showing, as he seems to elevate himself above Job. He tells Job, If I were you, I would appeal to God, because although God frustrates the wicked (vv. 11-13), God is good and delivers the helpless (vv. 14-15). God is the giver of life and the sustainer of life (5:10-13).[29] Job, you're suffering because God makes the rules and you have broken them. God brings about justice in the world (5:15), and you, Job, are on the receiving end of his justice because of your sin. Eliphaz is blissfully ignorant that the religious platitudes he is belching don't tell the whole story.

In fact, in verse 17 Eliphaz says Job should be happy God has shown such an interest in him to discipline him for sin! If he'll repent and seek God's forgiveness, God will forgive, heal, and protect Job once again. "Don't blame fate when things go wrong—trouble doesn't come from nowhere. . . . What a blessing when God steps in and corrects you. . . . The same hand that hurts you, heals you" (vv. 7,17,18 MSG).

Some comfort! At least Eliphaz got this much right: no matter how much you sin, God is a forgiving God (v. 19). But Eliphaz got it all wrong about Job since he based his advice on the premise that Job had sinned.

---

[28] The meaning of vv. 6-7 has been variously expressed. Some interpret it to mean just as sparks defy gravity and fly upward, sin leads to suffering. Another option is to interpret the Hebrew word usually translated "not" with the translation "surely." In this view, v. 6 would be translated something like "for affliction indeed comes from the dust, and trouble sprouts from the ground."

[29] Dunham, *Pious Sage*, 41–42, suggests that Paul appropriates the citation of Job 5:13 "as part of a rhetorical strategy of irony in 1 Cor 3:18-23."

Eliphaz attempts to impale Job on the horns of a dilemma: Either all suffering comes from God as retribution for sin, or if one has not sinned, then God is unjust to permit the innocent to suffer. The latter can't be the case according to Eliphaz, so the former must be true. Something has to give: either the justice of God or the integrity of Job. There are no other logical alternatives as far as Eliphaz is concerned. Eliphaz closes his speech by telling Job, repent and you will regain your material prosperity, have a long life, and obtain many children (vv. 24-27). In summary, Eliphaz says six things to Job: (1) Job's suffering is the result of his sin; (2) Job has no chance before God of being pure and innocent; (3) Job is a mortal being; (4) suffering is not accidental but retribution for sin or at least disciplinary in nature; (5) God is transcendent; and (6) if Job will submit to God and repent, God will restore his blessings on him (Zuck, *Job*, 35). If we were to summarize Eliphaz's counsel to Job, we might say he told Job four things: (1) be consistent with what you know to be true; (2) be realistic about being human; (3) be humble; and (4) be submissive to God's discipline (Ash, *Job*, 102).

We may note several things about Eliphaz's speech. First, he started well but quickly turned to condemnation of Job. This is all the more troubling since we know the true situation with Job based on the prologue. Eliphaz is overconfident in his knowledge and jumps to false conclusions.

Second, Eliphaz has a simple philosophy: good always comes to those who are good, and bad always comes to those who are bad. The operative word here is "always." It is often true that good comes to those who are good and bad to bad, but to universalize the maxim as Eliphaz did is to stray from the truth of life and the truth of Scripture. He doesn't believe there are exceptions to the ironclad retribution principle that he and the other friends attempt to foist on Job and his situation. Eliphaz begins from a wrong premise based on a false dichotomy, which leads him to make many bad conclusions here and in his other two speeches. For Eliphaz, Job has "become a superlative sufferer, he must of necessity be a superlative sinner" (Chappell, *Sermons*, 11).

Third, Eliphaz's viewpoint is based on his own experience: "I have seen . . ." (5:3 ESV). But experience alone cannot furnish the key to solving Job's problems. Because Eliphaz's perspective and observation are limited, he falls into the trap of universalizing a general principle.

All the human characters in Job grasp some aspects of God's truth and ways, but they all have blind spots. Job, the three friends, and Elihu occasionally affirm good theology, but they also are occasionally faulty in their application of that theology. "God's wisdom matches the right truth to the right situation at the right time and in the right Spirit; humans often fail to do so" (Estes, *Job*, 36).

Finally, Eliphaz doesn't offer Job any hope—a poor example of counseling. I've done my share of pastoral counseling through the years. I would estimate that more than 50 percent of all the people I have counseled suffer from the consequences of one of two sources: their own sin or the sin of others. Sometimes people are suffering as a consequence of their own sin. The hardest part at this point is getting people to recognize and admit their sin. Sometimes people suffer from the sins of others. This is especially true in the lives of children and teenagers. Many times my heart was grieved over a situation where someone's suffering was caused by the sins of other people, even members of their own family.

But the really difficult situation is when someone is suffering when there is no known reason for their suffering, either within themselves or others. That was Job's situation. Whatever the circumstances, I've learned the importance of giving people a sense of hope. Hurting people often can see nothing beyond their pain. They become myopic and tend toward hopelessness. Eliphaz strikes me as the guy who kicks Job while he is down instead of lending a true helping hand to lift him up.

If Eliphaz could have donned New Testament glasses and known of Jesus's teaching in John 9:1-3 concerning Jesus's healing of the man born blind, he would have learned that the retribution principle is not always in play. The disciples were trying to answer the "why" question. Why was this man born blind? Did he sin or did his parents sin? Charles Stanley speaks for us all when he writes,

> Like the disciples, we are prone to view adversity narrowly. We turn on ourselves and begin an often fruitless journey into our recent—and sometimes not-so-recent—past. Our purpose is to find the reason for the adversity we face. The thought may arise: *Surely this is God's way of paying me back.* If, however, we are convinced that nothing we have done merits the magnitude of our adversity, we have no choice, it seems, but to question the goodness and faithfulness of God.
>
> In his response to the disciples' question, Jesus revealed yet another error that plagued the theology of the day. But His

answer did much more than that. It enlightens us and offers a much broader perspective on suffering than that held by many. His answer brings hope to those who have thus far been afraid to ask *why*. It allows us to look beyond ourselves—and that is always an improvement!

. . .

Is it possible that adversity can originate with God? All of us would be more comfortable if Jesus had said, "This man is blind because he sinned, but God is going to use it anyway." That would be a much easier pill to swallow. But Jesus leaves us no escape. Sin was not the direct cause of this man's blindness; God was. (Stanley, *Victory*, 196–98)

Jesus points to a larger purpose in the life of the man born blind and explicitly denies that his condition was the result of his sin. The same is true of Job's suffering.

Job 5 teaches us several practical lessons. First, God is a trustworthy God (v. 8). Four things demonstrate his trustworthiness: God is love; God is a truthful God; God is infinitely capable; and God is a consistent God. Second, God is a wonder-working God. He works in general ways and in particular ways.

God can use affliction for good. God corrects the godly by affliction. God redeems the godly from affliction. God guards the godly in their affliction. God blesses the godly in the midst of their afflictions. God perfects and matures the godly by affliction. Therefore, when we suffer, we should ponder its origin, its necessity, its design, its tendency, and its goal (Thomas, *Problemata Mundi*, 76–79).

Job's Affirmations
JOB 6

In chapters 6–7 Job responds to Eliphaz. In summary, Job justifies his right to complain about his suffering, chiding his friends for offering no help at all and praying that God would simply let him die. Job is frustrated that Eliphaz doesn't seem to understand his suffering. Job is also frustrated with the level of his suffering and pleads for its limitation. He maintains his innocence and challenges Eliphaz for proof that his suffering is because of his sin.

Job Affirms the Reality of His Suffering (6:1-7)

When everything goes wrong at one time, many of us feel like the construction worker who filled out the following accident report:

> When I got to the building I found that the hurricane had
> knocked off some bricks around the top. So I rigged up a
> beam with a pulley at the top of the building and hoisted up
> a couple barrels full of bricks. When I had fixed the damaged
> area, there were a lot of bricks left over. Then I went to the
> bottom and began releasing the line. Unfortunately, the barrel
> of bricks was much heavier than I was—and before I knew
> what was happening the barrel started coming down, jerking
> me up.
>
> I decided to hang on since I was too far off the ground
> by then to jump, and halfway up I met the barrel of bricks
> coming down fast. I received a hard blow on my shoulder. I
> then continued to the top, banging my head against the beam
> and getting my fingers pinched and jammed in the pulley.
> When the barrel hit the ground hard, it burst its bottom,
> allowing the bricks to spill out. I was now heavier than the
> barrel. So I started down again at high speed. Halfway down
> I met the barrel coming up fast and received severe injuries
> to my shins. When I hit the ground, I landed on the pile of
> broken bricks, getting several painful cuts and deep bruises. At
> this point I must have lost my presence of mind, because I let
> go of my grip on the line. The barrel came down fast—giving
> me another blow on my head and putting me in the hospital. I
> respectfully request sick leave. (Swindoll, *Tardy Oxcart*, 21–22)

Job 6 is divided into four sections. In 6:1-7 Job questions why there seems to be no balance to suffering and grief: "If only my grief could be weighed and my devastation placed with it on the scales. For then it would outweigh the sand of the seas!" (vv. 2-3). Here Job employs hyperbole to emphasize his point. Job reasons, essentially, "Shouldn't God be my faithful protector? Instead he has become my enemy" (v. 4). In fact, he feels he has become target practice for God! Job's adversity is beginning to distort his view of God. This will become more and more evident in Job's responses to his three friends. Job implies that Eliphaz's words are like egg whites—tasteless food you can't eat without salt (vv. 6-7).

Job Pleads for Death (6:8-13)

Since his suffering is so intense, Job pleads for death. He longs for God either to bless him or crush him (God, why don't you just step in and squash me like a bug?) but not to leave him in the miserable condition he is in. In spite of his suffering, Job makes no overtures toward suicide. He wishes he were dead, but he doesn't think of taking his own life. Job knows two things about God: he is the one who brings trouble, but he is also the one who sustains life. He also knows two things about himself: he has no internal strength to solve his problem, and he has no other resources to overcome his suffering.

Job Accuses His Friends (6:14-23)

Job turns the tables on his three friends and accuses them of sin as well in the accusations they make against Job (vv. 14-23). He accuses his friends of being unsympathetic and disloyal (v. 14). In verses 15-20 Job uses a vivid word picture to express the dangerous and deceptive nature of his friends' counsel. The Middle Eastern streambed, or wadi, was well known in Job's day. In the rainy season, the wadi would be full of rushing water ("overflow"), but in the summer, when water was desperately needed, the wadi would dry up into parched ground. Caravans in need of water look for wadis, but when they find them, "they are disappointed" (vv. 19-20).

Job also accuses the friends of having a sense of fear themselves now that they have seen the extremity of his suffering (vv. 21-23). Are they afraid of showing sympathy, perhaps thinking that if they do so, God will be provoked at them for attempting to show it to someone whom God himself is judging? Do they fear guilt by association?

Job Desires His Friends' Sympathy (6:24-30)

Finally, Job pleads with his three friends to provide the evidence that suggests Job had sinned. "Where have I gone wrong?" Job asks. Eliphaz has not presented any evidence that would hold up in a court of law that would make his charge of Job's sinful behavior stick. This is insulting to Job; the accused should be presumed innocent until proven guilty. In his frustration Job turns the tables and accuses Eliphaz of being heartless and one who would gamble for orphans and "negotiate a price to sell [his] friend" (v. 27). Job's integrity is at stake (v. 29). He appeals to Eliphaz to consider his character and not rush to judgment and condemnation.

The Message paraphrases verses 24-27 well:

> *Confront me with the truth and I'll shut up, show me where I've gone off the track. Honest words never hurt anyone, but what's the point of all this pious bluster? You pretend to tell me what's wrong with my life, but treat my words of anguish as so much hot air. Are people mere things to you? Are friends just items of profit and loss?*

Job's Frustrations
JOB 7

Job's View: Existence Is Servitude (7:1-6)

Job 7 is divided into three sections: 1-6, 7-10, and 11-21. Job 7 could be summed up with a question and a plea to God. The question (vv. 1-10) is in essence, "Why do I matter?" The plea (vv. 11-21) is in essence, "Leave me alone!" (Ash, *Job*, 127).

In 7:1-6 Job astutely compares his life of suffering to that of a servant, slave, or hired hand. Human life is a life's sentence to hard labor. Existence is servitude, life is one large disappointment, days end without hope, and there is no rest even at night. He speaks of "troubled nights" (v. 3), indicating sleeplessness, and "months of futility," indicating that his suffering was at least several months in duration. In his suffering Job can only hope for release from his anguish.

Job's Petition (7:7-10)

Job despairs of life, but he does not pray for death here as he did in chapter 3. Life is brief, like a "breath" and a "cloud," and death is final. In verse 8 Job speaks of "the eye of anyone who looks on me," a reference to God made explicit when he speaks of "your eyes." Job speaks in verse 9 of going down to "Sheol," the Hebrew word used to speak of the place of the dead. At this point, for Job, "everything about Job's experience points to insignificance and transience. That is why he says in effect, 'You will look for me, but I will not be here anymore' (v. 8b)" (Ash, *Job*, 129). With shades of Gladys Knight as she sang about her guy leaving for Georgia, so Job thinks he will soon be on that midnight train to the grave.

Job's Complaint against God (7:11-21)

In verses 11-12 Job complains of being harassed by God, as if God were guarding him like some enemy. Job accuses God of frightening him with dreams (vv. 13-14) so that sleep is impossible. He wishes God would just leave him alone (vv. 16-19).[30] God is constantly bothering Job with his suffering, such that he doesn't even have time to swallow his saliva (v. 19)! Job felt God had become a cosmic Yoda who has turned to the dark side. Job wonders why God pays him so much hostile attention if he is as insignificant to God as he appears to be. In Scripture, God's watchful eye is a source of protection and hope, but for Job it feels just the opposite.

Job asks God for evidence of his sin. He cannot understand why it seems as if God had set Job up for target practice (v. 20)! "Why make me your punching bag, God?" Finally, Job says to God somewhat sarcastically, "You'll be sorry when I'm gone! Once I'm dead you'll have no one to toy with!" (v. 21, author's paraphrase). Job's words in this section are dripping with sarcasm. The word "forgive" in verse 21 is the translation of a related Hebrew word translated "burden" in verse 20. Sin is indeed a burden that needs to be lifted off and carried away.

Here is how Peterson renders Job 7:17-21 in *The Message*:

What are mortals anyway, that you bother with them, that you even give them the time of day? That you check up on them every morning, looking in on them to see how they're doing? Let up on me, will you? Can't you even let me spit in peace? Even suppose I'd sinned—how would that hurt you? You're responsible for every human being. Don't you have better things to do than pick on me? Why make a federal case out of me? Why don't you just forgive my sins and start me off with a clean slate? The way things are going, I'll soon be dead. You'll look high and low, but I won't be around.

Conclusion

We learn several practical lessons from Job 6–7. In the way Job was treated, we realize his sufferings were unappreciated and misunderstood by his

---

[30] In v. 17 the Hb word translated "set" in the KJV and ESV connotes fixing an idea of permanence, so "pay so much attention" (CSB) connotes unrelenting, concentrated observation.

friends, and this led to offensive speech in the form of false accusations by his friends. There are times when friends are desperately needed, and there are times when friends are terribly disappointing. Instead of showing compassion, they were unsympathetic. Instead of showing pity, they were intrusive and verbally abusive. Instead of offering condolence, their words were ungenerous and irrelevant.

Friendship misused . . .

is often an offence and an injury to men in trouble. It comes with a glib tongue, but with an icy heart: its words are often irrelevant, they never touch the point, and throw no light upon our darkness: not infrequently does it enter our chamber of affliction intrusively and unasked, and begin to criticize words that we have spoken in the wild fury of a nature wrapped in anguish. Mistaken friendship is sometimes as pernicious and irritating as false friendship. (Thomas, *Problemata Mundi*, 91)

Not only were Job's sufferings intolerable to his friends, but they were intolerable to Job himself. Yet in the midst of his almost unbearable pain, Job never contemplated suicide, remained mindful of his relation to God his maker, and realized life is transient and brief.

Whether we live with minimal suffering or maximal suffering, life according to Job is summed up as (1) hard servitude, (2) spent worthlessly, (3) physically afflicted, and (4) brief—"My days pass more swiftly than a weaver's shuttle."

Death is disruption. It reminds us of the folly of worldliness and the wisdom of spirituality. Death is easily accomplished. Our lives are fragile. The slightest thing could bring about death. Death is final with respect to this life. It is never remedied—"he will never return to his house"—except in resurrection!

Job can't figure out why God should afflict him at all, much less why God should afflict him so greatly in mind and body. Even at the end of the book, Job doesn't find out why. Likely, neither will we until we get to heaven.

The editors of *Christian Century* were aware that Martin Luther King Jr. had constantly received threats against his life. They urged him to comment on his view of suffering. He wrote,

Some of my personal sufferings over the last few years have
also served to shape my thinking. I always hesitate to mention
these experiences for fear of conveying the wrong impression.
A person who constantly calls attention to his trials and
sufferings is in danger of developing a martyr complex and
of making others feel that he is consciously seeking sympathy.
It is possible for one to be self-centered in his self-denial and
self-righteous in his self-sacrifice. So I am always reluctant to
refer to my personal sacrifices. But I feel somewhat justified in
mentioning them in this article because of the influence they
have had in shaping my thinking.

Due to my involvement in the struggle for the freedom
of my people, I have known very few quiet days in the last
few years. I have been arrested five times and put in Alabama
jails. My home has been bombed twice. A day seldom passes
that my family and I are not the recipients of threats of death.
I have been the victim of a near-fatal stabbing. So in a real
sense I have been battered by the storms of persecution. I
must admit that at times I have felt that I could no longer bear
such a heavy burden, and have been tempted to retreat to a
more quiet and serene life. But every time such a temptation
appeared, something came to strengthen and sustain my
determination. I have learned now that the Master's burden is
light precisely when we take his yoke upon us.

My personal trials have also taught me the value of
unmerited suffering. As my sufferings mounted I soon realized
that there were two ways that I could respond to my situation:
either to react with bitterness or seek to transform the
suffering into a creative force. I decided to follow the latter
course. Recognizing the necessity for suffering I have tried
to make of it a virtue. If only to save myself from bitterness, I
have attempted to see my personal ordeals as an opportunity
to transform myself and heal the people involved in the tragic
situation which now obtains. I have lived these last few years
with the conviction that unearned suffering is redemptive.

There are some who still find the cross a stumbling block,
and others consider it foolishness, but I am more convinced

than ever before that it is the power of God unto social and individual salvation. So like the Apostle Paul, I can humbly yet proudly say, "I bear in my body the marks of the Lord Jesus." The suffering and agonizing moments through which I have passed over the last few years have also drawn me closer to God. More than ever before I am convinced of the reality of a personal God. (Washington, *Testament of Hope*, 41–42)

Like Martin Luther King Jr. and Job, at the end of our suffering we must entrust ourselves to Jesus. Jesus promised he would never leave us or forsake us. Even when we don't sense his presence, he is near, and he is ready to come to our aid. "Therefore, let us approach the throne of grace with boldness, so that we may receive mercy and find grace to help us in time of need" (Heb 4:16). The cross of Christ has hallowed our suffering. We may not understand, but Christ has a purpose in our pain. Trust him!

Far more important than the *source* of our suffering is our *response* to it. Job never knew the source of his suffering. The author of Job records how Job responded to his suffering, warts and all. Regardless of the source of adversity, it is one of God's most effective tools to mold us into the image of Christ. Suffering deepens our faith. Suffering deepens our Christian commitment. The real question for us in our suffering is not "why." The real question is how will we respond?

One of the first books added to my little library shortly after being called to preach was a four-volume commentary on Romans by the great Donald Grey Barnhouse. The books were really more like sermons than a commentary. On one occasion during his ministry, Barnhouse was conducting a weeklong revival meeting at a church. The pastor and his wife were expecting their first child. On the last night of services, the pastor did not show up. Barnhouse assumed he was at the hospital with his wife, so he went ahead with the service. Toward the end, the pastor slipped in quietly and took his seat on the back pew. When the service concluded, the pastor made his way to the front of the church and dismissed the people.

Later, in his office, the pastor confided in Barnhouse that his child had been born and had Down syndrome. He told Barnhouse he did not know how he was going to break the news to his wife. Barnhouse then turned to Exodus 4:11 and read, "The LORD said to him, 'Who placed a mouth on humans? Who makes a person mute or deaf, seeing or blind?

Is it not I, the LORD?'" Then Barnhouse reminded the pastor of Romans 8:28: "We know that all things work together for the good of those who love God, who are called according to his purpose." The pastor left the office and returned to the hospital. His wife was distressed that the nurses would not let her see her baby. The young pastor took his wife by the hand, quoted Exodus 4:11, and told her that the Lord had blessed them with a Down syndrome child.

News of the birth spread through the hospital. The switchboard operator, who was not a Christian, listened in on the conversation when the new young mother called her own mother to break the news. She told her mother how the Lord had blessed her husband and her with a child with Down syndrome. The switchboard operator heard the young mother say that somehow this is going to be a blessing from God. The operator was shocked. She told everyone what she had heard, and soon the entire hospital was buzzing with the story.

The next Sunday the pastor was back in his pulpit to preach. In the congregation were the hospital telephone operator along with seventy nurses and staff members from the hospital. At the conclusion of the service when the pastor extended the invitation for those who had never come to Christ to believe on him for salvation, thirty nurses came forward to receive Christ as Savior (Stanley, *Victory*, 219–21).

> Down shadowy lanes, across strange streams,
> Bridged over by our broken dreams,
> Behind the misty caps of years,
> Close to the great salt fount of tears
> The garden lies; strive as you may,
>
> You cannot miss it in your way.
>   All paths that have been, or shall be
>   Pass somewhere through Gethsemane.
>
> All those who journey soon or late,
> Must pass within the garden's gate;
> Must kneel alone in darkness there,
> And battle with some fierce despair.
> God pity those who cannot say:
> "Not mine but thine;" who only pray,
> "Let this cup pass;" and cannot see
> The purpose in Gethsemane.

Gethsemane, Gethsemane,
God help us through Gethsemane.
(Ella Wheeler Wilcox, "Gethsemane")

Reflect and Discuss

1. How do you evaluate Eliphaz as a counselor?
2. What is Eliphaz's main point to Job regarding why he is suffering?
3. What do you discern is Eliphaz's personal "theology of suffering"?
4. What parts of Eliphaz's speech do you think are true, and what parts false?
5. What is the retribution principle?
6. Do you think Job has responded too harshly to his sufferings? Why?
7. How does Job's view of God differ from that of his three friends?
8. Does Job go too far in his criticism of God's lack of response to his suffering? Explain.
9. How do you respond when you feel abandoned by friends in the midst of your suffering?
10. How do you respond when you feel abandoned by God in your suffering?

Bildad's First Speech and Job's Response

JOB 8–10

Main Idea: Bildad asserts God's justice and Job's sin, but Job desires God to declare him righteous as he laments his innocence.

I. **Bildad's First Speech (8)**
   A. God's ways are just (8:1-7).
   B. Tradition and nature testify to God's justice (8:8-19).
   C. Conclusion: Character determines destiny (8:20-22).
II. **Job's Response (9–10)**
   A. Job considers a court case against God (9:1-12).
   B. Misgivings about arguing Job's case (9:13-24)
   C. God refuses to acquit Job (9:25-35).
   D. Job's lament (10:1-22)

Bildad's First Speech

JOB 8

Bildad illustrates the fact that "human beings are hardwired to think things ought to be fair" (Ash, *Job*, 133). We believe the bad guy should get what he deserves and the good guy should get what he deserves. This is why we cheer in a movie when the bad guy gets what's coming to him. Most people possess something of a sense of justice.

Bildad operates from the same basic theological reference point as did Eliphaz and offers the same basic counsel to Job: acknowledge your sin and God will forgive and restore.

God's Ways Are Just (8:1-7)

In verses 1-7 Bildad boldly and abruptly calls Job on the carpet for his response to Eliphaz and basically calls him a windbag. To add insult to injury, Bildad accuses Job of distorting God's justice and in essence of blaspheming God. Because God must be just, Job must not be. God justly punishes sin.

With an even greater cruelty, coldhearted Bildad asserts that Job's children sinned and Job's suffering is due to his children's sin (v. 4). No sympathy. No "I'm sorry you lost your children, Job." It is the height of presumption to conclude that Job's children sinned in the first place, unless Bildad knows something we don't know from the text. It is doubly so to conclude that Job's suffering is because of his children's sin. Bildad maintains that forgiveness and prosperity from the hand of God will come to Job if only he would repent (vv. 6-7).

Tradition and Nature Testify to God's Justice (8:8-19)

In verses 8-10 Bildad invites Job to check out history. History teaches two lessons: (1) your life is brief, and therefore your knowledge is limited; (2) the ancients possessed wisdom and believed suffering was due to sin. Job should listen to history. In the remainder of this chapter Bildad appeals to the traditions of past generations to support his argument (8:8-22). Whereas Eliphaz relies more on experience for his argument, Bildad leans more on tradition.

In verses 11-19, like a good preacher, Bildad employs two examples from plant life to prove his point. First, just as the papyrus plant cannot sustain itself without water, so the wicked cannot sustain themselves for lack of righteousness, and thus they lose their prosperity. Trying to protect oneself from ruin without righteousness is like depending on a flimsy spider's web for support (v. 14). Bildad seems to be insinuating that Job was dependent on his possessions for his security, something that couldn't be further from the truth.

Bildad's second illustration from botany occurs in 8:16-19. A green plant may thrive even in the hot sun when planted in moist soil, but if it is uprooted, it can no longer flourish, and another plant will take its place. Similarly, Job has been removed from the "soil" of his prosperity, and others will come along and take his place. An uprooted plant dies.

Conclusion: Character Determines Destiny (8:20-22)

Bildad's commitment to the concept of retributive justice is clear: God will not reject people of integrity, nor will he support the evildoer. Bildad's philosophy is simple: there is no way God will reject a good person, and there is no way he will help a bad person.

True enough, but Bildad's logic and conclusion that suffering is the result of sin in a cause-effect relationship are unfounded. Material prosperity for Bildad equals God's blessings. Loss of prosperity and suffering equals God's judgment. But as Paul Scherer said, "Life's tragic inequities grinned at all the glib talk about a just God" ("Book of Job," 974). Bildad's speech was a severe reproof for Job that contained truth and error. It contained some unquestionable truth ("Does the Almighty pervert what is right?" No, of course not). Yet it also contained a damnable lie—bilge from Bildad you might say (Your children are dead because of their sin). Truth from Bildad: If you will seek God, he will heal you. Error from Bildad: Inquire of the former age. Tradition, however, does not always render a valid verdict. But one thing Bildad got exactly right: "We were born only yesterday and know nothing."

According to David Thomas, we learn an eternal principle from Bildad: moral character determines destiny. The godly will never be deserted by God and will find true happiness even in suffering. The ungodly will never be helped by God and will in fact be destroyed by God. Psalm 1 confirms this eternal principle (*Problemata Mundi*, 106–17).

Job's Response

JOB 9–10

Job's response to Bildad comprises chapters 9 and 10. His response is actually more directed to God than to Bildad. The two chapters fall into four sections: 9:1-12; 9:13-24; 9:25-35; and 10:1-22.

Job Considers a Court Case against God (9:1-12)

Job agrees with Bildad—all who reject God are cut off. But Job cannot fathom why he is being punished because he has not rejected God. If God causes Job to suffer when he has not committed any sin to bring it on, then how can *any person* ever hope to stand before God? It is impossible to fight God and win, Job reasoned. His arms are to too short to box with God. God cannot be forced in any direction. Job acknowledges God's power over nature and the cosmos (vv. 6-9). "If he steals you blind, who can stop him? Who's going to say, 'Hey, what are you doing?'" (v. 9 MSG). Nature demonstrates the power of God. God is free to do what he wills (vv. 10-12).

Misgivings about Arguing Job's Case (9:13-24)

Job acknowledges God's sovereignty over all in such a way that is ultimately inexplicable by man. Job asks, What is man in God's eyes? In all things God is supreme in power; no human being has any ground to stand before God and contend with him. Even if Job could get God in court, he wouldn't have a chance against God. Though he is innocent, he would appear guilty no matter what and would be declared guilty and condemned. "If it's a question of justice, who'll serve him the subpoena?" (v. 19 MSG). What difference does it make if I'm guilty or innocent, Job reasoned. God destroys both the guilty and the guiltless (v. 22). Job feels the weight of the impossibility of his getting justice from God. Job realizes that his friends' theology of God's rewarding the good and punishing the wicked is false. In the end God destroys both.

According to Job, humanity is found guilty by God because of God's omnipotence and not necessarily because of any sense of fair play on God's part. Since no one can argue with God—he is all powerful—even if God is wrong in his guilty assessment of a human being, that person could not dispute with God anyway. Job's reasoning is true as far as it goes, but it fails to account for God's upright moral character. God is more than power without love, righteousness, justice, and such.[31]

This leads Job in 9:25–10:22 to declare that God is unfair. God refuses to acquit Job (9:25-35), continues to punish him (10:1-7), refuses to leave him alone (10:8-17), and, in the midst of it all, won't let Job die (10:18-22) (Zuck, *Job*, 49).

God Refuses to Acquit Job (9:25-35)

Job laments his helplessness, futility, and despair before God. No matter how much Job "cleaned himself up" in an attempt to exonerate himself (vv. 30-31), his divine adversary would still win out. He longs for a mediator, an arbitrator, an umpire, to intervene on his behalf to bring God and Job together to settle the case (vv. 32-35). The arbitrator Job speaks about would be one who would listen to both sides, come to a verdict, and pronounce the verdict. Job feels deeply the unfairness of

---

[31] "There can be no immorality like that of omnipotence and omniscience uncontrolled by goodness. Such Job feels to be the Immorality who governs the universe" (Peake, *Problem of Suffering*, 79).

the situation: he who should be his judge has become his prosecutor, and without cause as far as Job is concerned (Archer, *Book of Job*, 59). But God seems uninterested in Job's case. God will not "take [away] his rod" of affliction against Job (v. 34). Job's dilemma is expressed well in *The Message*:

God and I are not equals; I can't bring a case against him. We'll never enter a courtroom as peers. How I wish we had an arbitrator to step in and let me get on with life—To break God's death grip on me, to free me from this terror so I could breathe again. Then I'd speak up and state my case boldly. As things stand, there is no way I can do it. (9:32-35)

Job's Lament (10:1-22)

In 10:1-7 Job is frustrated with God. Laying everything on the table, he "give[s] vent to [his] complaint" to God for treating him like a criminal when God knows Job is innocent. He resentfully charges God with condemning him when he has done nothing wrong. "Declare guilty" means to render a legal judgment or formal verdict of condemnation. Job can't exercise his "right to remain silent," and he proclaims his innocence, though he feels everything he says can and will be used against him by God in a court of law. Job says to God, "You know good and well I'm not guilty!"

In verses 8-17 Job asks how God can show him such favor earlier but now reduce him to such suffering. The section divides into two paragraphs: 8-12 and 13-17. Until the onset of Job's suffering, God had cared for him in every way (vv. 8-12), but now God has somehow secretly prepared his current suffering and allowed his three friends to accuse him of conduct he never committed. Job uses a poignant word picture in 8-9 that is captured well in *The Message*:

"You made me like a handcrafted piece of pottery—and now are you going to smash me to pieces? Don't you remember how beautifully you worked my clay? Will you reduce me now to a mud pie?"

Finally, in 10:18-22, in words reminiscent of Job 3, Job questions why he was born and appeals to God for just a little relief before he dies, like a death row inmate having his last twenty-four hours of peace and quiet and his favorite meal before being led off to his death. To this point, each of Job's speeches ends on a gloomy note with a reference to death.

Job has lost his bearings on the sea of suffering. He needs to get back on an even keel. Hunt explains,

> If you ask any mariner, "What is the most important part of a sailboat?" you might get a variety of answers: "A sound hull for staying afloat." "A mast and a sail for catching the wind." "A rudder for steering the right direction."
>
> But to keep the boat upright during a storm, there is one indispensable part . . . the keel. It is unseen and hidden below the surface of the water, but without it a brisk breeze can blow a large sailboat over on its side or force it to stray off course. When sailing in a strong wind, you need a sturdy keel.
>
> On many boats, the keel resembles an upside-down shark's fin that slices through the water beneath the hull. When a forceful wind on the sail causes the craft to heel, to lean to one side, the keel provides a counterforce that prevents it from flipping over. It also keeps the boat moving forward instead of drifting sideways across the water's surface.
>
> Finally, the keel gives structural strength to the entire boat, holding it together when the swirling action of wind and waves could tear it apart. Traditional boat builders always begin construction with the keel because of its importance to the ship's overall design and integrity.
>
> Storms are inevitable in life. But when the winds begin to blow, your hope in the living God is your "keel" to keep you upright and moving in the right direction. Just like a boat's keel, hope isn't optional, but rather is an essential part of the Creator's design for your life.
>
> The following prayer from the Bible reflects a heart of hope based on God's promises: "Sustain me according to your promise, and I will live; do not let my hopes be dashed" (Ps. 119:116).
>
> You may not always feel that hope is at work when blustering waves are battering you on every side. But when your hope is in God, you can know He is holding you together . . . keeping you on course . . . assuring your safety . . . just as He promised. (Hunt, *Hope for Your Heart*, 101)

These two chapters teach important doctrinal and practical lessons. As to his nature, God is just, wise, and strong. As to his actions, God is almighty over his universe and punishes those who reject him. God is inscrutable in his essence and his works. God is unaccountable in that he does what he pleases and gives account to no human being. God is irresistible in what he does and is uninfluenced by people in his thoughts and actions. Job realizes that life is fleeting. Most of us die with unused influence and unfulfilled plans. Suffering is sometimes so great that our efforts of self-consolation are fruitless. Job concludes that our suffering is too deserved to justify any hope of relief. Such is his pessimism at the moment, but Yahweh has not come on the scene yet!

We who live on this side of the cross see things in a clearer light than Job. True enough, there may be no final relief of suffering in this life. There may be no final explanation of our suffering in this life. Nevertheless, we live in the light of the glorious promises of our Lord Jesus that suffering and death have been conquered by the cross! "Where, death, is your victory? Where, death, is your sting? . . . But thanks be to God, who gives us the victory through our Lord Jesus Christ!" (1 Cor 15:55,57).

John Stott reminded us that few men who lived in the twentieth century understood the reality of suffering better than Dietrich Bonhoeffer.

> He seems never to have wavered in his Christian antagonism to the Nazi regime, although it meant for him imprisonment, the threat of torture, danger to his own family and finally death. He was executed by the direct order of Heinrich Himmler in April 1945, in the Flossenburg concentration camp, only a few days before it was liberated. It was the fulfillment of what he had believed and taught. "Suffering, then, is the badge of true discipleship. The disciple is not above his master. Following Christ means *passio passiva* suffering because we have to suffer. That is why Luther reckoned suffering among the marks of the true Church, and one of the memoranda drawn up in preparation for the Augsburg Confession similarly defines the Church as the community of those 'who are persecuted and martyred for the gospel's sake' . . . Discipleship means allegiance to the suffering Christ, and it is therefore not at all surprising that Christians should be called upon to suffer. In fact, it is a joy and a token of his grace." (Stott, *The Message*, 53, quoting Bonhoeffer, *The Cost of Discipleship*, 80–81)

Reflect and Discuss

1. What is Bildad's approach to the retribution principle?
2. Why does Job question the justice of God?
3. How can a person be "blameless" even though he is a sinner?
4. In what way does Bildad appeal to tradition in his response to Job?
5. How can you be on guard against making bad application from good theology?

Zophar's First Speech and Job's Response

JOB 11–14

Main Idea: Zophar dismisses Job's complaints, accuses Job of sin, affirms God's wisdom, and calls on Job to repent. Job accepts God's sovereignty but rejects the retribution principle and pleads for God to reveal himself and declare Job innocent.

I. **Zophar's First Speech (11)**
   A. Accusation against Job (11:1-6)
   B. Affirmation of God's wisdom (11:7-12)
   C. Call to repentance (11:13-20)
II. **Job's Response (12–14)**
   A. Retribution not validated by experience (12:1-12)
   B. God's sovereign power (12:13-25)
   C. The friends' arguments are worthless (13:1-12).
   D. Job pleads for God to hear his case (13:13-28).
   E. Hardship, hopelessness, and death (14:1-22)

Zophar's speech in chapter 11 falls into three sections: 1-6, 7-12, and 13-20. No one who reads Zophar's first speech to Job can fail to be struck by its insensitive and harsh tone. Instead of offering any soothing balm for Job's suffering, Zophar pours in more vinegar.

Zophar's First Speech

JOB 11

Accusation against Job (11:1-6)

Don't you hate those annoying telemarketer calls that always seem to come at inopportune times? All leave the same perfunctory voice mail that I just immediately delete. Few things are more frustrating. Job's third friend, Zophar, approaches Job like a telemarketer. He is insensitive, brusque, and won't take no for an answer. He leaves the same message the previous two friends left with Job: Your suffering is because of your sin.

In 11:1-6 Zophar rebukes Job for protesting his innocence. He chastises Job for his verbosity (literally "a man of lips," that is, one who is "all mouth"), his boasting of innocence (Job had said he was not wicked in 10:7, not that he was "clean" in God's eyes), his self-justification, and his ignorance of God, his wisdom, and his ways. Zophar was convinced that if God did speak to Job, he would take Zophar's side. In essence, Zophar is saying to Job, "If God were to respond to you, then you would see just how stupid you are. You should be thankful: you're not getting half of what you deserve." Why is it that those who disagree with someone often try to paint the opponent in the worst light possible? Zophar piles his weight on top of that of the other two friends; it's three against one.

Affirmation of God's Wisdom (11:7-12)

Zophar proceeds to inform Job of the greatness of God as controller of creation. There are no limits to his power, nor can Job perceive the extremities of God, which are higher than the heavens, deeper than Sheol, the abode of the dead, longer than the earth, and wider than the sea. Zophar's description of God's greatness is on target. God is an incomprehensible being. As Matthew Henry said,

> We that are so little acquainted with the divine nature are
> incompetent judges of the divine providence. . . . Note, God is
> unsearchable. The ages of his eternity cannot be numbered,
> nor the spaces of his immensity be measured; the depths of
> his wisdom cannot be fathomed, nor the reaches of his power
> bounded; the brightness of his glory can never be described,
> nor the treasures of his goodness reckoned up. (*Job to Song of
> Solomon*, 53)

Job can't deceive God concerning his own iniquity. Job is like a spiritual idiot, who can no more gain wisdom than a donkey can give birth to a human being (v. 12).

Call to Repentance (11:13-20)

Zophar exhorts Job to repent. He also essentially offers a salvation by works. Get your heart right before God, stretch out your hand toward him in humility, reform your life, and don't let wickedness dwell in your tents (vv. 13-14). Job, change your life and then God will act, giving you a clear conscience, confidence, no more memory of trouble

("You'll forget your troubles; they'll be like old, faded photographs"; v. 16 MSG); you'll have joy, hope, rest, popularity, and restored leadership (vv. 15-19).

Zophar concludes in verse 20 with a brief summary of the doom of the wicked: "But the sight of the wicked will fail. Their way of escape will be cut off, and their only hope is their last breath."

The interesting thing about Zophar's counsel regarding returning to God when you have sinned is that it is good counsel! It just doesn't apply to Job. Look within and prepare your heart; look up and stretch out your hand to God in repentance; change what you were doing wrong, and don't do it anymore; and don't let injustice be seen anywhere in your sphere of influence (vv. 13-14).

Zophar's bedside manner leaves something to be desired. It is a wonder Job did not throw him out of the hospital room! Just as Satan argued that Job serves God because God has given him much, the friends argue the inverse: God has punished Job for his sin. In fact, Job's three friends believed "that anybody old enough to spell his own name knew that since God was just, he made bad things happen to bad people and good things happen to good people" (Buechner, *Peculiar Treasures*, 34–35).

Eliphaz, Bildad, and Zophar have now each spoken to Job and analyzed his suffering. In all three cases their basic assumptions were wrong, leading them to give Job bad counsel. Job's three friends could have benefited from reading Agur, an otherwise unknown character in Scripture, who wrote Proverbs 30. In verses 5 and 6 he stated, "Every word of God is pure; he is a shield to those who take refuge in him. Don't add to his words, or he will rebuke you, and you will be proved a liar." In light of this, Agur offered a prayer, the only one recorded in Proverbs:

> *Two things I ask of you; don't deny them to me before I die: Keep falsehood and deceitful words far from me. Give me neither poverty nor wealth; feed me with the food I need. Otherwise, I might have too much and deny you, saying, "Who is the LORD?" or I might have nothing and steal, profaning the name of my God.* (Prov 30:7-10)

Agur's first prayer is particularly applicable to Job's three friends. "Falsehood" translates a Hebrew term that describes deceit, fraudulence, and worthlessness. What Eliphaz, Bildad, and Zophar had done was to speak falsely to and about Job.

The lesson here is it is difficult to determine falsehood without God's help. We are sometimes easily deceived and can deceive others.

It would seem that Job's three friends played into Satan's hands. As a liar and the father of lies, he is more proficient at deceiving us than we are at recognizing his deception. We need God's wisdom in refusing his lies. The flip side to this is we cannot speak the truth without God's help. Like Agur, Eliphaz, Bildad, and Zophar should have been more careful to avoid deception and to avoid deceiving others. Divine assistance is the only way we can consistently speak the truth.

Job's Response
JOB 12–14

Chapters 12–14 constitute Job's first response to Zophar, the first half addressed to all three friends (12:1–13:19) and the rest addressed to God (13:20–14:22). Twice Job flatly denies that his friends have won the day with their shallow arguments (12:3 and 13:2). Having dispatched the false reasoning of his friends, Job's view of God becomes a little clearer. Whatever happens, God's character is such that he will not permit the just person to go unavenged (13:7-16). Job expresses little hope of acquittal, but sink or swim, he will embrace his sentence, whatever God may pronounce (13:14-22).

This speech is located "at the junction between the first and second cycles of speeches. It signals a climax in the progress of Job's emotions and lays down a marker for the future development of the plot of the work as a whole" (Clines, "Brief Explanation," 261). Job addresses the three friends in chapters 12–13 and gives them an earful. His tone is assertive and sarcastic. In chapter 14 Job offers an elegy on the human condition, with the exception of verses 13-17 where Job focuses on himself.

Retribution Not Validated by Experience (12:1-12)

Job begins his response with fierce irony: "No doubt you are the people, and wisdom will die with you!" (v. 2). Job defends his own intelligence and knowledge of the things his friends have spoken about: "I am not inferior to you" (v. 3). He reminds his friends that they don't hold a monopoly on knowledge or wisdom. Job has knowledge equal to theirs. Job chafed under the well-worn platitudes his friends had tried to drum into his ears. *The Message* captures Job's feelings at this point in 13:4-5: "You graffiti my life with lies. You're a bunch of pompous quacks! I wish you'd shut your mouths—silence is your only claim to wisdom."

In addition, Job presents facts of life inconsistent with the inadequate theology of his friends. Job's argument refutes the friends' false notions that material wealth is given by God for living justly, for even thieves receive material wealth (vv. 5-6).

Job acknowledges God as controller of creation. He controls animals and birds (v. 7), plants and fish (v. 8). All these things come from the "hand of the Lord,"[32] a Semitic concept of expressing God as Creator by means of his power (vv. 9-10).

God's Sovereign Power (12:13-25)

To those like Job's three friends who would pin their faith to the sleeve of tradition, Job points out that the sayings of the ancients are not to be accepted indiscriminately but should be examined (v. 11). Tradition is good; God's words are better. Job ascribes four attributes to God that people can experience: wisdom, strength, counsel, and understanding (v. 13). "True wisdom and real power belong to God; from him we learn how to live, and also what to live for" (MSG). Wisdom is to know what to do; strength is to have the power to carry it out.

In verses 14-16 Job affirms that the ultimate and inscrutable power of God shapes all events, both in the natural and in the human worlds. God's power is seen in nature: "When he withholds water, everything dries up, and when he releases it, it destroys the land" (v. 15). Both the "deceived" and the "deceiver" belong to God, Job asserts. "The deceivers make tools of the deceived, but the great God makes tools of them both" (Henry, *Job to Song of Solomon*, 59).

In verses 17-21 he traces God's power and control in the history of classes of people who themselves wield power on earth—counselors, kings, priests, elders, and princes. God controls those who control society.

In verses 22-25 Job asserts God's control on national communities and their leaders. God "makes nations great, then destroys them" (v. 23).

---

[32] Job 12:9 is the only place among the speeches in chapters 3–37 where the name *Yahweh* for God occurs. F. Delitzsch suggested that it occurs here because Job is quoting an old proverb (Keil and Delitzsch, *Job*, Kindle edition).

The Friends' Arguments Are Worthless (13:1-12)

Job 13:1-28 comprises three sections: 1-5, 6-17,[33] and 18-28. In the first section Job reminds the three friends that he sees and knows what they know: "I am not inferior to you" (v. 2). Job is not really interested in remonstrating with the friends but rather desires an audience with God to argue his case before him (v. 3). Job's friends "use lies like plaster" and are "worthless healers" (v. 4) ("idol-physicians, who can do me no more good than an idol can," as Matthew Henry put it; *Job to Song of Solomon*, 61). Job's words are more than just a schoolyard taunt. His three friends were trying to put a false face on the real truth of things, like diagnosing cancer as a minor ache or pulled muscle. (Note to preachers: I wonder in what ways we have been worthless healers in our preaching—rolling our thin veneers of a watered-down gospel to a sin-sick world?) Job concludes this section by wishing the friends would simply "shut up and let that be [their] wisdom" (v. 5). In these five verses Job asserts that he understands the issues as well as his friends, he would rather talk to God than the friends, and they deserve condemnation for their uncharitable and unjust treatment.

The second section, 13:6-17, is divided by the CSB between verses 12 and 13. In verses 6-12 Job charges his friends with being false witnesses for God. They are guilty of perjury. They speak deceitfully and with partiality. Their declaration of Job's guilt is groundless. Their only goal is to protect the reputation of God, which needs no protection. They have not listened to Job closely and have not known God or represented him correctly (Estes, *Handbook*, 66).

Job Pleads for God to Hear His Case (13:13-28)

In verses 13-17 Job begins with a direct imperative: "Be quiet, and I will speak." Job explicitly says he is less interested now in self-preservation and more interested in justice.[34] Job reasons in verse 16 that "no godless person can appear before [God]," and thus, if Job were granted an audience before God, that would be tacit evidence of his innocence.

---

[33] The CSB carries the section through v. 19 and begins a new section with v. 20 where Job addresses God directly.

[34] Verse 15 contains a difficult textual problem. Accessible summaries of the issues can be found in Ballentine, *Job*, 212; and Wharton, *Job*, 69–70.

Job concludes this subsection the way he began in verse 13: "Pay close attention to my words." In verses 18-28 Job begins by boldly declaring, "I have prepared my case; I know that I am right. Can anyone indict me? If so, I will be silent and die" (vv. 18-19). This section is well known for the trial metaphor and the legal language Job employs.[35] He proceeds by seeking from God two pretrial conditions: remove your heavy hand of affliction from me, and remove your frightening terror from me (vv. 20-21). Continuing in the courtroom scene, Job offers to serve as either the defendant or the prosecutor, whatever God chooses (v. 22). Job peppers God with five questions in this subsection, the first in verse 19 and four more in 23-25, when Job asks God to function as a prosecutor and enumerate his "iniquities," "sins," and "transgression" (v. 23). "Why do you hide your face and consider me your enemy?" (v. 24). "Will you frighten a wind-driven leaf? Will you chase after dry straw?" (v. 25). Could his troubles now be the result of his youthful "iniquities," Job wonders. Job feels God has imprisoned him ("You put my feet in the stocks") and obtained a divine FISA warrant to surveil his every move (You "stand watch over all my paths") (v. 27). The result? Job feels like he is rotting away like an old garment (v. 28).

Peterson renders Job 13:20-26 in *The Message* in a way that would be helpful to the preacher:

> *Please, God, I have two requests; grant them so I'll know I count with you: First, lay off the afflictions; the terror is too much for me. Second, address me directly so I can answer you, or let me speak and then you answer me. How many sins have been charged against me? Show me the list—how bad is it? Why do you stay hidden and silent? Why treat me like I'm your enemy? Why kick me around like an old tin can? Why beat a dead horse? You compile a long list of mean things about me, even hold me accountable for the sins of my youth.*

---

[35] "Perhaps the most significant single legal term used is the root [*rib*], which is used eleven times in Job (seven times as a verb—9:3; 10:2; 13:8,19; 23:6; 33:13; 40:2; and four times as a noun—13:6; 29:16; 31:13,35). As a verb in the Old Testament, it means 'to make a complaint or accusation (by engaging in hostile unilateral speech activity) against an aggrieving party.' As a noun, it denotes 'a complaint or accusation by an aggrieving party, one held responsible for a grievance.' Although the word [*rib*] in the Old Testament sometimes describes a dispute outside court, it is used in Job solely in a legal sense as a metaphor to portray a 'lawsuit' between Job and God" (Parsons, "Structure and Purpose," 29).

Hardship, Hopelessness, and Death (14:1-22)

Job 14 is the final chapter of Job's response to Zophar and the closure of the first cycle of speeches. It is composed of four sections: 1-6, where Job outlines the nature of human life—it is hardship and hopelessness; 7-12, where Job speaks of the possibility of hope for a tree that has been cut down but an absence of hope for humanity—death is the end; 13-17, where Job speaks of the illusion of hope—if a man dies, will he live again?; and 18-22, where the naturalistic erosion of land becomes a metaphor for gradual disintegration of all hope for humankind as represented by Job.

In Job 14:1-6, even though he is responding to Zophar, Job continues his direct address to God begun in 13:20. For Job, humanity is condemned to a brief and troubled life, like a flower that blossoms then withers or like a fleeting shadow (vv. 1-2). Job's rhetorical question in verse 3 leads to his statement that people must live within the limits God has prescribed for them, so that God has hemmed each person in and loaded him or her down with troubles squeezed into a brief life span. Life is like a hired laborer compelled to serve a harsh taskmaster. Happiness is a tiny island in an ocean of blood, sweat, and tears. Since this is the case, the least God could do is to grant some respite from his overbearing, relentless watchfulness so a person can stumble his way to his inevitable end without undue harassment (v. 6).

Job's despair continues in verses 7-12 with the stark reality that our mortality leads to death. A tree, when it is felled, at least has the hope that new shoots will sprout. But not so with humanity. When death comes, that's it. A person is like a lake or riverbed that goes permanently dry; death cannot be avoided.

In one of the most famous passages in the book of Job, Job asks in verse 14, "When a person dies, will he come back to life?" In verses 13-17 Job's hope is for a resurrection after death. After God's wrath subsides, Job longs for some semblance of reconciliation with God and resurrection. This is the first time in the book the question of life after death is raised. "Job sees, as it were, a light in the keyhole of the door in heaven which John the apostle saw opened full wide" (Harris, "Doctrine of God," 174). Job's question is answered by Jesus in John 11:25-26: "I am the resurrection and the life. The one who believes in me, even if he dies, will live. Everyone who lives and believes in me will never die." Alexander Maclaren expressed it well:

Job's question waited long for an answer. Weary centuries rolled away; but at last the doubting, almost despairing, cry put into the mouth of the man of sorrows of the Old Testament is answered by the Man of Sorrows of the New. (*Esther, Job*, 43)

Job speaks of "waiting" out the days of his "struggle" until his "relief comes" (v. 14). Job uses a metaphor for life as compulsory military service, with the weary soldier fighting battle after battle and finally, exhausted, lifting his eyes to see a fresh squadron of soldiers coming to relieve him. After it is all over, surely God will want his much-afflicted child back, and his sins will be covered over and sealed in a bag of forgetfulness (vv. 15-17). Imagine all your sins stuffed in a garbage bag, tied off at the top, and thrown away. This is what Job longs for in his desire for fellowship with God again.

Job's wishful thinking is once again overshadowed by his melancholy in the final section, 14:18-22. The years pass, our bodies decay, Job is all alone, death awaits, and there is no hope. As the mountains erode and are left in rubble, so God destroys Job's hope (v. 19). Death separates and ends all communication with people (v. 21). Job's final thought: "He feels only the pain of his own body and mourns only for himself" (v. 22). Job feels hopeless in the face of his sufferings. God is nowhere to be found.

The silence of God to Job's pleas at the end of this first speech cycle must have been deafening. Job cannot understand why God has not responded to him. Job must have felt like Paul Newman's character, the convict Luke in *Cool Hand Luke*, when he calls out to God in the pouring rain during a thunderstorm: "Let me know you're up there. Come on. Love me, hate me, kill me, anything. Just let me know it!" Or at the end of the movie in the old, empty church scene at night, when Luke, on the run from the law, asks,

> "Anybody here? . . . I know I got no cause to ask much, but even so you gotta admit you ain't dealt me no cards in a long time. It looks like you got things fixed so I can't never win out. . . . When does it end? What have you got in mind for me? What do I do now?"

What do you do in your life when you go through a period of time when God says to you, "No comment"? Most of us are acutely aware of

God's silence when we need him the most. "Just send me an angel, God, with some word! Say something! Anything!"

Although Job can't understand God's silence in his suffering, we know that the cross is God's megaphone (to adapt an illustration from C. S. Lewis about pain as God's megaphone). The cross loudly proclaims to us God's love and provision for our sins so that all suffering, whether the result of our sin or others' sins or God's will for our lives to glorify him, is answered.

Job's hopelessness does not have to be your hopelessness. Because of the cross of Jesus, we have hope. Remember—biblical hope is not an uncertain, wishy-washy thing like it is in our vocabulary. "I hope it doesn't rain." "I hope I make an A on that test." "I hope I get that raise at my job." Such hope is uncertain. But the biblical word *hope* means "a settled certainty and confident expectation based on the promises of God." The author of Hebrews describes this hope in Hebrews 6:19-20:

> We have this hope as an anchor for the soul, firm and secure. It enters the inner sanctuary behind the curtain. Jesus has entered there on our behalf as a forerunner.

Because of the cross, the resurrection, and the ascension of Jesus into heaven, our hope is certain and secure for all eternity. No matter what storms come our way in this life, Jesus is our hope anchor.

Job's hope for a resurrection is met in the reality of the resurrection of Christ. Mary and Martha were distraught at their brother Lazarus's death. When Jesus arrived in Bethany, he told Martha that Lazarus would one day be raised from the dead. Martha acknowledged that this was true—he will rise in the resurrection at the last day. But Jesus had something more immediate in mind for Lazarus. Jesus told Martha in John 11:25-26,

> "I am the resurrection and the life. The one who believes in me, even if he dies, will live. Everyone who lives and believes in me will never die. Do you believe this?"

Jesus then raised Lazarus from the dead.

No matter what happens to us in this life, including death, nothing can win the victory over us. The resurrection of Christ guarantees our future resurrection. Job can have hope in his suffering, and so can you and I, because of the death and resurrection of Christ!

Some things are so important to God that they are worth interrupting the happiness and health of his children in order to accomplish them. Jesus allowed Lazarus to die for the sake of his higher purpose in Lazarus's life. You can always count on two things being true in the midst of your pain and adversity. First, God knows and hurts with you. Jesus wept at the grave of Lazarus. He weeps with us over our sorrows as well. Second, whatever God is in the process of accomplishing in our lives through suffering will *always* be for our best interest. Trust him.

The first speech cycle ends with Job's suffering unchanged. And worse still, God continues to give Job the cold shoulder.

Reflect and Discuss

1. What evidence does Job point out in life that contradicts the retribution principle?
2. Do you think Job keeps a good balance between his adversity and God's sovereignty? Why?
3. How are God's ways sometimes different from what we expect?
4. How do you explain Job's vacillation between hope and despair?
5. What, if any, connection do you see between Job's suffering and that of Christ in the New Testament?

Eliphaz's Second Speech and Job's Response

JOB 15–17

Main Idea: Eliphaz insists Job is guilty of sin and deserves God's punishment; Job disputes his friends' account of his suffering, offers again his complaint against God, and laments his hopelessness in life and death.

I. **Eliphaz's Second Speech (15)**
   A. Rejection of Job's claim to wisdom (15:1-16)
   B. The woes of the wicked (15:17-35)
II. **Job's Response (16–17)**
   A. Job's dispute with his friends (16:1-5)
   B. Personal lament and complaint against God (16:6-17)
   C. The heavenly witness (16:18-22)
   D. Job's lament (17:1-16)

Like the first cycle of speeches, the second cycle follows the same alternating order, with each of the three friends speaking followed by Job's responses. In this cycle the dialogue becomes more strained and caustic. The three friends must have sounded like belligerent prosecutors determined to bring Job down. They move speedily from friendly persuasion to vehement indictment. They constantly parade before Job extended portraits of the wicked and hold them up to Job like mirrors for him to see himself as they see him and as God sees him.

Eliphaz's Second Speech

JOB 15

Eliphaz speaks in chapter 15, and Job responds in chapters 16 and 17. Eliphaz's speech contains two sections: verses 1-16 and 17-35. The first part is divided into two subsections: verses 2-5 and 6-16. The focus of verses 2-5 is how a man condemns himself by his speaking. The focus of verses 6-16 is a restatement of Eliphaz's confidence that Job has indeed sinned. In verses 17-35 Eliphaz addresses the fate of the wicked and continues to lecture Job that the retribution principle of sin and punishment is true and Job is getting what he deserves.

Rejection of Job's Claim to Wisdom (15:1-16)

Have you ever felt like God was against you? No matter what you say or do, your predicament is such that not only is God nowhere to be found, but he seems actually to be working against you behind the scenes! Job's complaint against God in this passage indicates that is exactly how he felt. On top of that, Job's three friends continue their relentless pursuit of criticism.

In verses 1-16 Eliphaz assaults Job with a barrage of no fewer than ten questions rhetorically designed to illustrate Job's sinful attitudes and actions. Eliphaz insults Job right out of the gate in verse 2: "Does a wise man answer with empty counsel or fill himself with the hot east wind?" The east wind that would blow off the Arabian desert was stifling. Job is full of hot air, according to Eliphaz.

The vocabulary of the first six verses centers on the notion of speech: "answer," "counsel," "argue," "useless talk," "words," "say," "language," "your own mouth condemns," and "your own lips testify." According to Eliphaz, Job's speech belies his sin; Job is condemned by his own testimony.

In verses 7-16 Eliphaz begins by asking Job if he thinks he is the epitome of wisdom (vv. 7-9). The wisdom teachers of old are on our side, Job, Eliphaz says in verse 10. He then somewhat equates his counsel to Job with that of "God's consolations" (v. 11). Your anger is "against God," not me, Eliphaz states in verses 12-13. In the final subparagraph, verses 14-16, Eliphaz concludes that even God's "holy ones," presumably angels, are not pure in God's sight, much less all humans, who deserve only divine judgment; how much more so then will one who is "revolting and corrupt" be deserving of God's judgment?

The Woes of the Wicked (15:17-35)

Eliphaz begins this section with a direct imperative: "Listen to me." Eliphaz assumes the role of the wise teacher with Job as the ignorant student. All the wicked, present and future, receive the judgment they deserve. Eliphaz proceeds to enumerate examples in life that bear out his conclusion: when the rich man is at peace, a robber attacks (vv. 21-22); he wanders about looking for food (v. 23); trouble and distress terrify him because he has opposed God (vv. 24-25); though his face is covered with fat (a sign of prosperity) and his waistline bulges, he will not prosper (vv. 26-29); as the shoots wither, branches don't flourish, vines drop unripe fruit, and the olive tree sheds its blossoms, so the wicked will not escape (vv. 30-33); the company of the godless will conceive trouble and give birth to evil (vv. 34-35). *The Message* expresses these last two verses in a graphic way: "They have sex with sin and give birth to evil. Their lives are wombs for breeding deceit."

Eliphaz appears to operate with a single goal—force Job to the only reasonable conclusion: your sin has brought God's judgment.

By way of summary, Eliphaz reproves Job for justifying himself and infers many evil things Job must have done (vv. 2-13). He then asks Job to humble himself before God and accept his shame (vv. 14-16). Eliphaz rehearses a long record concerning the woeful state of the wicked and their judgments (vv. 17-35) (Henry, *Job to Song of Solomon*, 69). Eliphaz's points about the judgment of the wicked are valid. They simply don't apply to Job.

Job's Response
JOB 16–17

Job responds to Eliphaz in chapters 16–17. His indignation and disgust with his friends and their arguments are now on full display.

Job's Dispute with His Friends (16:1-5)

Eliphaz's windbag insult in 15:2 is now thrown back in his face as Job insists Eliphaz is the real windbag. Job charges all three friends as "miserable comforters" with endless empty words—literally "words of wind" (v. 3). If the situation were reversed, Job says he would be a true comforter of his friends (vv. 4-5).

Personal Lament and Complaint against God (16:6-17)

Job says that whether he speaks or remains silent, his suffering remains unabated (v. 6). God's judgment has exhausted Job—shriveled, torn, and harassed him (vv. 7-9). Like a helpless animal thrown to a pack of wolves, Job feels God has "seized [him] by the scruff of the neck" and handed him over to the wicked. Job describes his predicament as being handed over by God to archers for target practice. As if a warrior had attacked and broken through Job's defenses, he is helpless before the onslaught (vv. 10-14).

Job's personal experience with suffering gives him something of a new perspective on God. Some of the images Job uses to describe God include an enemy, a ruthless taskmaster, a spy rather than a protector, a hunter rather than a healer, one who harasses humans, and a destroyer rather than a sustainer of order (6:4; 7:1-8; 9:5-13; 10:8-17; 12:13-25; and 16:9-14). Turning to his miserable condition, Job speaks of his "sackcloth" and burying his "strength in the dust" (v. 15). Though he mourns his plight, he maintains his innocence once again: "My hands are free from violence and my prayer is pure" (v. 17).

The Heavenly Witness (16:18-22)

Once again Job comes to the brink of despair, but at the last moment holds out hope that a "witness" and "advocate" who is "in heaven" will step in to plead his case. But if the help does not come soon, Job knows he will "go the way of no return" (vv. 18-22).

Job's Lament (17:1-16)

The CSB divides Job 17 into four sections: 1-2, 3-5, 6-10, and 11-16. Job is overwhelmed by the verbal abuse he has received from his friends so that his "spirit is broken," his "days are extinguished," and "a graveyard awaits" him (v. 1). Job describes his three friends as "mockers" who surround him, and he is forced to watch and listen to their accusations, which Job calls "rebellion" (v. 2).

In verses 3-5 Job longs for someone who will put up security for him and be his "sponsor" (v. 3). This is the language of ancient commercial law. In effect, Job is asking God to cosign for him—provide security and show up in court to defend him. Verse 5 may be an ancient proverb that is obscure to us, but the essence is that if one falsely denounces his friend for a price, their children will pay a price.

Sitting on his ash heap, Job has become an "object of scorn," like a mangy tramp people shun (v. 6). He has lost so much weight that his body has become "but a shadow" (v. 7). The "upright" and "innocent" are appalled at Job's misfortune, and they don't want to associate with him, yet Job refuses to yield to the accusations that he has sinned (v. 9). "Come back and try again, all of you," Job taunts his accusers. It is as if Job is in the boxing ring, getting pummeled by his opponents, but defiantly says, "Is that all you've got? Hit me with your best shot!" (see v. 10).

In verses 11-16 Job sinks back into despair. He was so near to death that he spoke of the grave as his father and the maggot as his mother or sister. Job expresses his hopelessness: "Where then is my hope?" Job pathetically pictures his plight as he, along with his companion hope, "descend together to the dust" (vv. 15-16). R. Laird Harris translates 17:13-16:

> *If I have hope, Sheol (the grave) is my house.*
> *I will spread my couch in the darkness.*
> *I have called corruption my father and the worm my mother and sister,*
> *Where then is my hope? and who will see my hope?*
> *When my hope goes down to Sheol (the grave) and we descend together*
> *to the dust.* ("Doctrine of God," 175)

In summary, Job's response in these two chapters is set to the same melancholy tune as previously. After upbraiding his friends for their unkindness toward him (16:1-5), he describes his situation as deplorable (vv. 6-16). However, he continues to maintain his innocence and appeals to God's righteous judgment from the unrighteous censures of his friends (vv. 14-22). In chapter 17 Job reflects again on the harsh censures from his friends and appeals to God to appear and declare him right in the face of his friends who have wronged him (vv. 2-7). He hopes that his condition, though a surprise, will not be a stumbling block to good people who see him abused (vv. 8-9). Job reflects on the empty hopes his friends had offered and states that his days are numbered and, along with his body, all his hopes would be buried in the dust of death (vv. 10-16). His only comfort is the grave (Henry, *Job to Song of Solomon*, 75, 78).

Where do you turn when you have lost all hope? Like Job, do you feel like a prisoner in your own dungeon of hopelessness? Hope for you is a mirage in the desert. You feel as if the drapes have been pulled closed forever on hope. But hope is not a bedraggled prisoner of circumstances. It is a strong soldier who marches side by side with faith. Only in Jesus do we find hope. Christian hope is not optimism based on what I see around me, but it is confident expectation of what I know is above me, regardless of the circumstances I see around me. No wonder Jeremiah could say, "The person who trusts in the LORD, whose confidence indeed is the LORD, is blessed" (Jer 17:7). Paul wrote of Christ as our hope. Peter encourages us:

> *Blessed be the God and Father of our Lord Jesus Christ. Because of*
> *his great mercy he has given us new birth into a living hope through*

the resurrection of Jesus Christ from the dead and into an inheritance that is imperishable, undefiled, and unfading, kept in heaven for you. (1 Pet 1:3-4)

Just like Job, you and I need to be reminded that our hope in Christ is grounded in the resurrection of Christ. We have an inheritance that awaits us that is death proof ("imperishable"), sin proof ("undefiled"), and time proof ("unfading")! We have victory in Jesus!

Reflect and Discuss

1. According to Eliphaz, what is the life of the wicked like? How does Eliphaz use this information to condemn Job?
2. How is sin a rejection of God's wisdom?
3. Do you agree with Eliphaz that all humans are inherently sinful? Why?
4. Why is Eliphaz wrong in his condemnation of Job?
5. Compare and contrast Eliphaz's first speech with this speech. How do they differ?
6. What do Job's words reveal about his emotions concerning his friends?
7. What imagery does Job use to describe how he feels God is treating him?
8. In what way might Job have expected God to be his "witness" and "advocate"?
9. When have you felt like Job, in his oscillation between discouragement and hope?
10. If God is all good and all powerful, then why do bad things happen to good people?

Bildad's Second Speech and Job's Response

JOB 18–19

Main Idea: Bildad argues once again for the retribution principle and says Job is suffering because of his sin; Job expresses frustration with his friends and with God, and he pleads for ultimate vindication.

I. Bildad's Second Speech (18)
  A. Complaint against Job (18:1-4)
  B. Description of the wicked and their fate (18:5-21)
II. Job's Response (19)
  A. Job's continued frustration with his friends (19:1-6)
  B. Job's complaint about God's enmity (19:7-12)
  C. Job's separation from human love (19:13-22)
  D. Job's plea for ultimate vindication (19:23-27)
  E. Job's warning to the three friends (19:28-29)

Job 18 contains the second speech of Bildad. It essentially contains two parts: Job's failure to show respect for his friends whom he should be heeding (vv. 1-4) and a description of the wicked and their fate (vv. 5-21). Bildad must have been listening in on the previous exchange between Eliphaz and Job, since he makes use of many of the same terms and arguments as in chapter 15.

Bildad's Second Speech

JOB 18

Complaint against Job (18:1-4)

Are you a survivor? Not in the sense of having survived a car accident, a shipwreck, or a plane crash. I mean, are you a survivor, an overcomer, when you face the hard trials of life, even when death is staring you in the face? One of the most important lessons to grasp in life is this: "It's not about me." You will never be a survivor until you learn this lesson. Bildad's question to Job in 18:4 hits us right between the eyes: "Do you want the world redesigned to suit you? Should reality be suspended to accommodate you?" (MSG). Until we learn to look beyond ourselves and the grave that awaits us, we will never be overcomers. Just when Job was about to be overcome by it all, he exclaims in 19:25, "I know that my Redeemer lives." It's not about me; it's about Christ!

Bildad offers not a word of encouragement for Job in this second speech. He sharply reproves Job as haughty and obstinate (vv. 1-4). Bildad begins his second speech where his first left off and describes the misery of the wicked and their certain destruction (vv. 5-21). Basically, Bildad says to Job, "This is the condition of a wicked man, and therefore you are one" (Henry, *Job to Song of Solomon*, 82).

In verse 3 Bildad asks Job, "Why are we regarded as cattle, as stupid in your sight?" The Hebrew word translated "stupid" in the CSB might also be translated "unclean." Judaism goes into some detail in determining which animals are to be considered "clean" and which "unclean." One category of unclean animals is any animal that has been "torn," a Hebrew word that is customarily used as the opposite of *kosher*. Bildad employs a play on words in the next line when he says, "You who tear yourself in anger," probably a reference to 16:9 where Job says, "His anger tears at me," using the same Hebrew word. The gist of what Bildad expresses is, "How can you, who are self-admittedly unclean by virtue of being torn (though you blame it on God rather than yourself), keep on treating us as unclean animals?" (Wolfers, *Deep Things*, 92). Bildad essentially asks in verse 4, "Who do you think you are, Job? Do you think God will alter the course of nature just for your benefit?" For Job to be right, in Bildad's mind, the moral order of the universe would have to be overturned.

Description of the Wicked and Their Fate (18:5-21)

Bildad offers a description of the fate of the wicked. The light in the tents of the wicked will be extinguished. There will be no light and no fire, symbolizing no prosperity (vv. 5-6). The ungodly are tripped up by their own schemes (vv. 7-11). Bildad uses six words for "trap" in verses 8-10 ("net," "mesh," "trap," "noose," "rope," and "snare"), emphasizing that no matter which way Job tries to run, he will be caught. His strength is depleted, and disaster causes him to stumble (v. 12). Diseases were sometimes known as "death's children" because they serve death's purposes (v. 13). Verses 14 and 15 depict a nomadic tent-dwelling encampment, where evildoers and their possessions are removed from the security of their tents. In verse 16 Bildad uses the metaphor of a decaying tree with roots dying from lack of water and branches withering. The name and memory of the ungodly perish (v. 17). He is "driven" and "chased"; he has no survivor carrying on the family name where he used to live (vv. 18-19). The fate of the wicked is so calamitous that people everywhere ("those in the west . . . those in the east") are appalled (v. 20). Bildad concludes, "Indeed, such is the dwelling of the unjust man, and this is the place of the one who does not know God" (v. 21). Job fits the description of "the wicked," so Bildad concludes Job is suffering for his sin. No prosperity, no place to hide, no foundation, no name, no children, no friends, no hope in life or in death—this is Bildad's assessment of Job. Same song, second verse; a little louder, a little worse.

Job's Response
JOB 19

Job 19 contains five sections: Job expresses his ongoing frustration with his friends (vv. 1-6); he turns to God (vv. 7-12); he feels separated from human love (vv. 13-22); he believes God will vindicate him ultimately (vv. 23-27); and he warns the three friends because he may be right and they will be punished (vv. 28-29).

Job's Continued Frustration with His Friends (19:1-6)

Job responds to Bildad with a question: "How long will you torment me and crush me with words?" (v. 2). When Job uses the phrase "ten times now," he is not speaking literally but employing an idiom meaning "often" (v. 3). Job does not accept Bildad's theory that he has sinned in any way to deserve his suffering, but he says to Bildad, "Even if it is true that I have sinned, my mistake concerns only me" (v. 4), which implies, "You have no reason to stick your nose in my business!" Job's friends are intruding in an area where they do not belong. Bildad had spoken about how the wicked have their feet caught in a net of their own making (18:8); now Job says, "No, that's not it; God himself has caught me in his net" (v. 6).[36] Job overtly speaks of God's injustice toward him when he says, "It is God who has wronged me" (v. 6).

---

[36] The Hebrew word for "net" in this verse is different from the six words used in Job 18 for nets and traps. The word here connotes being driven and caught in a hunter's net.

His own perception of God's injustice kept C. S. Lewis from becoming a Christian for some time. How could there be a God who allowed so much evil in the world? Lewis explained his pilgrimage in his famous book *Mere Christianity*:

> My argument against God was that the universe seemed so cruel and unjust. But how had I got this idea of just and unjust? A man does not call a line crooked unless he has some idea of a straight line. What was I comparing this universe with when I called it unjust? If the whole show was bad and senseless from A to Z, so to speak, why did I who was supposed to be a part of the show, find myself in such violent reaction against it? . . . Of course I could have given up my idea of justice by saying it was nothing but a private idea of my own. But if I did that, then my argument against God collapsed too—for the argument depended on saying that the world was really unjust, not simply that it did not happen to please my private fancies. (*Mere Christianity*, 38–39)

Job's Complaint about God's Enmity (19:7-12)

Job speaks to and about God. Job feels God has been unjust: "I cry out, 'Violence!' but get no response; I call for help, but there is no justice" (v. 7). Job feels God is violating his own rules by how he has treated Job, so Job throws a penalty flag on God! Yet he gets no response from God— just the cold shoulder, as if God were saying, "Talk to the hand, Job; I'm not listening to you." In the remainder of this section, God ("he") is the subject of every main verb as Job enumerates ten ways in which God has been unjust in his treatment of Job: (1) "He has blocked my way," (2) "he has veiled my paths with darkness," (3) "He has stripped me of my honor," (4) he has "removed the crown from my head," (5) "He tears me down on every side," (6) "He uproots my hope like a tree," (7) "His anger burns against me," (8) "he regards me as one of his enemies," (9) "His troops advance . . . against me," and (10) "camp around my tent" [i.e., besiege me] (vv. 8-12).

Job's Separation from Human Love (19:13-22)

Job laments that all his relatives, friends, and servants have turned their backs on him. Loss of family and social fellowship devastated Job. The list includes "brothers," "acquaintances," "relatives," "close friends," "house guests," "female servants," "my servant," "my wife," "my own family," "young boys," and "my best friends" (vv. 13-19). Job's outward emaciated appearance indicates the dire situation he is in (v. 20). The final two verses are Job's pathetic appeal where he pleads with his three friends: "Have mercy on me, my friends, have mercy, for God's hand has struck me." The repetition of "mercy" in the Hebrew text places particular emphasis on Job's pleading.

Job's Plea for Ultimate Vindication (19:23-27)

Job 19:23-27 is the most well-known part of the entire book. Verses 23-24 express Job's desire to have his innocence inscribed on a scroll or chiseled in stone. Job would write something like, "I, Job, do solemnly swear that I have committed no sin to warrant the catastrophe that has befallen me!" (Archer, *Book of Job*, 74).

Verses 25-27 merit greater attention in this section, for it is likely the peak of Job's confidence in his future vindication, and that by God himself.[37] Job says, "I know that my Redeemer lives" in verse 25. Who is this Redeemer? His identity is not clearly stated in the text. There are two basic views. Some say Job is referencing a human arbiter such as he had requested previously, as in 9:33 and 16:19. Others identify the Redeemer as God himself, or Christ, since Job says in verse 26, "I will see God in my flesh."[38] These verses are used in Handel's *Messiah* as a prediction of the coming of Christ.

The Hebrew word translated "Redeemer" is used forty-four times in the Old Testament. The root meaning of the verb is "to lay claim to a person; to free or deliver." "A redeemer in the Old Testament was a person who provided protection or legal preservation for a close relative who could not do so for himself" (Zuck, *Job*, 89). The word is used of Boaz, who "redeemed" Ruth because he was her *go'el*, her "kinsman-redeemer."

The Hebrew of verse 25 is emphatic: "I, even I, know . . . ." "At the end" this "Redeemer" will "stand on the dust." The phrase *at the end* is actually an adjective in the Hebrew text describing the Redeemer as "the last one" or "he who comes last." In other words, God will have the final say. The word translated "dust" can also be translated "soil."

---

[37] The text is also complicated by textual and hermeneutical issues of uncertainty that cannot be discussed in detail here. Consult the exegetical commentaries on Job for details.

[38] Both Jerome and Gregory think Job saw Christ in his resurrection (Gregory, *Morals*, xiv.67).

Job's Redeemer is living and will stand on the earth and testify. The Redeemer will have the final word.

The time of this event is stated in verse 26: "Even after my skin has been destroyed, yet I will see God in my flesh." This verse is notoriously difficult to translate. The Hebrew word translated "destroyed" could be translated "flayed" in the figurative sense of Job's skin peeling because of his epidermal disease, as a picture of slow death. The verb means "to be stripped off" and is so used of underbrush in Isaiah 10:34.

The meaning of verse 26b is also complicated: "I will see God in my flesh." Again the question of timing is raised. Does Job mean he will see God while still alive, or does he mean he will see God at some point after his death, perhaps from the vantage point of a resurrection body? The latter is the most likely because of the Hebrew parallelism of the two propositions in verse 26. The first part of verse 26 speaks of "after" Job's death, so the parallel second part speaks of a time after death also. This is a remarkable affirmation of life after death that repudiates the errors of annihilationism or soul sleep.

So certain was Job that he would see God that he repeats the point in verse 27. "He himself would see God, face to face, and he would not be a stranger or enemy to Job, as he was then" (Zuck, *Job*, 91). The God whom Job expects to see after his death in his resurrection body will be no stranger to him but rather the faithful, redeeming God he has always known (Archer, *Book of Job*, 76). Job's final statement, "My heart longs within me," expresses his emotional exhaustion and yet exhilaration of the future prospect of such an encounter with God himself.

Did Job's expectation of seeing God mean after death and in a resurrected body or after death but not in a resurrected body? The text does not say. Only through New Testament revelation can we know that Job would indeed see God in a resurrected body. Zuck's analysis of the important questions in this text is worth noting:

> After he was dead, then Job would **see God**. He would continue in a conscious existence; he would not be annihilated or sink into soul sleep. But how could he say he would see the Lord **in his flesh** after **he had** just said he would die? Either he meant he would receive a resurrection body . . . or he meant he would see God "apart from" any physical flesh at all, . . . that is, in his conscious existence after death but before the resurrection. . . . This gazing on God for all eternity

will be **with** his **own eyes** (either the eyes of his resurrected
body, or figuratively the eyes of his soul). Job would no longer
be like a stranger to God, for God would be on his side. ("The
Certainty," 280; emphasis in original)

Job's Warning to the Three Friends (19:28-29)

In the final two verses Job returns to addressing his friends directly. He
offers a warning and a reason for the warning. We might paraphrase
what Job says in verses 28 and 29 this way: "If you think the root problem
is Job [and it's not], and you try to convince him it is, then beware and
know that you are placing yourselves in harm's way of God's judgment
in the same way you are accusing Job of being under the wrath of God
for his sin."

In summary, Job asserts that his "comforters" added to his affliction
(vv. 2-7). Yet Job identified God as the source of his affliction (vv. 8-12).
Because of his severe suffering, his family and friends were standoffish
(vv. 20-22). Job's only comfort is his hope of happiness in the other world.
He desired that his confession of faith might be recorded as evidence of
his sincerity (vv. 23-27). Finally, Job cautions his friends not to persist in
their hard censures of him (vv. 28-29) (Henry, *Job to Song of Solomon*, 85).

Like Job, who said because his Redeemer lives he will see God after
his resurrection, we know that death is not the end. The resurrection
of Christ guarantees my resurrection. Whether I die young or live to be
a hundred, whether I suffer on a bed of pain or die peacefully in my
sleep, either way Christ guarantees my being ushered into his presence
for all eternity. Like Job, I know that my Redeemer lives! And, as the
song says, . . .

Because He lives I can face tomorrow;
Because He lives all fear is gone;
Because I know He holds the future,
And life is worth the living
Just because He lives.

And then one day I'll cross the river;
I'll fight life's final war with pain;
And then as death gives way to vict'ry,
I'll see the lights of glory and I'll know He lives.
(Bill and Gloria Gaither, "Because He Lives")

Reflect and Discuss

1. How do you think Bildad's approach to Job and suffering marginalizes God's activity in his world?
2. What does Bildad think of God's involvement in human life? How personal is God in our lives?
3. Does every act, good or bad, receive the same consequence? Explain your answer.
4. "Wicked people always receive adversity, and adversity only comes on the wicked." What are the operative words in this sentence that make it incorrect?
5. How does Bildad's assessment of Job contradict God's assessment of Job in the prologue?
6. What is the meaning of the "kinsman-redeemer" Job refers to?
7. Would you equate the "Redeemer" here with God, Jesus, or someone else?
8. When Job says, "I will see God in my flesh," what does that imply he believes about the resurrection?
9. How does the resurrection of Christ impact our future resurrection?
10. What lessons about counseling those who are hurting do you glean from this chapter?

Zophar's Second Speech and Job's Response

JOB 20–21

Main Idea: Zophar asserts the retribution principle: the wicked will be judged and perish; Job demonstrates that the wicked do not always suffer though they ultimately die for their sins.

I. **Zophar's Assertion of the Retribution Principle (20)**
   A. The wicked will perish forever (20:1-11).
   B. The wicked will experience God's wrath (20:12-19).
   C. The wicked will be destroyed (20:20-29).
II. **Job's Response (21)**
   A. Job appeals for a sympathetic hearing (21:1-6).
   B. Job describes the prosperity of the wicked (21:7-16).
   C. Job affirms that the wicked ultimately die for their sins (21:17-22).
   D. Job asserts that death is the great equalizer (21:23-26).
   E. Job concludes that the wicked sometimes escape judgment in this life (21:27-34).

It always depresses me when I see a movie where the good guy gets shafted in the end and the bad guy gets off scot-free. In this world sometimes the wicked don't get what they deserve. There was never a more inequitable ending than what happened to Jesus when he died on the cross. Here was the perfect Son of God who never sinned, yet he was sentenced to capital punishment. Ironically, if he had not died, then all of us *would* die—not only physically but eternally.

Zophar's Assertion of the Retribution Principle
JOB 20

Job 20 is Zophar's second speech. In his first speech he sought to diagnose Job's problem as God's judgment due to sin, and he exhorted Job to repent. The second speech begins with a vitriolic, impatient diatribe followed by a discourse on the brevity of life the wicked experience and the consequent judgment the wicked bring on themselves. Zophar charges Job with rejecting God himself because Job criticizes God's administration of justice in the world.

The Wicked Will Perish Forever (20:1-11)

The chapter is divided into three sections: verses 1-11, 12-19, and 20-29. In verses 1-11 Zophar argues that history testifies the wicked will come to a speedy end and will be swept away, leaving nothing.

Zophar caustically asserts that Job should know that history reveals that the celebration of the wicked is short-lived (vv. 4-5). The height of success and influence the wicked one achieves will be matched by the depth of his fall, where "he will vanish forever like his own dung" (v. 7). The wicked one will vanish "like a dream" (v. 8), and he will be seen no more (v. 9). His children will be affected as well, becoming like beggars (v. 10). Though he be vigorous physically, he will ultimately die (v. 11).

The Wicked Will Experience God's Wrath (20:12-19)

Employing the metaphor of a sour stomach, Zophar likens the wicked person to one who enjoys the sweet taste of evil, but it becomes like "cobras' venom inside him" and he will "vomit it up; God will force it from his stomach." The poison of his evil deeds will kill the wicked (vv. 12-16). Then Zophar shifts the metaphor slightly to say the wicked will not enjoy "the fruit of his labor" or "the profits from his trading" (vv. 17-18). The "rivers flowing with honey and curds" (curdled milk) refers to the delicacies of the Middle East and serve as symbols of prosperity. The reason for this judgment from God is the wicked person's oppression of the poor (v. 19). Zophar concludes this section by telling Job that his impoverishment is God's judgment on Job for impoverishing the poor.

The Wicked Will Be Destroyed (20:20-29)

Zophar concludes his speech with a rhetorical tirade against the insatiable craving of the wicked for more riches, resulting in the loss of all prosperity. The wicked finds himself a fugitive who cannot escape the avenging arrows of God's justice. "A fire unfanned by human hands" (v. 26) consumes the wicked. Heaven and earth will expose his wickedness, and his possessions will be removed in the day of God's anger (vv. 27-28). Verse 29 provides the summary of Zophar's second speech (which will be his last): "This is the wicked person's lot from God, the inheritance God ordained for him" (v. 29).

In this last verse we see clearly Zophar's theological viewpoint: the law of retribution—God is judging Job for his sin. As far as Zophar is concerned, the suffering and evil that have befallen Job are directly from the hand of God, and the reason for such suffering is Job's sin. Whereas previously Job's friends left him with no hope, here Zophar leaves him with no escape—God's judgment is inevitable. Job will have no place to hide.

For Zophar, there are no special cases with God. If someone suffers, he has sinned and is being condemned. There is no "innocent until proven guilty" with Zophar. It's all cut-and-dried. It's that simple. Zophar no longer pleads with Job to repent. All Job can expect is certain and total destruction.

In summary, Zophar's long harangue is monotone: the misery and ruin of the wicked. The wicked person's prosperity is short and his ruin sure (vv. 4-9). Job's misery is exemplified by . . .

> a diseased body, a troubled conscience, a ruined estate, a
> beggared family, an infamous name and that he himself should
> perish under the weight of divine wrath: All this is most curiously
> described here in lofty expressions and lively similitudes; and it
> often proves true in this world, and always in another, without
> repentance (v. 10-29). (Henry, *Job to Song of Solomon*, 90)

Job's Response
JOB 21

The second cycle of speeches comes to a close with Job's response to Zophar. The content of his response is interesting when compared to Zophar's speech in Job 20. There are numerous parallels where Job counteracts Zopher's every assertion (Zuck, *Job*, 98). Here Job summarizes his counterarguments to all three of his friends in this second speech cycle. The chapter is divided into five sections: verses 1-6, 7-16, 17-22, 23-26, and 27-34.

Job Appeals for a Sympathetic Hearing (21:1-6)

Job requests that his friends listen carefully and remain silent so he can speak. That would be a comfort to him. "Then after I have spoken, you may continue mocking," Job sarcastically remarks (vv. 2-3). As Buechner said, Job's friends were a bunch of theological quacks, and the smartest thing they could do was shut up, but they were too busy explaining things to listen (*Peculiar Treasures*, 34).

Job said his complaint was with God, not his friends, and because God did not respond, why shouldn't Job be impatient (vv. 3-4)? One look at Job in his emaciated condition brought on by suffering should silence the three friends. Job himself was certainly "terrified" when he thought about his situation (vv. 5-6).

Job Describes the Prosperity of the Wicked (21:7-16)

The fact is the wicked do sometimes prosper. Honesty is not always the policy that succeeds, and crime sometimes pays. Job makes the point that if one can cite instances of the wicked experiencing success, then God's justice is not always demonstrable in these cases. Job paints the picture of some wicked people who enjoy living to a ripe old age, experience prominence, enjoy children and grandchildren, live in security, possess fertile herds, enjoy the merriment of music, live in peace, and die peacefully. Though they experience all these good things, Job says the wicked have no desire to know or serve God, and in fact, they deliberately reject him. Bildad had claimed in 18:21 that the one who did not know God suffered; Job turned the tables on him and demonstrated that sometimes the one who rejects God does *not* suffer (vv. 14-15)! Job rightly concludes that the prosperity of the wicked is "not of their own doing" but comes from the hand of God. Finally, Job clearly states that he does not affirm the wicked or their lifestyle in any way (v. 16).

Job Affirms that the Wicked Ultimately Die for Their Sins (21:17-22)

Job affirms that the wicked, regardless of station in life, ultimately die for their own sins. Their sins are not necessarily punished in the wicked person's children. Job asserts a dead person would not know what his children were suffering anyway, nor would he care. The wicked should suffer retribution for their own sins (vv. 19-21). Job pointed out the error of his friends in that they thought they could "teach God knowledge," meaning tell him what to do. He judges all people, even the universe, from his lofty position in heaven (v. 22).

Job Asserts that Death Is the Great Equalizer (21:23-26)

The next section is Job's claim that death is the great equalizer—all come to judgment regardless of whether or not they suffer in this life. Your lot in life is no foolproof determiner of your character. "Job's opponents should not seek to tell God to judge a person's life by his bank account or his medical chart" (Zuck, *Job*, 100).

Job Concludes that the Wicked Sometimes Escape Judgment in This Life (21:27-34)

The final section is Job's closing point, that Zophar needs to face the facts: even foreign travelers who have seen the world testify to the fact that the wicked sometimes become wealthy, are influential, live with success, and die with honor. There are too many exceptions to Zophar's theological rule of retribution. Zophar has failed to convince Job of his own sin, much less that a narrow theology of retribution is true. So ends the second cycle of speeches.

In summary, Job agrees that sometimes God passes judgment against the wicked in this life, but sometimes he does not. The wicked are sometimes hardened by prosperity (vv. 14-16). Job describes their ultimate ruin, but only after a long reprieve (vv. 17-21). Job finds variety in God's providence toward humanity in general and the wicked in particular (vv. 22-26). He defeats the friends' arguments by showing that when it comes to the wicked, they often escape judgment in this world and only receive their just punishment in the next (vv. 27-34) (Henry, *Job to Song of Solomon*, 94).

What good would it do for you to have a fortune yet not be able to access it? That is the ultimate condition of all who die without Christ. Regardless of their earthly wealth, position, or power, without Christ they face an eternal destiny separated from God.

Stefan Thomas, a resident of San Francisco, had seen his Bitcoin account grow to about $220 million. He had the treasure locked on a hard drive that would erase its data after ten password attempts. Unfortunately, Stefan lost the paper where he wrote down the password! He attempted to input the correct password eight times without success. Stefan told an interviewer, "You sort of question your own self-worth. What kind of person loses something this important?" Great question. But the loss of $200 million is nothing compared to the loss of your own soul in eternity. Without God's password, Christ, there is no salvation and no heaven for you.

Since we live on this side of the cross of Christ, we understand what Job could not know during his day. Christ's suffering on the cross holds the key to understanding our own suffering. Life is unfair in many ways. But Jesus took on all the unfairness, along with all the sin as well, when he died on the cross. He rose again and demonstrated the defeat of suffering and death by means of suffering and death!

The Golden Gate Bridge in San Francisco is a magnificent sight. Engineers who constructed the bridge had to take into account three loads, or stresses: the dead load, the live load, and the wind load.

> The dead load is the weight of the bridge itself. The live load is the weight of the daily traffic that the bridge must carry. The wind load is the pressure of the storms that beat on the bridge. The designer plans for bracings that will enable the bridge to bear all these loads.
>
> In our lives, too, we need bracings that make it possible to carry the dead load of self, the live load of daily living, and the wind load of emergencies. When we place our trust in Christ, he gives us the strength we need to withstand these various stresses. He thus gives our lives usefulness, stability, and durability. (Swindoll, *Tardy Oxcart*, 578–79)

Like Job, though we may be innocent of some specific sins we are falsely accused of, the fact is none of us is completely innocent. We are all guilty sinners in need of God's grace and redemption. Grace and redemption have come to us through Christ Jesus. Suffering is real; life is sometimes unfair. But by the stripes of Isaiah's Suffering Servant, Jesus, we are healed! Jesus provides the bracings we need for the bridge of life.

Reflect and Discuss

1. How much of Zophar's depiction of the wicked is true?
2. Why does Zophar's depiction of the wicked not apply to Job?
3. Does Zophar think Job will receive divine condemnation no matter what? What part of Zophar's speech leads you to that conclusion?
4. Why do you think Zophar refrains from calling Job to repent?

5. Compare Zophar's approach to Job with Romans 6:23.
6. How does Job's description of the wicked compare to that of the three friends?
7. How does Job's description of God's ways in the world differ from that of his friends?
8. What does Job reject that his friends accept?
9. In what way, if any, is the retribution principle valid?
10. Summarize the arguments of each of Job's friends to this point.

Conclusion of the Second Cycle of Speeches

JOB 15–21

Little new ground is broken during this second cycle of speeches, as the friends repeat essentially what they said in the first cycle but with a more caustic and condemning tone. They maintain the retribution principle with respect to suffering in Job's case. Job must be guilty of great sin.

> To Job's friends, theology is a lens through which to examine reality, and for this reason they tend to see only the way things *ought to be*. . . . Against the systematic tidiness that Job's friends try to impose upon this chaos, Job asserts a healthy belief in the present rein of anarchy. (Mason, *Gospel according to Job*, 232; emphasis in original)

Their focus is single-minded: a terrible fate awaits the wicked, and this will be Job's end if he does not repent.

Job continues to maintain his innocence before God and firmly rejects their calls to repentance. Job's responses to his friends sometimes contain elements of rebuttal to their logic, but they always express his desire to hear from God. Although God has final veto power over everything Satan does, for the time being God seems to exercise his veto erratically (Mason, *Gospel According to Job*, 234). At least that's how Job sees it. "Life is unfair not because God is, or because he is nonexistent. God holds back his fairness for a future dispensation" (Mason, *Gospel According to Job*, 236).

Eliphaz's Third Speech and Job's Response

JOB 22–24

Main Idea: Eliphaz accuses Job of sin and calls on him to repent and return to God; Job affirms God's sovereignty and justice against injustice but laments he cannot find God anywhere in his suffering.

I. **Eliphaz's Third Speech (22)**
   A. Eliphaz accuses Job (22:1-11).
   B. Eliphaz explains how God relates to the wicked (22:12-20).
   C. Eliphaz calls on Job to repent and return to God (22:21-30).
II. **Job's Response (23–24)**
   A. Job desires to present his case to God (23:1-7).
   B. Job can't find God but remains confident (23:8-17).
   C. Civil injustice—the poor (24:1-12)
   D. Criminal injustice—the rebels (24:13-17)
   E. The final fate of the wicked (24:18-25)

The third cycle of speeches (22–27) is similar to the other two with three exceptions. First, in this cycle Zophar does not speak. Second, only Eliphaz calls on Job to repent and return to God. Third, Eliphaz and Bildad attack Job with accusations of specific sins they presume he has committed.

Eliphaz's Third Speech

JOB 22

Most commentators place Job 22:1-5 together as a paragraph unit, but the CSB places 1-3 together and begins a new paragraph with verse 4. Following the introductory verse 1, verses 2-5 contain six questions followed by Eliphaz's answers in verses 6-11. Thus, we could take 1-11 together as one paragraph unit. The other two sections are 12-20 and 21-30.

Eliphaz Accuses Job (22:1-11)

When I was a child, I loved to play the game hide-and-seek. It was especially fun when all the kids in the neighborhood got together at dusk to play. If you could find a really good place to hide, no one could find you! In this section Job feels like God is playing hide-and-seek with him. Job longs to present his case of innocence to God, but it is as if God is hiding from him. On the other hand, Job wishes he could hide from his three friends. Once again Eliphaz accuses Job.

Eliphaz sees things this way: Since a person's goodness in no way adds to God's use or profit, God would not send prosperity on some and suffering on others for his own advantage. The cause of either prosperity or suffering must lie in those who receive them from God (vv. 1-3). Eliphaz draws the logical conclusion that it must be Job's sins that occasioned his suffering (vv. 4-5).

In verses 6-11 Eliphaz produces a trumped-up laundry list of Job's sins that have somehow remained secret until now. He essentially says, Job, you have used power unjustly; you have been uncharitable; you have shown partiality to the wealthy; and you have not acted in a socially just way with the underprivileged.

> Job must have withheld pawned clothing from his penniless relatives, denied water to the thirsty and food to the starving and victimized widows and orphans for such severe judgments to have befallen him from the Lord. (Archer, *Book of Job*, 78)

How Eliphaz knows that these are Job's sins we are not told by him or the narrator. Certainly Job has confessed to none of these things.

Eliphaz Explains How God Relates to the Wicked (22:12-20)

Eliphaz turns from his laundry list of Job's supposed sins to Job's attitude of insolence against God. He reminds Job that God sees and knows all the evil deeds of people, even when they think God does not see, and in time he brings judgment against them. Zuck captures well the irony and error of Eliphaz's words in 12-14:

> Eliphaz trumped up a falsehood, for Job had never questioned God's omniscience (see 21:22). His justice, yes; but not His knowledge. In fact, God's awareness of all things—with

apparent indifference—was what frustrated Job. Furthermore, Job had not questioned God's *ability* to judge; he challenged God's *failure* to judge. (*Job*, 105; emphasis in original)

Thus, Eliphaz asserts Job is not only ethically wrong in his behavior (vv. 6-11) but theologically wrong in his beliefs (vv. 12-20) (Estes, *Job*, 134).

Eliphaz repeats Job's words from 21:16—"The counsel of the wicked is far from me!"—in a possible jest at what Job had said coupled with Eliphaz's own disavowal of the counsel of wicked people (v. 18). The righteous rejoice when God condemns the wicked (vv. 19-20).

Eliphaz Calls on Job to Repent and Return to God (22:21-30)

The final section of Eliphaz's speech urges Job to repent and promises him if he returns to God, then God's goodness will come to him (v. 21). Eliphaz employs several direct imperatives and conditional clauses introduced by "if" to encode imperatival intent to urge Job to repent. The phrase "come to terms" in verse 21 means "yield." Eliphaz urges Job to "be at peace," "receive instruction," "place his sayings in [his] heart," "return," "banish injustice," and "consign [his] gold to the dust."[39] If Job does these things, then

> "the Almighty will be [his] gold. . . . Then [he] will delight in the Almighty. . . . [He] will pray to him, and he will hear [Job], and [Job] will fulfill [his] vows. When [he makes] a decision, it will be carried out, and light will shine on [Job's] ways." (vv. 21-28)

In other words, Eliphaz assured Job if he would repent of his sin, he would experience four results: wealth, spiritual fellowship with God, success, and influence. Archer summarizes Eliphaz's final words in verses 29-30: "Best of all, your new life of godliness will make you a real influence for good in restoring others who have likewise fallen into sin" (*Book of Job*, 79).

---

[39] The location of Ophir, the source of gold in v. 24b, is debated, but it was known for its high-quality gold; Estes, *Job*, 137.

Job's Response
JOB 23–24

In chapters 23 and 24 Job makes his third reply to Eliphaz. Job's frustration and desperation continue to intensify. Job longed for an opportunity to present his case to God (23:1-7), but God remained silent in spite of Job's repeated claims of innocence (23:8-17). In chapter 24 Job laments that God remains inactive and silent in the face of injustice, where Job, one who is innocent, is punished, while others who are guilty seem to evade God's judgment.

Job Desires to Present His Case to God (23:1-7)

Job is convinced that if he had an opportunity to plead his case before God, God would act justly. Job would act as his own defense attorney and argue his case persuasively, then listen to God's response. Job's brick wall is that he knew his own innocence and therefore refused to confess guilt where none existed. Even more problematic is that Job cannot even find God to plead his case of innocence. Job must have wondered, "Why is God playing a cosmic game of hide-and-seek?"

Job Can't Find God but Remains Confident (23:8-17)

Job 23:8-17 is composed of two subsections: 8-12 and 13-17. In verses 8-12 Job expresses his frustration that he cannot find God no matter where he turns. He makes a crucial statement in this passage that sheds light on the problem of undeserved suffering: "Yet he knows the way I have taken; when he has tested me, I will emerge as pure gold" (v. 10). The "testing" of which Job speaks indicates a legal background. Gold is a symbol of purity and righteousness. When you put New Testament glasses on, this is precisely one of the reasons for suffering in the lives of God's people (1 Pet 1:6-7). In verses 11-12 Job asserts he has walked with the Lord in obedience and has "treasured the words from his mouth more than . . . daily food." As Archer writes, "No higher standard than this could be set for a New Testament believer!" (*Book of Job*, 80).

> A little piece of wood once complained bitterly because its
> owner kept whittling away at it, cutting it, and filling it with
> holes, but the one who was cutting it so remorselessly paid
> no attention to its complaining. He was making a flute out of
> that piece of ebony, and he was too wise to desist from doing

so, even though the wood complained bitterly. He seemed
to say, "Little piece of wood, without these holes, and all this
cutting, you would be a black stick forever—just a useless piece
of ebony. What I am doing now may make you think that I am
destroying you, but, instead, I will change you into a flute, and
your sweet music will charm the souls of men and comfort
many a sorrowing heart. My cutting you is the making of you,
for only thus can you be a blessing in the world." (DeHaan,
Broken Things, in Swindoll, *Tardy Oxcart,* 547)

Job asserts two key things in verses 13-17. First, God is sovereign and
does what he pleases (vv. 13-14). Though things are out of control in
Job's life, he still believes God is in control. Therefore, Job is "terrified"
and "afraid" of God the "Almighty" (vv. 15-16). God indeed does intend
that people "fear" him in the sense of reverence, respect, and obedience. But there is an aspect of God that properly engenders a sense of
terror as well. Yet in spite of all this, Job affirms he is not "destroyed" by
the darkness that currently enshrouds him and keeps him from understanding what God is doing (v. 17).

Civil Injustice—the Poor (24:1-12)

In chapter 24 Job continues his response to Eliphaz. He decries the
slowness with which God deals with the wicked in this life, although in
the end they meet their doom by God's judgment. Oppressors carry out
their oppression on the defenseless—the poor, indigent day laborers,
widows and orphans, and debtors who sell themselves into slavery—yet
God leaves the oppressor "undisturbed and unpunished" (Archer, *Book
of Job,* 81). All of this social injustice occurs openly, yet God does not
respond (vv. 1-12).

Criminal Injustice—the Rebels (24:13-17)

Even worse, the murderer, the adulterer, and the burglar all commit
their crimes under the cover of darkness and seem to get away with their
evil (vv. 13-17).

The Final Fate of the Wicked (24:18-25)

Verses 18-25 appear on first reading to contradict what Job just stated
about the wicked. Previously, the wicked seem to get away with their sin;

here they do not get away but end up being punished—a punishment they cannot escape.[40] Although it may appear for a time that God is not passing judgment on the wicked, the big picture indicates God always does condemn wickedness. The word pictures in this paragraph depict the fragility of life and the certainty of punishment: foam on the surface of water, unproductive land, snow that melts, the womb that gave him birth would forget him and the worm would devour his decaying body at death, the tree that has been cut down. God does not forget to punish the wicked. Death comes to them along with judgment.

In the final verse Job challenges Eliphaz and the friends to prove him wrong (v. 25).

Reflect and Discuss

1. Why do you think the speeches in the third and final cycle are shorter?
2. What kind of sin does Eliphaz accuse Job of?
3. What do you think of Eliphaz's appeal to Job in 22:26-27?
4. What does Eliphaz get wrong about God?
5. What does Eliphaz get right about God?
6. What evidence is there that Job is gaining confidence in his struggle of suffering?
7. What does Job say about God's relationship with the wicked?
8. What are the two views concerning the fate of the wicked that Job proffers?
9. What is Job's attitude about God allowing injustice to exist in the world?
10. Do you think God will correct all injustices before Jesus returns to the earth or after?

---

[40] Many theories have been proposed to alleviate this apparent contradiction. Some suggest these are actually Zophar's words and not Job's. There is no textual evidence for this. Some see this paragraph as Bildad's words, but again there is no textual evidence for this. Another approach is to insert the words "you say" and place quotation marks around vv. 18-20 to indicate these are the words of one of the three friends, or the gist of all of their argument, and thus Job offers a rebuttal in vv. 21-25. However, the best approach is to take this section as part of Job's speech. Job recognizes that the wicked do indeed come to judgment, if only in eternity. Job never said that the wicked never suffer and the righteous never prosper; instead, he said they both suffer and they both prosper. This is a different argument from that made by the three friends. See Anderson, *Job*, 213–14.

Bildad's Third Speech and Job's Response

JOB 25–27

Main Idea: Bildad asserts humans have no hope in standing before God; therefore, Job is guilty because of his suffering. Job praises God's omnipotence, avows his own innocence, and longs for God to bring him justice.

I. **Of Moon, Man, and Maggots: Bildad Asserts Job's Guilt (25).**
II. **A Case of Mistaken Identity: Job Is Not One of the Wicked (26–27).**
    A. Job rejects Bildad's counsel (26:1-4).
    B. Job praises God's great power (26:5-14).
    C. Job avows his innocence (27:1-6).
    D. Job asserts that God administers the moral law against enemies (27:7-12).
    E. Job warns that the wicked will be punished by God (27:13-23).

The brevity of Bildad's reply to Job in chapter 25 may indicate that the three friends are finally running out of steam in the argument. After extoling God's greatness and sovereignty—dominion is his, he establishes harmony in his heights, his "troops" (probably a reference to his angels) cannot be numbered, and his light shines on everyone (vv. 2-3)—Bildad wonders aloud, "How can a human be justified before God? How can one born of woman be pure?" (v. 4). The moon and stars shine with brilliance yet are still insignificant in God's sight, how much less so is a mere human being? If creation, as magnificent as it is, is inferior to God's majesty, then surely man, a mere creature himself, must be sinful.

Bildad compares a human being to a "maggot" and a "worm" (v. 6). The first term connotes putrefaction, and the latter term suggests weakness. Moon, man, and maggots—that's Bildad's way of trying to demonstrate Job's worthlessness in God's sight. As Anderson put it, "On this disgusting and hopeless note, the words of Job's friends end" (*Job*, 215).

A Case of Mistaken Identity: Job Is Not One of the Wicked

JOB 26–27

Job's third reply to Bildad extends through Job 31. Though some interpreters think Job 28 is a textual interpolation, there is really no good reason for not attributing this chapter to Job as well. In the first two chapters of this large section, Job asserts two primary things: God shows wisdom and sovereignty in his punishment of the wicked, and God's punishment does not occur in the stereotypical way presented by the three friends.

Job Rejects Bildad's Counsel (26:1-4)

Job 26 is divided into two sections: 1-4 and 5-14. The first section contains Job's sarcastic excoriation of Bildad's final outburst.[41] As a counselor, Bildad has turned out to be a miserable failure.

> Instead of encouragement to the depressed or understanding
> insight for the dejected he has offered only unfeeling
> bombast, denunciation devoid of God's spirit of compassion!
> (Archer, *Book of Job*, 82)

Job accused Bildad of merely speaking off the top of his head concerning things he knew nothing about. No one would say the things Bildad had said to Job. Bildad was all theory and no practical application. Even worse, his theory was wrong. Job turns Bildad's attempt to belittle him back on Bildad.

Job Praises God's Great Power (26:5-14)

Job lets Bildad know that he himself knows something of God's majesty too. God is sovereign and controls the universe. "Rahab" in verse 12 refers to a mythological creature possessing power over the seas, or it may be interpreted as a reference to the primordial surging seas themselves. Job's reference to Rahab does not indicate his own belief in the reality of a mythical creature. He is most likely employing a metaphor from the common culture of the time to make his point. The "fleeing serpent" in verse 13 may refer to the same mythological creature. The

---

[41] Note the singular "you" in vv. 2-4. In Job 27–31 Job's reply includes all three friends (note the plural "you" in 27:5,11,12).

stirring of the sea in verse 12 is sometimes rendered "quieted" in the sense of "to restrain," which would fit the context as well. "By his breath the heavens gained their beauty" probably refers to the wind that clears the sky of clouds.

One should be cautious as to how much such metaphorical language—as found in verse 7 ("He hangs the earth on nothing") and verse 10 ("He laid out the horizon on the surface of the waters")—should be used to suggest scientific conformity with the notion of the earth being suspended in space and the circular shape of the earth. But let it be noted that such language in no way contradicts modern science in these aspects of astronomy and meteorology. The Bible is not a science book, but when it speaks about such things, even in metaphorical language, it does not contradict true science and speaks with accuracy. The "pillars" that hold up the sky is a reference to the mountains.

For Job, whatever we can know of God is "but the fringes of his ways" and a faint word we hear of him (v. 14). The staggering greatness of creation is but the tip of the iceberg of God's majesty, power, wisdom, and sovereignty.

Job Avows His Innocence (27:1-6)

Job 27 is divided into three sections: 1-6, 7-12, and 13-23. In verses 1-6 Job returns to his reaffirmation of his own integrity and innocence. God's character is also intact, even though the three friends have attempted to defend God's justice via their unjust arguments. Their construal of retributive justice just doesn't conform to God's providence or the way things are in the world. Job will not relent: he is innocent. In verses 5-6 Job sounds like an Old Testament Martin Luther:

> "I will never affirm that you are right; I will maintain my integrity until I die. I will cling to my righteousness and never let it go. My conscience will not accuse me as long as I live!"

Job never changes his story. He is a one-note guy, and that note is "innocent!"

Job Asserts that God Administers the Moral Law against Enemies (27:7-12)

God does not hear the wicked in their times of distress, since that is the only time they call on him. In verses 8-10 Job asks three questions intended to convey three truths: (1) the godless person has no hope when God cuts him off, (2) the godless person has no answer to his cries for help when he is in a difficult situation—"distress" (v. 9)—and (3) the godless person does not delight in God himself, thus demonstrating that person's true godless character (v. 10). In verses 11-12 Job asserts he will teach his friends since they have been trying to teach him. They know God's power as well as Job does. Therefore, "why do [they] keep up this empty talk?" (v. 12).

Job Warns that the Wicked Will Be Punished by God (27:13-23)

Some attribute verses 13-23 to Zophar for one or more of the following reasons: Job seems to contradict his early statements; several statements here are similar to Zophar's previous statements; and this would give Zophar a final third speech in the structure of the book. Zuck, however, presents five reasons Job is likely the speaker of these words: (1) the section is consistent with Job's desire that his enemy (the three friends) become as the wicked; (2) Job never denied that the wicked would be punished; he questioned why they continued to prosper; (3) frequently Job used his friends' own words and arguments against them; (4) the absence of a speech by Zophar is consistent with the fact that the speeches become progressively shorter, suggesting Job's verbal victory over a tacit Zophar; and (5) Job 28 is a continuation of Job 27 (*Job*, 121).

Job opines that the wicked suffer the loss of children from war and famine (vv. 14-15) and the loss of wealth (vv. 16-23). This is their "lot" and "inheritance" from God himself. The security wealth brings is temporary. Life is full of fears including the fear of the unknown. The wicked person's house will be as unstable as a moth's cocoon or the temporary shack-like shelter constructed by the farmer at harvest time to guard the crops (v. 18). The wind will come and take away the wicked. Here the wind is personified as "clapping" and "hissing" at the wicked (v. 23). There is no place to escape God's judgment in the end.

Counselors like Job's three friends are full of spiritual diagnosis and prescription, but after all their help, we often feel worse instead of better. Some of the answers Job received from his friends are true to a point, at least technically so. Job's counselors methodically and pedantically recite their bookish precepts to Job and then slap their conclusions onto Job's life like labels on a specimen bottle. But they horribly mislabeled Job—so much so that God would have to chastise them in the end for their counseling malpractice.

Thankfully, we don't have to depend on human counselors. Jesus is our "Wonderful Counselor," as Isaiah describes him in Isaiah 9:6. In Jesus "are hidden all the treasures of wisdom and knowledge" (Col 2:3). Human counselors are helpful at times, but as in Job's case, they are not infallible. We need an infallible guide through life. Only Jesus can fulfill that need. He is wisdom incarnate. He has given us the Holy Spirit of truth to indwell us. He has given us his written Word, the Bible, to guide us. Thanks be to God for his Wonderful Counselor!

Reflect and Discuss

1. What parallel continuities and contrasts appear in Bildad's short speech?
2. What does the brevity of this speech suggest about the debate at this point?
3. How does Bildad view people in relation to God?
4. Why do you think Bildad focuses so much on the transcendence of God?
5. Where is the God of love in Bildad's speeches and theology?
6. How should we as Christians respond to God's mysteries in his way of working in the world?
7. In light of God's ways, how can we as Christians trust in God when we suffer?

Job's Monologue—Got Wisdom?

JOB 28

Main Idea: Humans cannot find wisdom; it resides only with God.

I. **Human Skill in Mining Technology (28:1-11)**
II. **Human Skill Is Inadequate to Find Wisdom (28:12-19).**
III. **God Alone Knows the Path to Wisdom (28:20-28).**

At this point in the narrative, we would expect to have a final speech from Zophar to complete the third cycle of speeches, but for some unknown reason Zophar does not speak again. From his previous two speeches, we know Zophar's theology well. He is a one-note counselor: Though we cannot always be sure why God is punishing someone, we can be sure that when they are suffering, God is punishing them for some reason—never without reason (Clines, "Shape and Argument," 133).

Since from this point forward we don't hear anymore from Job's three friends, a quick, final summation of their counsel is in order. When they first arrived and spent seven days of silence and grief with Job, things were fine. Then they decided they needed to try to help Job "fix" his problem. Sufferers attract fixers the way roadkill attracts vultures (Peterson, *Led by Suffering*, 7). No matter how insightful our friends may be, they don't really understand the full depth and breadth of our suffering. Job's friends may have originally meant well, but they ended up only adding to Job's pain.

Chapters 28–31 create some consternation among interpreters as they attempt to discern whether chapter 28 is an interpolation or the words of Job. Suggestions include attributing it to Zophar, to Bildad, to a poem that was added later to the book, or perhaps to God himself as the speaker. On first blush, Job 28 appears distinct from the previous and subsequent context. It is clearly a discourse on wisdom, but it reads like an interlude, something like a break in a TV program: "And now a word from our sponsor!"

No good reason exists for rejecting this chapter as coming from Job himself. In light of the previous chapters where Job's friends have constantly pushed their refrain that they themselves know the ways of God, Job 28 affirms what Job has himself already stated, namely, that it is not possible to discern the imponderables of God. Ultimately, wisdom is the domain of deity.

In the final three chapters before Elihu speaks, Job expresses a longing for the good old days when life was calm and coherent (ch. 29); he describes the harsh present incoherence of his sufferings (ch. 30); and he mounts a final defense of his innocence by covering the gamut of personal and social offences (ch. 31), in each case declaring himself "not guilty."

Job 28 can be divided into three sections: 1-11, where Job compares mining for precious metals in connection with the difficulty of discovering the hidden treasure of wisdom; 12-19, where Job employs a series of rhetorical questions highlighting the preciousness and inaccessibility of wisdom; and 20-28, where more rhetorical questions introduce and answer the question of where wisdom can be found.

Human Skill in Mining Technology
JOB 28:1-11

Most people talk to themselves. When there is no one to talk to, sometimes you wind up having internal conversations! That's what happened to Job. In the silence following the speeches of Job's three friends, and in the dark night before the morning of God's coming to Job, through the space of four chapters, Job talked to himself in soliloquy fashion. Psychologists tell us that self-talk aids in emotional control and gaining emotional objectivity, especially during stressful situations. Job knows that he needs wisdom in the crisis he is in. He rightly concludes that the fear of the Lord is the source of wisdom.

In Job 28:1-11 Job illustrates the fact that there is no trodden path to wisdom. On the earth's surface, no precious metals are found. Only when miners work beneath the surface do they discover treasure.

Human Skill Is Inadequate to Find Wisdom
JOB 28:12-19

In spite of humanity's technological ability to mine precious metals, wisdom remains elusive (vv. 12-19). Even worse, if a person could find wisdom, he could not purchase it even with the precious metals he has mined from the earth (vv. 15-19).

God Alone Knows the Path to Wisdom
JOB 28:20-28

In verse 20 Job repeats the question of verse 12: "Where then does wisdom come from?" Job answers that only God knows where wisdom is to be found (v. 23), for only God is omniscient (v. 24).

Because God himself has established the winds, the waves, and the lightning and rain of the thunderstorm (vv. 23-26), he alone knows what wisdom is and where it is to be found. Verse 25 speaks of the weight of the wind, which expresses the maximum force that it cannot exceed.

True wisdom consists in two things: the fear of the Lord and departing from evil (v. 28). Job's point is that true wisdom is God's gift. As in the other Wisdom literature of the Bible, "fearing God" does not connote primarily terror but respect, honor, and obedience. Fearing God is an attitude that leads to right living. To fear the Lord means to order our lives in accordance with his standards of holiness as outlined in Scripture. Job's linking of these two things—fear of God and avoidance of sin—makes clear that a proper understanding and description of true holiness is characterized by an avoidance of sin demonstrated in righteous living. Interestingly, this is how the book of Proverbs summarizes the fear of God: "The fear of the LORD is the beginning of knowledge" (1:7); "To fear the LORD is to hate evil" (8:13); and "The fear of the LORD is the beginning of wisdom" (9:10). It is also identical to how Solomon concludes Ecclesiastes 12:13: "Fear God and keep his commands, because this is for all humanity." The essence of all wisdom is to fear God and do what he says. Job's conclusion in verse 28 is a fitting segue to chapters 29–31.

Structurally, Job 28:28 uses the identical terminology used to describe Job himself in 1:1, thus forming what is called an *inclusio*, a form of bookends where the same or similar word or phrase is found at the beginning and end of a section or an entire book.

In preaching or teaching Job 28, we might use the following outline:
1. The Celebration of Human Wisdom (28:1-11)
2. The Limitation of Human Wisdom (28:12-19)
3. The Revelation of All Wisdom—God (28:20-28)

Job 28 begins a crucial turn in the book. To this point Job's search has been for a reason for his suffering. Now Job turns to a search for true wisdom. The point of Job 28 is simple: God alone knows where wisdom is (Murphy, *Tree of Life*, 41). Ultimately, Job discovers and asserts that only God knows the pathway to true wisdom. This leads him to shift his search from an answer to his questions to God himself. Job wants to see God face-to-face in order to prove his innocence. God's "face" is a pivotal theme in several of Job's speeches (see chaps. 13 and 23).

Job's three friends, for all their counsel, couldn't produce a thimble full of wisdom to help Job in his suffering. Not much has changed from Job's day to ours. The subtitle of C. John Sommerville's book *How the News Makes Us Dumb* sums up our situation: *The Death of Wisdom in an Information Society.* At no time in history have we been better and more quickly informed than we are today. Yet for all this information, we are none the wiser when it comes to the ultimate questions of life.

I find it interesting that Job speaks of mining for treasure under the earth's surface. Part of the purpose of the book of Job is to teach us where our real treasure is.

Joel Ruth was walking on a Florida beach when he came across 180 near-mint-condition silver coins. The coins were from a Spanish fleet of about a dozen ships destroyed in a hurricane in 1715. Two hundred and eighty-nine years later, Hurricane Jeanne altered the shoreline to where it had once been back in 1715 and uncovered a portion of this treasure that had washed ashore. The storm exposed a treasure. God allows storms in our lives to lead us to hidden spiritual treasure.

In 1 Corinthians 1:30 Paul tells us that Christ "became wisdom from God for us." In Colossians 2:2-3, Paul informs us,

> *I want their hearts to be encouraged and joined together in love, so that they may have all the riches of complete understanding and have the knowledge of God's mystery—Christ. In him are hidden all the treasures of wisdom and knowledge.*

Our search for wisdom can only be satisfied in Christ. Wisdom is not what you know; it's who you know! When you know him who is wisdom incarnate, you may not have all the answers to your questions, but you have the answers that matter. Got wisdom?

Reflect and Discuss

1. What is the difference between knowledge and wisdom?
2. How does the Bible define and describe wisdom?
3. How can we find wisdom today?
4. In what way is Christ our wisdom today?
5. How does Job 28 function in the overall structure of the book?

Job's Summary Defense—the Good Life I Once Had

JOB 29–31

Main Idea: Job recalls his former blessings and status, describes his feelings of rejection, and denies that he has sinned.

I. **Job's Soliloquy (29)**
   A. Job's longing for former blessings from God (29:1-6)
   B. Job's longing for former respect (29:7-10)
   C. Job's striving for justice (29:11-17)
   D. Job's longing for a long life (29:18-20)
   E. Job's remembrance of his days of counsel and leadership (29:21-25)
II. **Job's Lament (30)**
   A. Job's mockers and their mockery (30:1-15)
   B. Impact of suffering on Job (30:16-19)
   C. Impact of God's harsh treatment on Job (30:20-23)
   D. Job's personal lament (30:24-31)
III. **Job's Oath of Innocence (31)**
   A. List of sins denied (31:1-34,38-39)
   B. Job's oath of innocence (31:35-37)

It is common for us to look back at times in our lives and yearn for the good old days, especially when times are hard. Hard times bring a longing for yesteryear when things were easier. In war we long for the days of peace. In a messy divorce we long for the happy days of the early years of marriage. In sickness we long for the previous days of health.

In the Beatles' 1965 album *Help*, Paul McCartney sang what would become the most played song on the radio. "Yesterday" has more cover versions than any song ever written—more than three thousand!

For many people today, yesterday always seems better. Somehow it seems the weather was better, the pressure lesser, the prices lower, the traffic slower, the currency stronger, the trees greener, the atmosphere cleaner, the youth kinder, the music softer, and the world safer.

The Beatles sang about yesterday. Country singer Don Williams sings about tomorrow (Andrews, "Yesterday and Today"). Job yearned for yesterday, thinking his today would never change, and thus he would have no tomorrow.

This longing for the good old days is especially acute when we find ourselves in a situation of suffering that is not the result of our own sin or mistakes. When there is no answer to the question "Why?" and especially the question "Why me?" it is easy to sink into despair.

In these three chapters we hear Job's concluding summary of his case as if he were in a courtroom. Job is not addressing his three friends specifically or God. Rather, his speech is something of a soliloquy.

In chapter 29 Job rehearses his past as evidence that he did indeed fear God. In chapter 30 Job describes his present condition and treatment. Then in chapter 31 Job recounts his innocence with respect to numerous kinds of sins, demonstrating he also "turned from evil." At the end, he looks to the future: "If only I had someone to hear my case" (31:35).

Job's Soliloquy

JOB 29

The CSB divides Job 29 as follows: 1-6, 7-17, 18-20, 21-25. In verses 1-6 Job recounts the past blessings he has enjoyed; in 7-17 the honors he had received and the good deeds he had done; in 18-20 how he thought his life would turn out; and in 21-25 his past influence on others. Job's résumé is impressive. He had it all!

Job's Longing for Former Blessings from God (29:1-6)

"If only I could be as in months gone by, in the days when God watched over me" (v. 2) is Job's longing for the good old days when he sensed God's constant presence and blessing. Those were days of plenty for Job: "[His] feet were bathed in curds and the rock poured out streams of oil for [him]" (v. 6). Cream and oil are commodities Job names to indicate he had plenty of everything in those days.

Job's Longing for Former Respect (29:7-10)

Job was well known and respected, such that when he arrived in the city square, "young men . . . withdrew" and "older men stood to their feet"

(vv. 7-8). In the ANE the city gate was the center of community life. Here was the marketplace, the city court, and the place of exchange of ideas. Only the most prominent citizens received the deferential treatment accorded Job.

Job's Striving for Justice (29:11-17)

City officials and noblemen stopped talking among themselves to honor Job (vv. 9-11). Why? Everyone knew Job was a man concerned with social welfare and mercy. He "rescued the poor" and the "fatherless," "the widow," and "the needy" (vv. 12-16). "[Job] shattered the fangs of the unjust and snatched the prey from his teeth" (v. 17).

Job's Longing for a Long Life (29:18-20)

Job's just actions caused him to feel he had earned a good conduct medal from God. "So I thought . . ." (v. 18). Job thought he would live to a ripe old age and die quietly in his bed (vv. 18-20). Job felt security and confidence in those days. There was peace in the valley, and all was well.

Job's Remembrance of His Days of Counsel and Leadership (29:21-25)

In addition to all his other accomplishments, Job hung out a shingle, "Job's Counseling Service": "Men listened to [him] with expectation, waiting silently for [his] advice" (v. 21). People found Job's counsel to be like the dew (v. 22). "[He] lived as a king among his troops, like one who comforts those who mourn" (v. 25).

Job's reminiscing trip down memory lane of the "good ol' days" in chapter 29 reminded him of what he once enjoyed and likely would never have again, making his current pain and suffering all the more difficult to bear.

Job's Lament

JOB 30

Both Archer (*Book of Job*, 86–87) and the CSB divide Job 30 into five paragraphs: 1-8, 9-15, 16-19, 20-23, and 24-31. Actually, 1-15 is a unit, with verse 9 picking up and reiterating what Job stated in verse 1 with the repetition of "mock": "Now I am mocked by their songs." Notice the repetition of "now" introducing three of these paragraphs: 1, 9, and 16. If chapter 29 summarizes what Job possessed in the past, chapter 30 summarizes what Job has lost in the present. Disrespected by young people, whom Job calls "foolish men, without even a name" and "rabble" (vv. 1-15), he also felt disregarded by God (vv. 16-23), leading him to despondency because of his physical and mental suffering (Zuck, *Job*, 129).

Job's Mockers and Their Mockery (30:1-15)

In verses 1-8 Job laments that even wandering desert riffraff—men younger than Job whose fathers Job would not have deigned to employ with his sheepdogs and whom society deemed the dregs of humanity and therefore despised and banished (vv. 1-5)—now mock Job in his sufferings. Job describes them as "foolish men, without even a name" (v. 8). This section is primarily a description of these foolish men. Job has sunk so low that even the lowest of society treat him with contempt.

Verses 9-15 continue to describe the activity of these foolish men who mock Job. They alternate between keeping their distance and spitting in his face. They no longer fear Job because now he is a helpless suffering shell of his former self (vv. 10-11). With word pictures drawn from military action, Job speaks of "the rabble" who "rise up," "trap [his] feet," "construct their siege ramp against [him]," and "advance as through a gaping breach" (vv. 12-14). Job's "dignity" and "prosperity" have been chased away "like the wind" and "like a cloud" (v. 15).

Impact of Suffering on Job (30:16-19)

Job turns to consider the agony of his suffering caused by his disease in verses 16-19. He says, "Days of suffering have seized me" and "night pierces my bones" (vv. 16-17). Job's clothing is "distorted," and he personifies his disease as one who "chokes [him] by the neck of [his] garment" (v. 18). Job has been cast down "into the mud" and has become like "dust and ashes" (v. 19), utterly hopeless.

Impact of God's Harsh Treatment on Job (30:20-23)

Job laments God's silence when Job cries out for help (v. 20). God's silence for Job turns to cruelty and harassment (v. 21). Job feels as if God has tossed him to the wind and scattered him in the storm (v. 22). Job fully expects the end result to be death, the final "place appointed for all who live" (v. 23).

Job's Personal Lament (30:24-31)

In the final paragraph, verses 24-31, Job bemoans how he would always help others when they were in trouble, but now no one is found to help him, not even God. He is met with indifference and neglect by all: "No one would stretch out his hand against a ruined person when he cries out to him for help because of his distress" (v. 24). In the past Job had felt deep emotion for those who had fallen on hard times, but now that he himself "hoped for good" and "looked for light," evil and darkness have come (v. 26). His suffering creates such physical and emotional distress that he is "churning within" (v. 27). Whatever skin disease Job had, he describes his skin as "blackened" and "flaking off" (vv. 28,30). Job is reduced to mourning and weeping. Musical instruments like the lyre and flute, usually associated with joyful occasions, are now reduced to playing mournful dirges (v. 31).

The *Titanic* was dubbed "unsinkable." Her special design with watertight compartments was supposed to keep her afloat even if some of the compartments were damaged. But when she struck an iceberg, too many of the watertight compartments were breached, and the *Titanic* was doomed to sink to the bottom of the ocean.

Like the *Titanic*, Job's ship of life has been hit by an iceberg of suffering, and he is sinking fast. He has all but lost hope. Without hope we all will sink under the weight of our suffering.

Off the coast of Saint Johns, Newfoundland, Canada, is the Hibernia oil platform. Enormous resources and time have been invested to build a structure that is said to be indestructible. Residents and workers on the platform go about their day-to-day routine without fear and full of hope. The Hibernia's meticulous design incorporates a GBS (gravity base structure) system that anchors it to the North Atlantic seabed two hundred and sixty-five feet below the water. The total structure from the ocean floor to the top of the derrick is 738 feet high, with construction costs of over six billion dollars.

> Simply stated, the structure is *immovable*. It has to be! It sits in the middle of "iceberg alley," where icebergs can be as large as ocean liners. Sixteen huge concrete "teeth" surround the Hibernia. These teeth were expensive additions, designed to distribute the force of an iceberg over the entire structure and into the seabed, should one ever get close. Radio operators plot and monitor all icebergs within twenty-seven miles of the

oil rig. Any icebergs that come close are "lassoed" and towed away from the platform by powerful supply ships. Smaller bergs are simply diverted by using the ship's propeller wash or high-pressure water cannons. As rugged and as strong as this platform is, and as prepared as it is for icebergs to strike, the owners have no intention of allowing an iceberg anywhere near Hibernia. But if something unpreventable comes its way, the Hibernia is anchored, rooted, and ready. Built to withstand a million-ton iceberg, designers claim it can actually withstand a six-million-ton iceberg, and even then it will still be functional. (Statistics indicate that a million-ton iceberg occurs only once every five hundred years, and supposedly one as large as six million tons comes around once every ten thousand years.)

As sturdy and secure as the massive Hibernia is, know that you have a source of protection that far exceeds any defense built by human hands. When storms rage in your life, the Lord Himself is your Anchor . . . your staunch and steady hope. When trouble like a massive iceberg threatens you, remember this: Because Jesus is your Anchor, He will give you *an anchored life*. He is your help and your hope. He will sustain you, and He will hold you . . . safe and secure. The Bible promises: "you will be secure, because there is hope; you will look about you and take your rest in safety" (Job 11:18). (Hunt, *Hope for Your Heart*, 87–88; emphasis in original)

From Job's perspective, he is disdained, defenseless, devastated, disregarded, and defeated physically and emotionally. Job has yet to learn that it will be his experience of suffering that will bring him into a new relationship with God.

Malcolm Muggeridge once wrote,

Contrary to what might be expected, I look back on experiences that at the time seemed especially desolating and painful with particular satisfaction. Indeed, I can say with complete truthfulness that everything I have learned in my seventy-five years in this world, everything that has truly enhanced and enlightened my existence, has been through affliction and not through happiness. In other words, if it ever were to be possible to eliminate affliction from our earthly existence by means of some drug or other medical mumbo jumbo, as Huxley envisaged in *Brave New World*, the result would not be to make life delectable, but to make it too banal and trivial to be endurable. This, of course, is what the Cross signifies. And it is the Cross, more than anything else, that has called me inexorably to Christ. (*Twentieth Century Testimony*, 35)

When I think of suffering overcome by faith in God, I think of the amazing story of Joni Eareckson Tada.

At age seventeen Joni had everything going for her—an attractive personality, good looks, and natural athletic ability. She was a tennis player and swimmer, and her physical gifts distinguished her as a true athlete.

But that would all change one hot July afternoon in 1967 when she splashed about in cool waters . . . for the last time.

A self-described risk-taker, Joni positioned herself for a refreshing dive, jumped, and in an instant her body was rocked from head to toe. It was a tragic miscalculation . . . the water was far too shallow. Her head hit bottom, and her neck snapped on impact, leaving Joni paralyzed in all four limbs.

The months that followed were filled with dismay and depressing adjustments to life in a wheelchair . . . and the realization that she would never again do all the physical activities she'd enjoyed before the accident. She found herself having suicidal thoughts, even asking friends to help her end her life.

Thankfully, she had brought to her teen years a Christian faith that had been nurtured in childhood. She admits that her faith was not strong at the time of her accident, but God moved in her life and caused the kind of security in him that would sustain her through countless challenges.

And there were plenty of daunting disappointments too. She and her family and friends prayed many times for miraculous healing. At one point she decided to attend a healing service. She had hoped to walk away from the healing service, but instead she was *whisked away*.

That day Joni Eareckson Tada, wheelchair-bound but holding out hope for a miracle, believed her moment had come. At some point during the service, perhaps while testimonies were shared or choruses were sung, she surely would sense a powerful surge permeating and restoring her body, prompting her to walk away from her wheelchair *forever.*

But the words of an usher soon dashed expectations, not only for Joni but also for about forty others in wheelchairs or on crutches who were hoping for healing. "Let's escort you all out early so as not to create a traffic jam," he directed as other ushers joined in to assist in the exodus. It was a very solemn stream of individuals who left the arena that day. The service droned on behind them, and Joni remembers thinking, *Something's wrong with this picture.* Another moment of hopefulness had been dashed.

After years of praying for healing and wrestling with Scripture, Joni has found peace and a resolute commitment to the lordship of Jesus Christ in her life. "Suffering is that good sheepdog, always snapping at my heels and driving me into the arms of my Shepherd. For that, I am so grateful. I am so grateful." "I'd rather be in this wheelchair knowing Him than on my feet without Him." (Hunt, *Hope for Your Heart*, 147–48; emphasis in original)

Job's Oath of Innocence
JOB 31

Job 31 is the conclusion of Job's final speech. It contains Job's solemn oath of innocence. The chapter is divided as follows: 1-4, 5-8, 9-12, 13-15, 16-23, 24-28, 29-34, 35-37, and 38-40. Crucial to note in this chapter is Job's recurring use of the "if guilty" oath in verses 5, 7, 9, 13, 16, 19, 20, 21, 24, 25, 26, 38, and 39.

List of Sins Denied (31:1-34,38-39)

In verses 1-4 Job makes a crucial statement concerning the cause and effect of sin and judgment: "Doesn't disaster come to the unjust and misfortune to evildoers?" (v. 3). Job himself recognizes that, as a general rule, the principle of retribution is valid. In this he agrees with his three friends. But Job staunchly maintains his innocence and does not believe the principle of retribution applies to him personally.

Job begins his final defense by asserting his fidelity to God's law at a point of temptation common to men: sexual lust. He says, "I have made a covenant with my eyes. How then could I look at a young woman?" (v. 1). Job had made a covenant and affirmed he had not broken the covenant. Furthermore, Job begins with inner motive and attitude before he moves to speak about outer conduct. Not only was Job not guilty of adultery (vv. 9-12); he was not guilty of lust.

Job invites us to inspect his life. He begins with his business life in 5-8. He affirms his total honesty in business dealings. The balance scale was a common tool to measure fair value in the market. Job invites God to "weigh [him] on accurate scales, and he will recognize [his] integrity" (v. 6). Job speaks of his "step," his "heart," and his "hands" as being pure. If not so, he says, "let someone else eat what I have sown, and let my crops be uprooted" (v. 8).

Job referred to a young, unmarried woman in verse 1. Now in 9-12 Job affirms his moral blamelessness and especially his commitment to his wife by swearing he has never been guilty of adultery (v. 9). Adultery was considered a serious moral crime punishable in court. If his oath to his faithfulness is untrue, Job states, "Let my own wife grind grain for another man, and let other men sleep with her" (v. 10). In Job's day the grinding of corn by hand with millstones was a menial task of female servants. It is unthinkable that a man would subject his wife to such labor. Job considers adultery to be a "disgrace," "an iniquity deserving punishment," not only by the courts but punishment inherent in the sin itself: "For it is a fire that consumes" (vv. 11-12).

In verses 13-15 Job explains his relationship to his employees and servants. He recognizes that he must act and has acted justly in this area for two reasons: because he must give an account to God (v. 14) and because "Did not the same God form us [all] in the womb?" (v. 15).

Job now turns to his treatment of the "poor" and the "needy" in 16-23. In every situation he asserts he has acted with justice and compassion toward society's disadvantaged. Whether the poor, widows, or orphans, Job has acted justly for two reasons: because of God's impending judgment on those who do not practice justice ("Being terrified by God's ability to destroy wrongdoers was a deterrent against wrongdoing!"; Zuck, *Job*, 137), and "because of his majesty [Job] could not do these things" (v. 23).

Job moves on to consider his attitude toward materialism and idolatry in 24-28. In verses 24-25 he never trusted in his bank account or prided himself in his wealth. Job refused to be an idolater and worship the sun or the moon (vv. 26-28),[42] for to do so would "be an iniquity deserving punishment, for [he] would have denied God above" (v. 28). In verses 29-34 Job relates to us his perspective toward his enemies and strangers. He never rejoiced over his enemy's distress (v. 29). Job does not sin against those who have wronged him, as Proverbs 24:17-18 says. Job's inward heart and outward actions were congruent. Strangers who traveled through Job's territory found a hospitable welcome at his hands (vv. 31-32). It is difficult in our culture to understand the role hospitality played in the ANE. Hospitality to strangers was considered a solemn duty, and Scripture makes clear God's attitude in this matter (e.g., Gen 18:1-8; Rom 12:13; and Heb 13:2). Job serves meat, typically reserved for celebrations (Estes, *Job*, 191), to the traveler who temporarily resides in his home.

Job's avowal of his unhypocritical lifestyle is stated in verses 33-34: "Have I covered my transgressions as others do by hiding my iniquity in my heart?" (vv. 33-34). Job is making clear that *if* he were to be made conscious of personal sin, he would not play the hypocrite and attempt to hide it.

Job's Oath of Innocence (31:35-37)

In the chapter to this point, Job has pled not guilty to a variety of common sins and wrongs, both personal and social. He now returns to the courtroom metaphor and earnestly and eagerly pleads for someone to hear his case. He calls for anyone to submit specific written accusations against him. Let the charges be specified! Job figuratively submits his signature to the legal document, his oath of purity (v. 35). Once again, Job calls on God ("the Almighty," "[his] Opponent") to answer him and "compose his indictment" (v. 35). "Here is my signature," God! See you in court! Job would present to God "an account of all [his] steps" and "approach him like a prince," meaning he would approach God confidently (v. 37). Job would like to talk to God in order to set him straight. Job rhetorically attempts ancient parliamentary procedure in

---

[42] In the ANE the sun was often worshiped as a god. Scripture records that idols were often kissed (1 Kgs 19:18; Hos 13:2), but since the sun and moon could not be kissed, the worshiper would kiss his hand and extend it toward the objects of worship.

an attempt to engage God. Job expects God the Judge to acquit him based on the evidence.

Finally, in verses 38-40 Job claims that his righteous behavior extends to how he treated his farmland and tenants. He never defrauded his tenants by withholding their pay. His last oath and imprecation on himself are for unproductive, worthless land: "If my land cries out against me . . . let thorns grow instead of wheat and stinkweed instead of barley" (vv. 38,40). This curse formula reminds one of Genesis 3–4 and the account of Cain and Abel: the land will cry out.

Job 31 plays a key role in the structure and development of the book. In the ANE the concept of an oath was used to challenge God. Here Job swears to his innocence. The entire chapter is Job's oath. "Job throws caution to the wind. Over and over he explicitly calls upon himself every conceivable punishment if what he says is not true" (Tsevat, "Meaning of the Book," 193).

Edwin Good provides a helpful chart of the structurally interesting points of Job 31:

1. Questions: retribution (vv. 1-4)
2. Curses and statements (vv. 5-12)
   a. Curse without result: fraud (v. 5)
   b. Statement: integrity (v. 6)
   c. Curse with result (vv. 7-8)
   d. Curse with result: adultery (vv. 9-10)
   e. Statement with "for": crimes (vv. 11-12)
3. Curses, questions, and statement (vv. 13-18)
   a. Curse without result: justice for slaves (v. 13)
   b. Questions: God and common origin (vv. 14-15)
   c. Curse without result: aloofness (vv. 16-17)
   d. Statement: care for the poor (v. 18)
4. Curses and statement (vv. 19-23)
   a. Curse without result: clothing for the poor (vv. 19-20)
   b. Curse with result: fairness (vv. 21-22)
   c. Statement: fear and disaster (v. 23)
5. Curses and statement (vv. 24-28)
   a. Curse without result: wealth (v. 24)
   b. Curse without result: power (v. 25)
   c. Curse without result: idolatry (vv. 26-27)
   d. Statement: crimes (v. 28)

6. Curses and statement (vv. 29-34)
   a. Curse without result: arrogance (v. 29)
   b. Statement: curse (v. 30)
   c. Curse without result: food (v. 31)
   d. Statement: hospitality (v. 32)
   e. Curse without result: hypocrisy (vv. 33-34)
7. Statement and curses (vv. 35-40)
   a. Statement (exclamation): challenge to trial (v. 35)
   b. Curse without result: pride (vv. 36-37)
   c. Curse with result: soil (vv. 38-40) (Good, "Job 31," 338)

Job 23 should be compared with Job 31 in that they both assert two things: Job's desire to stand before God and Job's formal declaration of innocence. At the beginning of Job 23, the order is Job's desire followed by his declaration of innocence. At the end of Job 31, the order is Job's declaration of innocence followed by his desire to stand before God.

The narrator closes this section with the terse statement, "The words of Job are concluded" (v. 40). Indeed. No more verbosity from his talkative friends; continued silence from God. This is where Job stands at the end of Job 31. He will not speak again until 40:3.

In the ever-changing vicissitudes of life, we need to remember that whether it was the good old days then or the bad days we now live in, "Jesus Christ is the same yesterday, today, and forever" (Heb 13:8). Because he never changes, he is there to help us keep our balance when the rugs are pulled out from under us and when the limbs on which we are sitting are sawed off beneath us. As Hebrews 7:25 reminds God's children, Jesus "always lives to intercede for [us]." Regardless of our circumstances, Jesus is praying for us right now! Though I cannot seem to find him in the midst of my suffering, he is there. Though the darkness surrounds me, he is my light and my salvation. I need not fear suffering or lose heart in my suffering because he will never leave me or abandon me.

You can sing with Paul McCartney, "I believe in yesterday," or with Don Williams, "Don't think about tomorrow," but only with Jesus, who is both the Suffering Servant and the risen Savior, can you sing, "Because he lives, I can face tomorrow" (Andrews, "Yesterday and Today").

Reflect and Discuss

1. What area of Job's life, if any, has been untouched by his suffering?
2. In what way does Job's suffering point to Jesus's suffering?
3. What do you think about Job's oath of innocence? Would you describe your current Christian life with such an oath?
4. In light of all you have learned in the book of Job to this point, how does Job's experience compare to ours?
5. In light of all you have learned in the book of Job to this point, how does Jesus help us in our suffering?

Summary and Conclusion of Job 3–31

The long cycle of speeches between Job and his three friends has come to an end. As far as the text goes, the friends fade from the scene and never speak again. We may summarize the speeches of Eliphaz, Bildad, and Zophar this way (see Clines, "Arguments," 272–74):

- In his first speech (Job 4–5), Eliphaz takes the position that even the innocent suffer, since perfect innocence is never found in humanity. Since Job is suffering, he need only be patient and commit his case to God.
- Bildad's first speech (Job 8) assumes Job is guilty of sin and that the death of his children is proof. If you are suffering, it is due to sin. If Job is pure, he will be delivered eventually by God.
- Zophar's first speech (Job 11) commences as did Bildad's: Job is suffering, so he must be a sinner. Job does not acknowledge his sin. If Job will repent, God will forgive and restore.
- The second speech of Eliphaz (Job 15) stresses Job's lack of wisdom in failing to acknowledge his sin. Suffering can only be expected, but Job is not destined for ultimate disaster.
- Bildad's second speech (Job 18) focuses on the fate of the wicked. Presumably, this will be Job's fate if he does not repent.
- Zophar's second speech (Job 20) likewise focuses on the fate of the wicked as developed in three themes: brevity of the rejoicing of the wicked (vv. 4-11), sin's self-destructive nature (vv. 12-22), and the sudden end of the wicked (vv. 23-29). Presumably, this is Job's expected fate if he does not repent.
- In Eliphaz's third speech (Job 22), he pulls out all the stops and goes for the jugular. Job's wickedness must be great because his suffering is great. Job is hiding his guilt since he will not admit it or confess it.
- Bildad's third speech (Job 25) focuses on all humanity being unclean before God and falling short of God's wisdom and power. God will deal with uncleanness through suffering.

Several immediate lessons come to mind from Job 3–31. Here is a short list:

1. Suffering is real and can never be fully fathomed as to its source or its course. Neither Job nor his three friends can plumb the depths of suffering's grand question: Why?

2. Not all suffering is due to personal sin. Job's three friends maintain the retribution principle like a dog refusing to release a bone. If you sin, then you suffer. If you suffer, you are a sinner. The solution is simple: repent. Job's rebuttal to their accusations demonstrates the emptiness of their traditional theology at this point. Some suffering is indeed due to personal sin, as Job admits. But Job himself knows that he is innocent of all he has been accused of. Job may not know the reason for his suffering, but he knows one thing: it is not because of his sin. Job's friends think the problem has to do with Job. They are mistaken. Job thinks the problem has to do with God. He is mistaken, too.

3. Job may nudge the borderline of assaulting God's character as unjust in his quest for self-vindication, but by the end of chapter 31, Job seems to have realized that even in the depths of his suffering, God's character never changes. God is not unjust. Job will learn this truth even more by the end of the book.

4. Job's three friends must be assessed on two fronts: their counsel and their attitude. Regarding their counsel, although some of what they said is no doubt true, the gist of their accusation against Job is false. Job had not sinned as they presumed. The retribution principle to which they were unalterably wedded and its validity they refused to question set them on a trajectory that missed Job's real situation by a thousand miles. They operated from a faulty theology that undergirded the security of their smug system. Though peers with Job socially and ideologically, their relentless embrace of the retribution principle and Job's relentless claims that his suffering was undeserved led to a yawning chasm between them.

Regarding their attitude, their hard and fast determination that their traditional theology was correct made them terrible counselors. Their bedside manner was atrocious. Where do they attempt to identify with Job in his pain? Job complained of their failure in this way in 12:4-6. They were quick to offer criticism and platitudes but slow to offer empathy and understanding.

It is not their accusations that provoke the anger of Job so much as their vacant platitudes, their superficial maxims, their sorry attempts to solve new problems by obsolete methods, their blind pedantic orthodoxy. (Peake, *Problem of Suffering*, 78)

Job's consciousness of his own integrity is incommunicable to his friends. They simply won't listen. "It is natural that Job's friends should sacrifice their friend to their theology" (Peake, *Problem of Suffering*, 77).

I find it interesting that there is no record of any of the three friends offering to pray with or for Job. The only prayers in the book come from Job's lips.

Although we are the involuntary spectators to Eliphaz, Bildad, and Zophar's long, hot, dusty, verbal ride through Ulcer Gulch, we already knew everything we needed to know about Job's character and integrity from the prologue in chapters 1–2. God told us. From the beginning we knew we could never side with Job's three counselor-theologian friends.

Here are some of the mistakes Eliphaz, Bildad, and Zophar made in their speeches to Job (Littleton, "Job's 'Comforters,'" 253–60):

- They had good intentions but bad bedside manners.
- They supported an unsupportable argument: the retribution principle always applies.
- They made mistakes based on human wisdom: Job must have sinned based on assumptions and incomplete evidence. When Job argued with them, they became indignant, forgot their original purpose, and became accusers.
- Their bad theology became a reason for them to reject Job, who was hurting. Such a theology and approach divide and punish people. It's like the law of karma—people get paid in this life for sins committed in a previous life. The caste system in India illustrates what happens when people follow this approach to the logical conclusion. "All the hurting people are set aside as gross sinners. Their pain becomes a reason to reject them rather than to care about them." (Littleton, "Job's 'Comforters,'" 257)
- They turned God into an arbitrary gift dispenser.
- Their theology lends itself to creating a "good works to please God" mentality.
- Their approach does not promote true accountability.
- They end up limiting the person and power of God.

5. Even though Job is righteous, and he knows he is not guilty of the sins he has been accused of, he does not know the true measure of either his righteousness or his love for God unless . . . he suffers a fate befitting the wicked. Greenberg perceptively noted that until his suffering, Job's prosperity kept him from even noticing the rift in the universe, "the crying contradiction," between the notion of a just order of how things should be and the reality of his own individual destiny. But good news: Even though "the orderly fabric of his life has been irreparably rent, yet his relation to God persists" (Greenberg, *Book of Job,* xvii–xix). Job may be confused, angry, frustrated, in the dark, hurting, ready to throw in the towel—yet he is no atheist.[43] His tidy system lies in ruins in the garbage dump outside his city, yet Job still somehow believes in God. Job's final challenge to God is, "Let the Almighty answer me" (31:35). When Job calls God's bluff, as it were, he oversteps his bounds of humble faith. Job is ready to defy God rather than deny his integrity (Habel, "Literary Features," 118).

A. W. Tozer once said, "God never uses a man greatly until he has hurt him deeply." God allowed Job to be hurt deeply. And from Job's pain and recovery to this day, God has used Job greatly. The great Puritan John Rutherford once said, "Praise God for the hammer, the file, and the furnace." Tozer elaborated on these three tools of God in our lives:

> The hammer is a useful tool, but the nail, if it had feeling and intelligence, could present another side of the story. For the nail knows the hammer only as an opponent, a brutal, merciless enemy who lives to pound it into submission, to beat it down out of sight and clinch it into place. That is the nail's view of the hammer; and it is accurate except for one thing: The nail forgets that both it and the hammer are servants of the same workman. Let the nail but remember that the hammer is held by the workman and all resentment toward it will disappear. The carpenter decides whose head shall be beaten next and what hammer shall be used in the beating. That is his sovereign right. When the nail has

---

[43] Recently we have seen the rise of the so-called new atheism. The book of Job raises the same arguments against God that atheists use to deny God's existence. See Brown, *Job: The Faith,* 343–47.

surrendered to the will of the workman and has gotten a little glimpse of his benign plans for its future it will yield to the hammer without complaint.

The file is more painful still, for its business is to bite into the soft metal, scraping and eating away the edges till it has shaped the metal to its will. Yet the file has, in truth, no real will in the matter, but serves another master as the metal also does. It is the master and not the file that decides how much shall be eaten away, what shape the metal shall take, and how long the painful filing shall continue. Let the metal accept the will of the master and it will not try to dictate when or how it shall be filed.

As for the furnace, it is the worst of all. Ruthless and savage, it leaps at every combustible thing that enters it and never relaxes its fury till it has reduced it all to shapeless ashes. All that refuses to burn is melted to a mass of helpless matter, without will or purpose of its own. When everything is melted that will melt and all is burned that will burn, then and not till then the furnace calms down and rests from its destructive fury. (*The Root of the Righteous*, as quoted in Swindoll, *Tardy Oxcart*, 581)

The Elihu Speeches

JOB 32–37

Main Idea: Elihu declares four major truths to Job: God is not silent, God is not unjust, God is not uncaring, and God is not powerless. He concludes Job must necessarily be suffering for his sin.

I. **Introduction of Elihu (32:1-5)**
II. **Elihu's Apology to the Friends for Entering the Discussion (32:6-22)**
III. **Elihu's First Speech: God Is Not Silent (33).**
IV. **Elihu's Second Speech: God Is Not Unjust (34).**
V. **Elihu's Third Speech: God Is Not Uncaring (35).**
VI. **Elihu's Fourth Speech: God Is Not Powerless (36–37).**

I wonder if God ever gets tired of being accused of things he never did and not getting credit for things he does? It's bad enough when non-Christians treat God this way, but it's worse when Christians do. Scripture reveals God and how he interacts with his creation. God is not silent; he speaks and reveals himself. God is not unjust; he acts justly according to his nature. God is not uncaring; not only does he care for his creation such that not a single bird falls to the ground apart from his consent, but even the cattle of Nineveh at the end of the book of Jonah fall under his care. Jesus reminds us to ask if our heavenly Father cares for these, how much more does he care for us (Matt 10:29-31)? God is not powerless; his awesome power is expressed in nature and in our lives in countless ways.

In the extremity of Job's suffering, he sometimes mistakes the silence of God for the indifference of God to his plight. Job concludes that God is unjust in his dealings with him since he has done nothing wrong to deserve his suffering. Job assumes, since God does not respond to all of his cries for help, then God must be uncaring. Although Job knows God is all powerful, he cannot fathom why God has not exerted his power to remedy his suffering.

The provenance and role of the Elihu speeches in the overall narrative of Job continues to be a matter of debate. Many interpreters of

Job conclude that the four Elihu speeches found in Job 32–37 are later additions to the original text. The evidence adduced to support this conjecture is slim.[44] The Elihu speeches actually prepare the way for God to speak in Job 38. Note how Elihu repeats the word *answer* nine times in his speech. Elihu is something of a mediator between Job and the three friends, as well as between Job's words and God's response to come. We shall see some of Elihu's basic ideas developed by God in his speeches in chapters 38–42.

Introduction of Elihu

JOB 32:1-5

In Job 32:1-6a the poetic section (3:3–42:6) is broken to insert this introduction of Elihu[45] and his speeches. In 32:1 the narrator informs us that the ash heap trio had fallen silent and thrown up their hands because Job "was righteous in his own eyes." Elihu was a silent listener present during the back-and-forth between Job and his three friends. He became angry at Job and rebuked him for his pride that developed because of his suffering and for justifying himself at the expense of God's integrity (v. 2). Elihu is right that Job has overlooked the possibility that God may permit his suffering for good and wise purposes and that Job's proper response should be humility and submission to God's will. Job has failed

---

[44] For an accessible survey of the evidence, see Zuck, *Job*, 140–42. Arguments for the removal of the Elihu speeches include the following: (1) Given the ANE's reverence for age and Elihu's youth, Elihu really has nothing to contribute to the discussion but blurts out his response from youthful enthusiasm. (2) Elihu is not mentioned anywhere in the prologue or epilogue. (3) He addresses Job by name, yet he does not know Job as the three friends do. (4) The context seems to break the train of thought in the narrative. (5) The language in this section includes many Aramaic words and loan words, hence the supposition that it is a late addition. (6) Job does not respond to Elihu as he did to the three friends. Answers to these objections can be easily presented: (1) Elihu actually does contribute something new to the discussion. (2) His absence in the prologue and epilogue is an argument from silence. (3) The fact that he addresses Job by name proves nothing. (4) The Elihu section is actually a bridge between Job's final speech in Job 31 and God's response to Job beginning in Job 38. (5) We now know that Aramaic words can be found as far back as 2000 BC, if not earlier. (6) Job's lack of response to Elihu is again an argument from silence.

[45] Elihu is the "son of Barachel the Buzite from the family of Ram" (32:2). According to Genesis, Buz was the brother of Uz and the son of Nahor, Abraham's brother (Gen 22:20-21). "From the family of Ram" may suggest Elihu was an ancestor of David (Ruth 4:19-22).

to realize that "his resentful attitude toward God manifests an insubordination bordering on arrogance" (Archer, *Book of Job*, 91).

On the other hand, Elihu was angry with Eliphaz, Bildad, and Zophar and rebuked them for failing to make their case against Job to convince and convict him of his personal sinfulness (32:3). The three friends claimed Job was suffering because he had sinned. Elihu turned this on its head and claimed Job was committing the sin of pride because he was suffering. In spite of Elihu's "occasional unfairness in his criticism," Archer believes Elihu's "insights prove to be valuable as a critique of both sides of the controversy and as a theological preparation for the speeches of Yahweh in chapters 38–41" (*Book of Job*, 90).

Elihu speaks four times to Job, with each speech designed to correct Job's faulty picture of God as Elihu perceives it: God is not silent (chap. 33); God is not unjust (chap. 34); God is not uncaring (chap. 35); and God is not powerless (chaps. 36–37) (Lawson, *When All Hell Breaks Loose*, 201). Elihu is like the young preacher "fresh out of seminary who hasn't lived long enough to be cynical and hasn't hurt enough to be quiet" (Max Lucado, *Eye of the Storm*, 160).

Elihu's Apology to the Friends for Entering the Discussion
JOB 32:6-22

Hearing all of the exchanges and finding fault on both sides, Elihu could stand it no longer. What he had kept bottled up inside now came pouring forth. He had kept quiet and patiently waited to speak in deference to Job, Eliphaz, Bildad, and Zophar, all of whom were older (and supposedly wiser) than him.

Elihu's first speech formally begins in 33:1. Job 32:6-22 is an introduction by Elihu of why he feels compelled to speak at this point. He respects the three counselors (vv. 6-10) but considers their attempts to convince Job a total failure (vv. 11-14) and affirms his desire to speak (vv. 15-22). He weaves together the threads of his youth being the reason he was "timid and afraid" to speak up at first, with the inability of the three friends who "are dismayed and can no longer answer; words have left them" (v. 15). He says, "Age should speak and maturity should teach wisdom" (v. 7). But understanding comes from God, and not only the old are wise, according to Elihu (vv. 8-9). So, in verse 10, Elihu states that he should be heard because, to paraphrase a chorus by *The Monkees*,

"He's the young generation, and he's got something to say." Throughout Elihu's four speeches, watch how often he employs the phrases "listen to me" and "let me speak"—at least ten times by my count. Elihu is correct when he asserts that none of the three friends succeeded in proving Job wrong (v. 12) and that his response to Job will not be with the arguments employed by Eliphaz, Bildad, and Zophar (v. 14). Turning his attention directly to Job in verses 15-22, Elihu declares, "I am full of words, and my spirit compels me to speak" (v. 18). We might take note that being "full of words" does not necessarily mean one is full of wisdom. Caution here—he declares impartiality in the matter (v. 21). His will be a new approach.

In summary, Elihu's five self-assigned qualifications for speaking were: The Spirit of God was in him, he had waited for the three counselors to finish, he had different and better arguments, he had a lot to say, and he was impartial and nonflattering. (Zuck, *Job*, 144)

Elihu's First Speech: God Is Not Silent
JOB 33

Elihu's first speech is directed specifically to Job. The CSB divides the chapter into three sections: 1-7, 8-11, and 12-33. Contrary to Job's complaint of injustice on God's part, Elihu defends God as being perfectly just in his treatment of Job: "I tell you that you are wrong in this matter, since God is greater than man" (v. 12). Elihu also refers to Job's complaint about God's silence and explains that God does speak "time and again, but a person may not notice it" (v. 14). In particular, Elihu says that God sometimes speaks through pain—not by causing the pain but by providing his grace in the midst of the pain (33:19-28).

In verses 1-7 Elihu addresses Job and exhorts him to "pay attention" to what he is about to say. Elihu informs Job he will speak sincerely and from his heart (v. 3). Elihu challenges Job to "refute" him if possible (vv. 4-5), asserts his equality with Job before God (v. 6), and concludes that Job should have no "fear of [him]" or experience "pressure" in the interchange (v. 7).

In this paragraph Elihu makes three claims: (1) He has a sincere heart (v. 3). Sincerity may not be a virtue, but insincerity is certainly a sin (Thomas, *Problemata Mundi*, 368). (2) He has a knowledgeable mind with ideas he wishes to declare clearly (v. 3). (3) He shares a common humanity with Job (vv. 4-6).

In verses 8-11, Elihu repeats Job's plea of innocence and his charge that God has treated him unfairly. Elihu says in verse 9 what he thinks he has heard Job say, namely, "I am pure, without transgression. I am clean and have no iniquity." But there is a problem. Nowhere in the book of Job do we read Job saying this. Job says he is not guilty *of what the three friends have accused him of,* but he never says he is totally sinless—totally innocent. Here it would seem Elihu has engaged in exaggeration. Job gave him an inch, and Elihu has stretched it into a mile. Elihu has taken a molehill and made it into a mountain. Putting words into the mouths of those with whom we disagree is a common fault.

In verses 12-14 Elihu affirms three things about God: (1) he is superior to all others; (2) he is unaccountable to all others; and (3) he is ever communicating to humanity.

In verses 12-33 Elihu proceeds to explain to Job why he is wrong in his assessment of God and in God's treatment of him? Job had charged that God remains silent. Elihu counters that God does indeed speak, loud and clear. God speaks through dreams (vv. 13-18), and he speaks through pain (vv. 19-28).

God sometimes warns us through dreams with the intention of deterring us from contemplated sin and of suppressing our pride (vv. 15-18). God spares the soul from the "Pit," the first of five references to death as the Pit (vv. 18,22,24,28,30).

God's second way of warning people is through sickness (vv. 19-28). Physical pain and sickness cause loss of appetite (v. 20), which causes loss of weight (v. 21), which brings one nearer to death (v. 22). In verses 23-30 God sends an "angel" or "mediator" to speak to the sick person "what is right for him and to be gracious to him" by sparing him from death (v. 23). Elihu is essentially saying, "Job, don't think of your pain as an unwelcome intruder but as a friend sent from God to lead you to repentance and keep you from death." The angel has "found a ransom" (v. 24), a difficult phrase to interpret since the term *ransom* is unspecified. The word is probably being used metaphorically in this context, either referencing the repentance of the sick person (as compared in context to v. 27) or some form of atonement provided by the angel, the result of which is health (vv. 24-25). The result is spiritual renewal and preservation from physical death (vv. 26-30).

In verses 31-33 Elihu concludes with imperatives similar to those he used in 1-3. "Pay attention," "listen to me," and "be quiet" are three imperatives followed by the reason for them: "for I would like to justify you" (vv. 31-32). Archer catches the meaning of these verses when he paraphrases,

> If I have said anything so far that is unfair to you or inappropriate to your case, please tell me now. Otherwise let me continue and try to convey the wisdom the Lord has taught me in this matter. (*Book of Job*, 94)

Job 33:19-33 teaches us at least three important truths regarding discipline in our lives. First, it often involves great suffering. Affliction renders a valuable service—it forces us to turn our attention to the spiritual realities of life that really matter. One of the reasons God allows adversity in our lives is to get our attention. We easily get caught up in our own activities and agendas and lose sight of God. We develop a certain spiritual insensitivity. Like the thunderstorm in nature, God shows up in our suffering and prunes our lives by shaking free the dead wood from our trees and purifies our spiritual atmosphere.

Second, suffering is a great teacher—it teaches us God's righteousness. Third, the school of suffering brings us back from the "Pit" and into God's presence and fellowship.

Elihu's Second Speech: God Is Not Unjust

JOB 34

Elihu challenges the three friends' inability to answer Job's complaint that God was unjustly punishing him (34:5). Turning to Job, Elihu refutes his claim of God's injustice by pointing out that God's nature makes injustice impossible (vv. 10-12) and that God is the author of justice and never shows partiality (vv. 16-20). Finally, Elihu states that God's justice is complete and perfect because he is omniscient and doesn't need to make any inquiries into any situation (vv. 21-30).

The CSB divides Job 34 into the following sections: 1-9, 10-15, 16-20, 21-30, and 31-37. In verses 1-15 Elihu speaks to the three friends, as is evidenced by the plural "you" and the reference to "wise ones" (v. 2). In verses 16-37 Elihu speaks directly to Job, as evidenced by the shift to the singular "you."

The first section, 1-9, itself comprises three subsections: 1-4, 5-6, and 7-9. The first four verses make up Elihu's appeal to the three friends to listen to him, examine his argument, and decide whether Job was right or wrong to indict God of being unjust in defense of his own righteous conduct.

At this point Elihu sides with the three friends against Job. Job had declared, "I am righteous, yet God has deprived me of justice" (v. 5). Elihu then proceeds to deride Job:

> What man is like Job? He drinks derision like water. He keeps company with evildoers and walks with wicked men. For he has said, "A man gains nothing when he becomes God's friend." (vv. 7-9)

This scathing denunciation needs special comment because it simply does not represent Job fairly. Elihu makes a serious mistake when he accuses Job of keeping company with wicked people. God himself makes this clear in the prologue. Job likewise makes this clear, at least in his speeches where he defends his character and conduct. But Job merits criticism on one key point:

> So far as Job's overall assumption is concerned—that he is competent to find fault with God's administration of justice, or with the constancy of his love—Job is grievously in error to imagine for even a moment that he who is a mere creature, deriving from his creator any comprehension of righteousness or love that he may possess, could possibly rise above the source from which he received them. This grossest of fallacies—into which any of us may fall whenever we ask of God the rebellious question, "Why me?"—must be exposed for its folly and be completely rejected! (Archer, Book of Job, 95)

In verses 10-15 Elihu continues to address the three friends. In verses 10-12 Elihu asserts and defends God's holiness and justice. God "repays a person according to his deeds, and he gives him what his conduct deserves" (v. 11). No one, Elihu states, has given God authority over the earth; he alone is supreme in the universe (v. 13). God sustains all living beings; if he did not do so, "mankind would return to the dust" (vv. 14-15).

Elihu returns to address Job personally in verses 16-20. He exalts God's sovereignty and asserts that God is beyond our criticism with respect to the enforcement of justice. Even kings are judged by God without partiality or favoritism. God removes the mighty when he pleases "without effort" (v. 20).

In verses 21-30 Elihu proceeds to explicate how human judges may be deceived but no one can hide from God's gaze or deceive him with false evidence. God dethrones and replaces unworthy and wicked rulers. God watches the ways of all people (v. 21). There is no place to hide from God (v. 22). God does not need to haul anyone into court to examine him concerning his life; he already knows all. "He shatters the mighty" and "overthrows" them because he heard the cry of the needy and responded to the injustice done to them (vv. 24-28). God watches over "individuals and nations" and intervenes when he wills "so that godless men should not rule or ensnare the people" (vv. 29-30). Injustice never gets the final word.

In verses 31-37 Elihu concludes this speech with a hypothetical situation: suppose someone who has been punished for sins he did not know he had committed were to approach God and demand that God reveal to him the sins of which he himself is unaware, whereupon the sufferer would cease and desist from his sins (vv. 31-32). Elihu's follow-up answer to this hypothetical situation is in verse 33: "Should God repay you on your terms when you have rejected his? You must choose, not I! So declare what you know."

If there is an alternative way of running the universe, Job must tell Elihu what it is. Elihu informs Job that wise men would inform Elihu, "Job speaks without knowledge" (v. 35). Job needs to be tested "to the limit" because his words reveal he is a wicked man, since "his answers are like those of wicked men" (v. 36). Finally, Job "adds rebellion to his sin" and acts arrogantly "in [their] presence, while multiplying his words against God" (v. 37).

Once again, it appears Elihu has misconstrued or misinterpreted what Job had said about God. "To ignore so completely the many affirmations that Job has expressed concerning the wisdom and holiness and ultimate justice of God is decidedly unfair and uncalled-for" (Archer, *Book of Job*, 97). In order to defend God, Elihu had fallen into the same trap as Job's three friends—he had to assume Job was lying about his innocence.

Elihu's Third Speech: God Is Not Uncaring
JOB 35

In chapter 35 Elihu explains to Job that God remains silent during a man's pleas for relief from suffering because those pleas are basically selfish. For Elihu the bottom line is this: God refuses to break his silence to Job because Job is only interested in proving God wrong and himself right. Job needs to just sit tight, and God will act when and how he sees fit.

The CSB treats all sixteen verses in Job 35 as a unit. Elihu quotes Job in verses 1-3 and then seeks to refute him in verses 4-16. Elihu's quotation of Job is actually not a statement Job himself ever made but more Elihu's interpretation of what Job has said in so many words before. "Do you think it is just when you say, 'I am righteous before God'? For you ask, 'What does it profit you, and what benefit comes to me, if I do not sin?'" (vv. 2-3). Zuck gets at the heart of Elihu's complaint: "How could you assert a righteous position before God when at the same time you asked what advantage there was to be innocent over being sinful?" (*Job*, 153).

Elihu proceeds to answer Job and the friends as well (v. 4). Whether Job sins or is righteous, either way God remains unaffected (vv. 5-7). Because God is transcendent, he is neither adversely affected by human sin nor benefited by human righteousness. Sin or righteousness affects only other human beings (v. 8). God's actions, whether justice in the face of transgression or beneficence in the face of righteousness, are not man centered or man determined.

Zuck summarizes Elihu's argument in this way:

> Job, you reasoned that because you are suffering as the wicked do, there is no point to your being righteous. But there is an advantage to holy living. God does judge impartially and does not alter His standards by what man does or does not do. Your wickedness or righteousness may influence or bribe others, but not the sovereign God. (*Job*, 154)

In verses 9-16 Elihu offers a second argument for why God does not answer Job's cries for help—pride. Pride keeps the suffering person from turning to God in true humility to learn the reason for his suffering. Such a person is like those in the animal kingdom who have no cognizance of the reason for suffering. They know not because they ask not. They ask not because of pride (vv. 9-12).

Charles Spurgeon preached one of his most famous sermons on verse 10: "But no one asks, 'Where is God my Maker, who provides us with songs in the night?'" Spurgeon asks about the meaning of this verse and suggests two answers. First, in the night of our suffering, God is our only song. Second, only God can inspire us to sing "songs in the night" ("Songs in the Night," 21–22).

Job interpreted the silence of God as the indifference of God. Elihu basically says to Job, "Be patient; you'll get what you deserve from God in due time." It is interesting to note that the cry for help to God without the corresponding answer from God is something of a repeated theme in the Old Testament. Two things stand out in this vein. First, the cry for help should be legitimate and based on repentance when sin is involved. Second, some people cry out to God because they got caught, not because they are genuinely repentant. Elihu seems to assume that Job's cry for help is an empty appeal, more like the latter. To his mind, Job simply has no theological basis for what he says (vv. 15-16).

Again, it seems Elihu has misrepresented Job's argument. Job's basic point has been that, in some cases, there is no visible retribution from God for sin up until a person dies. As Archer perceptively noted,

> It may well be that Job needs to repent for some of the things
> he once or twice affirmed in a way discreditable to God's
> justice and derogatory to His faithful love. But he never
> asserted that God is truly indifferent about the moral behavior
> of man, as Elihu has mistakenly inferred. (*Book of Job*, 98–99)

Elihu's Fourth Speech: God Is Not Powerless
JOB 36–37

Elihu's final speech comprises chapters 36–37. Somewhat surprisingly, Elihu claims to speak with divine authority (36:1-4). He proceeds to describe God's justice and warns Job of three things: (1) not to add to his sin by resentment against God; (2) not to desire death in the midst of his suffering; and (3) not to turn to evil (36:5-21). Beginning at 36:22, Elihu describes God's power and sovereign control over nature. God always has reasons for what he does. No human being can comprehend or explain those reasons or duplicate God's mighty works. The only proper response of anyone to God's sovereign control is complete trust and reverence (36:22–37:13). Finally, Elihu concludes his fourth speech by highlighting God's works of "wonder" in nature, which leads to the final truth—God's ways and works cannot be fathomed and are beyond us: "The Almighty—we cannot reach him—he is exalted in power!" (37:23).

The CSB divides chapter 36 into the following sections: 1-4, 5-7, 8-12, 13-15, 16-21, 22-33. In verses 5-15 Elihu speaks generally concerning the meaning and purpose of suffering. In verses 16-21 he moves to apply his theology to Job personally. God is judging you, Job, because you misused justice (vv. 16-17). God shows himself to be exalted by his power over nature (vv. 22-33). Notice that the subparagraphs that begin at verses 5 and 22 begin with "Yes" or "Look" (Hb *hen*). Twice more "Yes" or "See" occurs in the final subparagraph 22-33; verses 26 and 30.

Elihu begins with his somewhat deferential introduction: "Be patient with me a little longer, and I will inform you, for there is still more to be said on God's behalf" (v. 2). Elihu says he gains his knowledge from "a distant place" (a reference to the range of his knowledge) and he will "ascribe justice to [his] Maker" (a reference to his intent to justify God in the face of Job's arguments) (v. 3). With a bit of a braggart tone, Elihu claims "complete knowledge" (v. 4).

In verses 5-7 Elihu claims that though God is mighty, "he despises no one" and "understands all things" about all people (v. 5). God destroys the wicked and brings justice to the oppressed (v. 6). God watches the righteous continually and honors them (v. 7).

In verses 8-12 Elihu has two baskets into which all those who suffer fall. In basket one are those who have listened to God's conviction and correction for their sin and who, if they repent and return to serve the Lord, "will end their days in prosperity and their years in happiness" (vv. 9-11). In basket two are those who suffer but who don't listen to God's correction. They will "die without knowledge" (v. 12).

In verses 13-15 Elihu again mentions the two alternatives for the one who suffers. He asserts the ungodly will not cry to God for help in their time of distress. Instead, they have "a godless heart" and "harbor anger" when God afflicts them. They die young "among male cult prostitutes" (v. 14), which in Job's culture suggests a shameful and premature death (Zuck, *Job*, 157). On the other hand, "God rescues the afflicted by their affliction; he instructs them by their torment" (v. 15). God uses suffering to bring the ungodly to godliness by means of his teaching.

In verses 16-21 Elihu directly addresses Job once again. With a series of questions and imperatives, Elihu warns Job not to question God's justice regarding what Job is suffering. Job is obsessed with "judgment and justice" (v. 17). Perhaps this refers to Job's seeming preoccupation with why God does not immediately punish the wicked. Job wants this to occur on his timetable and not God's. "Job, God wants to rescue you, but you are hindering him" is what Elihu seems to be saying. Don't let your riches keep you from humbling yourself before God, Job (vv. 18-19). Don't long for death amid your misery, Job (v. 20). Don't turn to evil, Job (v. 21). Elihu concludes that the reason Job has been "tested by affliction" is because he has not turned from iniquity. Job is guilty of sin, and his suffering is judgment for that sin.

The final subsection is 22-33, where Elihu reminds Job that God is not subject to criticism or performance ratings by humanity. His management of nature and humanity is above Job's pay grade; thus, Job should cease and desist in his wrangling with God.

God's power demonstrates his exalted status. Who is a teacher like God? Who has determined what God must do and how he must do it? Who can declare to God, "You have done wrong?" God is the supreme sovereign of the universe and is answerable to no one (vv. 22-23). All humanity understands these truths, Job, and you should join them in praising God's works (vv. 24-25). God is exalted "beyond our knowledge" and is, in fact, eternal (v. 26). In verses 27-33 Elihu illustrates this by God's power in nature over waterdrops, clouds, thunder, and lightning. The elements of the storm illustrate God's power but also his means of bringing productivity to the land.

It would have been better if no chapter break existed between 36 and 37. Or at least it would have been better if the break had come earlier, perhaps before 36:22. Job 37 continues Elihu's fourth speech, with the focus remaining on the thunderstorm as an example of God's power over nature.

In the terrible lightning flashes and the deafening thunderclaps that follow, Elihu depicts in 37:1-3 "the mighty voice of the Creator addressing his puny creatures" (Archer, *Book of Job*, 101). God's "rumbling" voice is described as "thunderous." God does "great things that we cannot comprehend" (vv. 4-5). The snow and the rain "serve as his sign to all mankind, so that all men may know his work" (vv. 6-7). The windstorm, cold, and ice all accomplish "everything he commands them over the surface of the inhabited world" (vv. 8-12). Elihu lists three purposes why God causes these events of nature to occur: "for punishment, for his land, or for his faithful love" (v. 13).

In verses 14-24 Elihu concludes by telling Job, "Listen to this, Job. Stop and consider God's wonders" (v. 14). Elihu essentially has four final things to say to Job: (1) he should be awed by God (vv. 14-18); (2) he cannot approach God (vv. 19-20); (3) he cannot find God due to God's transcendence and power (vv. 21-23); and in spite of these latter two and because of the first, (4) he must fear God (v. 24) (Zuck, *Job*, 160).

The words of Elihu conclude. The next voice we hear will be God's.

In closing this section on Elihu's speech, two commentators separated by more than three hundred years, the seventeenth-century Scottish Presbyterian James Durham and the twentieth-century Old Testament scholar Gleason Archer, sum things up nicely.

> How sweet a thing it is to see in everything the sovereignty of God commanding, his power and greatness in ordering, his goodness in sending it for a good end, his wisdom in guiding it right, his justice in sending it, whiles for correction, and his mercy in sending it for a blessing; and to see this in every shower. And when so much of God is to be seen in these common and little things, which may be called so comparatively, how much of God may be seen in greater things? (Durham, *Lectures*, 218)

> [Elihu] has shown Job that God may send misfortune upon the innocent for benevolent purposes: to humble his pride, to intensify his sensitivity toward sin, to heighten his feelings of gratitude to the Lord for his faithful love, and above all—in Job's case—to purge him of all arrogance and self-defensiveness toward God. The right use of suffering leads to a complete and unreserved surrender to the will of God without rebellion or willfulness of any kind. The extensive references to the awesome power of the wind and lightning and storm appropriately pave the way for the speeches of Yahweh Himself. (Archer, *Book of Job*, 101–2)

If we listen carefully to what Elihu has told Job, we find not only that his words prepare Job for his encounter with God in the final section of the book but also that what he tells Job about God has parallels to the words and deeds of Jesus in the New Testament. Elihu told Job he should be awed by God because of his mighty deeds in nature. In the Gospels the disciples were awed by Jesus's miracles over nature, disease, even death. John, in his Gospel, describes these miracles as "signs" demonstrating the true nature of Jesus, his deity, and his mission. These signs were evidences of the true character and nature of Jesus so that we might believe in him. Elihu told Job that he could not approach God. Yet the Gospels record Jesus saying, "Come to me, all of you who are weary and burdened, and I will give you rest" (Matt 11:28). The inaccessible God has become accessible in Jesus, and we are invited to know him, trust him, and love him. Elihu said Job cannot find God due to his transcendence and his power. But in the Gospels Jesus has brought the transcendent One into immanence. The Word has become flesh and dwelt among us. Jesus is our "Immanuel," God with us! He is the God-man who has come seeking us so that we may know him. Elihu said Job must fear God. In the Gospels Jesus teaches us to love him and to love God. He says, "If you love me, do the things I command you." This is how we demonstrate our love and trust in Jesus—by keeping his commands. But how can we fulfill such a lofty goal? By abiding in Christ. Jesus said, "The one who remains in me and I in him produces much fruit" (John 15:5). Jesus has given us everything we need to walk with him, live for him, love him, and serve him.

Job's counselors mostly got it wrong but occasionally got some things right. Still, they certainly prepared Job to listen to the voice of God.

> Lord, I am willing
> To receive what You give
> To lack what You withhold
> To relinquish what You take
> To suffer what You inflict
> To be what You require.
> And, Lord, if others are to be
> Your messengers to me,
> I am willing to hear and heed
> What they have to say. Amen.
> (Nelson Mink, *Pocket Pearls*, in Swindoll, *Tardy Oxcart*, 552–53)

Arthur Gordon relates the story of how he was stricken with polio at age three. His parents, probably Depression-poor and overwhelmed, had abandoned him at a New York City hospital. Taken in by a foster family, he was sent to stay with their relatives in Georgia when he was six, in hopes that the warmer climate would improve his condition. What improved his condition, though, was Maum Jean, an elderly,

African American woman who took that "frail lost, lonely little boy" into her heart. For six years, she daily massaged his weak legs; administered her own hydrotherapy in a nearby creek; and encouraged him spiritually with her stories, songs, and prayers. Gordon writes,

> Night after night Maum Jean continued the massaging and praying. Then one morning, when I was about twelve, she told me she had a surprise for me. She led me out into the yard, placed me with my back against an oak tree; I can feel the rough bark of it to this day. She took away my crutches and braces. She moved back a dozen paces and told me that the Lord had spoken to her in a dream. He had said that the time had come for me to walk. "So now," said Maum Jean, "I want you to walk over to me." My instant reaction was fear. I knew I couldn't walk unaided; I had tried. I shrank back against the solid support of the tree. Maum Jean continued to urge me. I burst into tears. I begged. I pleaded. Her voice rose suddenly, no longer gentle and coaxing but full of power and command. "You can walk, boy! The Lord has spoken! Now walk over here." She knelt down and held out her arms. And somehow, impelled by something stronger than fear, I took a faltering step, and another, and another, until I reached Maum Jean and fell into her arms, both of us weeping. It was two more years before I could walk normally but I never used the crutches again. (Arthur Gordon, "A Touch of Wonder," in Swindoll, *Tardy Oxcart*, 583–84)

Debilitated by his suffering, Job thinks he will never walk again. But one far greater than Maum Jean is about to place Job's back against a tree and teach him how.

Reflect and Discuss

1. In what ways does Elihu differ from the three friends in his approach to Job?
2. Do you view Elihu positively, negatively, or neutrally in light of what he says to Job?
3. How does Elihu's view of suffering differ from that of the three friends?
4. Do you think Elihu offers a viable answer to Job's suffering? Why?
5. Why do you think neither Job nor God responds to Elihu?

"All Creatures of Our God and King"—God Speaks

JOB 38–41

Main Idea: God speaks to Job and poses questions about nature to demonstrate Job's incapacity to understand, his inability to run the universe, and thus his inability to know how God dispenses justice.

I. Yahweh's First Speech (38:1–40:2)
II. Job's Response (40:3-5)
III. Yahweh's Second Speech (40:6–41:34)

In the movie *Robin Hood: Prince of Thieves*, Kevin Costner plays the irascible character who thwarted the evil plans of the sheriff of Nottingham in the absence of King Richard, who was away fighting in the Crusades. Having himself returned to England from the Crusades, Robin Hood fell in love with his childhood friend, Maid Marion, the king's cousin. After the defeat and death of the evil sheriff, Robin Hood and Marion are about to be married by Friar Tuck. He says, "Any man who has any reason why these two should not be joined, let him speak now, or forever hold his peace." There is a pause, and then Friar Tuck continues: "Then I now pronounce you . . . ," but before he can complete his sentence, a regal voice from off camera exclaims, "Hold! I speak!" The camera pans to a retinue of soldiers on horseback slowly approaching, and to the surprise and delight of the wedding attendees, and the movie audience, King Richard, played by Sean Connery, has just arrived to the happy occasion! Suddenly every knee bows in the presence of the king, who approaches the happy couple to give away the bride in marriage.

After all of the wrangling back and forth between Job and his three friends, suddenly now at the end, the previously silent King's regal voice is heard by Job: "Hold! I speak!"

Job 38:1–42:6 constitutes the final part of the poetic section of Job. Here God himself speaks. With the exception of three verses—40:3-5, where Job makes an ever so brief first response to God—four entire chapters are God's speech to Job. Job's final response to God is recorded in 42:1-6.

God's speech in these chapters is nothing short of extraordinary! There is nothing else like this in all of Scripture. Job has been demanding an audience with the Almighty so he can prove his innocence. Now he gets his chance. God's silence is broken.

Let's take the aerial view of the passage at ten thousand feet, and then we can swoop down for some row-by-row crop dusting. The overall speech is structured in two sections: 38:1–40:2 and 40:6–41:34. The first section focuses on God's creative and sustaining power in his creation. After challenging Job's ability to debate him (38:1-3), God peppers Job with a series of questions focusing on God's creative powers (38:4-38) and his care for the animal kingdom (38:39–39:30). God then demands that Job answer his questions (40:1-2), but Job cowers in silence: "I am so insignificant. How can I answer you?" (40:3-5).

In the second section God issues another brief challenge for Job to "get ready to answer [him] like a man" (40:6-7). Here God unveils Job's main problem: his condemnation of God in order to justify himself (v. 8). God challenges Job regarding whether he is able to dispense justice on the earth (vv. 10-14).

God then offers two lengthy illustrations to demonstrate Job's lack of wisdom and power, the two things he would need in order to begin to understand how God operates his universe with justice. The first illustration is Behemoth, possibly a reference to the hippopotamus if an extant creature is in view (vv. 15-24). This powerful animal is beyond the ability of Job to understand or control. In 41:1-34 God describes a terrifying creature called Leviathan, perhaps a reference to the crocodile. Both of these creatures testify to the wonderful, marvelous wisdom and ways of God that are beyond Job's comprehension. God uses these two animals to demonstrate to Job his own utter incapacity to know, understand, or act in any way commensurate with God himself.

The section ends with Job's response recorded in 42:1-6. Job no longer stays quiet, but he begins to acknowledge how little he really knows and comprehends (42:1-3). Job has now come face-to-face with God himself and realizes the utter futility of his attempts to engage God on the subject of God's justice, wisdom, power, and sovereignty (42:4-6).

Yahweh's First Speech
JOB 38:1–40:2

God's speech begins with a simple statement of setting: "Then the LORD answered Job from the whirlwind" (v. 1). God's opening introduction to his speech consists of a rebuke of Job followed by a challenge. The rebuke: "Who is this who obscures my counsel with ignorant words?" (v. 2). The challenge: "Get ready to answer me like a man; when I question you, you will inform me" (v. 3). The Hebrew word for "counsel" here means wise counsel. Job had neither seen the issue of his suffering clearly nor spoken correctly about it. Job did not have all the facts, particularly the fact of the heavenly encounter between God and Satan. Job's false inferences concerning his suffering and his God kept him in darkness, paradox, and puzzlement. We might paraphrase God's rebuke to Job as, "Who do you think you are? Who would be so foolish as to muddy up my plans when they know absolutely nothing about them?"

God's challenge to Job is essentially, "Man up! Stand and deliver, Job!" In the Hebrew this is expressed in the picturesque way of "gird up your loins." In order to do strenuous work, run, or fight, men had to tuck their long robes into a belt or sash. The figure of speech in Hebrew suggests Job should be alert and ready to engage God.

Job has been looking for answers. Instead of answering Job's questions, God asks questions! The God who comes with the answers poses questions. For the next four chapters, God peppers Job with a series of questions; seventy-seven to be exact. You might call these chapters "God's Science Quiz," including questions of cosmogony, astronomy, oceanography, meteorology, zoology, and two specific creatures: Behemoth and Leviathan. The divine professor sits Job down in his class and schools him with a lecture consisting mostly of questions that seem to have little to do with Job's suffering. Each question highlights the sovereign power, majesty, wisdom, and awesomeness of almighty God. Each is designed to question Job's competence to pass judgment on God's providential operation of the universe. God essentially says to Job, "Let me see your qualifications. I have a list here of several questions I would like to ask to see if you are competent to understand how things are. If you are able to handle these basic, elementary questions, then we will talk."

For the entire book of Job, the five key players—Job, his three friends, and Elihu—have all bantered about the question of divine justice. It was their all-consuming concern. Yet God virtually ignored it. Job had wanted a legal trial with God on the witness stand. But now it is Job on the witness stand. Job the plaintiff has suddenly become Job the defendant (Zuck, *Job*, 165)!

In 38:4-11 God questions Job concerning his knowledge of the creation of the earth (vv. 4-7) and the oceans (vv. 8-11). "Where were you when I established the earth?" (v. 4). Of course, Job was nowhere. "Who fixed its dimensions? Certainly you know! Who stretched a measuring line across it?" (v. 5). Job, are you capable of measuring the earth in its circumference? Of course not. Job, are you capable of explaining the earth's foundations when God's angels sang together and shouted for joy at its creation (vv. 6-7)? No, you're not. Job, you are unable to do any of these things; thus, how can you possibly be in a position to advise God concerning them? Job, since you don't know how the earth originated, you are disqualified from commenting on how it is governed.

Who set the boundaries for the seas when they were created (vv. 8-11)? In this section God uses the imagery and poetic language of childbirth to describe the creation of the oceans. The shoreline is pictured as "gates" that keep the waters in their place. The clouds are the baby's garments and the darkness its swaddling clothes. "The sea, born clothed and confined to its cosmic playpen, is now given the paternal command never to cross the appointed boundaries" (Habel, *Book of Job*, 205). Job could not answer because he was a nonparticipant in creation. So far, he is flunking God's science quiz.

Surely, if Job is to criticize God's governance of the world, he should at least know something about the rotation of the earth on its axis such that light and darkness appear every twenty-four hours. Surely Job, you have the wherewithal to bring about the morning dawn (vv. 12-15). But, unfortunately, Job has never organized and launched a new day; therefore, how can he speak about the governance of the universe? Can Job administrate justice in such a way that the wicked may be broken in their power in the same way that tectonic forces shape the face of the earth (vv. 13-15)? Job remains silent.

In verses 16-18 God queries if Job knows things he has never seen, like the source of the waters of the sea, the depths of the oceans, the gates of deep darkness, the extent (width) of the earth. What say you, Job? Silence.

In verses 19-24 God asks Job if he understands the source and nature of light and darkness, where snow and hail are stored, and the source of the "east wind." In verses 25-30 God asks Job who cleared a path in the atmosphere for the rains and floodwaters to fall on the earth so that vegetation may grow (vv. 25-27). God questions Job concerning the origin of rain, dew, ice, and frost (vv. 28-30).

God asks Job in 38:31-35 whether he is sufficiently up on his astronomy and meteorology. To be qualified as God's critic, surely Job is able to sustain the constellations Pleiades, Orion, or the Bear (the Big Dipper), right? Does he understand the "laws of heaven," the principles by which the sun, moon, and stars are governed? Does Job have control over nature such that he could command the clouds to rain or the lightning to flash ("Do they report to you: 'Here we are'?") (v. 35)?

In verses 36-38 Job is asked, "Who put wisdom in the heart, or gave the mind understanding?" Who has the wisdom to number the clouds or cause the rain to fall on the hard, parched ground?

In 38:39-41 and continuing through 39:30, God shifts his focus to the animal kingdom. In this tour of a living museum of natural history, God queries Job about six different animals and four kinds of birds. The apparent randomness of God's choice of examples includes everything from the ferocious to the helpless; from the shy to the strong; from the bizarre to the wild. Yet there seems to be a reason for God's choices. The ten examples occur in five groups of two.

> Questions about the first two animals pertain to providing food for them; questions about the next two relate to their giving birth to their young; the queries about animals five and six have to do with freedom, the next two with out-of-the ordinary ways, and the last two with flight. It is fitting that the list begins with the lion, the king of the beasts, and concludes with the eagle, the king of the birds. (Zuck, *Job*, 170–71)

All these specimens exhibit God's creative genius and providential care of his creation.

In 38:39-41 God begins by asking Job about the lioness and the raven. Does Job know how to provide food to sustain them? He does not.

Job 39:1-4 continues God's tour of the zoo with mountain goats and wild deer. Does Job know how to provide for either species as they give birth to their young and while their offspring learn to take care of themselves without the aid of human help?

In verses 5-12 God continues his questioning of Job's zoological knowledge. Wild donkeys roam the hinterlands and are notoriously difficult to domesticate. Did the freedom the wild donkey has to avoid the city and roam the desert come from Job? No, his survival is dependent on God's provision (vv. 5-8). The same situation occurs with the wild ox. The wild ox is mentioned nine times in the Old Testament and is known for its strength and powerful horns. It is distinguished from the domesticated ox and resists domestication, making it unusable for plowing. If Job cannot handle the wild donkeys and oxen, he certainly can't govern God's universe of nature (vv. 9-12).

God moves to discourse about the ostrich in verses 13-18. Interestingly, in this section God asks not a single question but only employs declarative sentences. The ostrich is a weird-looking bird weighing up to three hundred pounds and reaching to a height of eight feet. She is the only bird with two toes and eyelashes, and though she is winged, she can't fly but can run at speeds up to forty miles per hour, taking giant strides of twelve to fifteen feet. She builds her nest in the sand and, like a poor parent, often leaves her eggs unprotected in a way that seems careless. Arabic culture has long considered the ostrich to be characterized by stupidity. God's creation of the ostrich demonstrates his sovereign creativity: the bird is inferior to other animals in wisdom but superior in other ways. There is no way for Job to explain God's reason or purpose in creating the ostrich, so how can Job have the wisdom to run all of nature?

In 39:19-25 God turns his attention to the warhorse in a vivid description. The warhorse is fitted for battle and seems to enjoy charging the opposing enemy line fearlessly! God's point in this paragraph seems to be a comparison of Job's inferiority to the horse, which naturally leads to the conclusion that Job is inferior to the horse's maker.

God turns to the beautiful and graceful hawk in its migration flight to the south (v. 26). Finally, Job's quick tour of God's zoo concludes with the majestic eagle (vv. 27-30). In the inaccessible mountain crag, the eagle builds her nest. With her keen eyesight, she spots her food from a great distance and swoops down to capture it for her young. God's point seems to be that he is the one who knows how to create, equip, and meet the needs of such wonders of nature. Are you able to do this, Job? No, he is not.

God ends his first speech in Job 40:1-2 as he had begun in chapter 38—with a challenge: "Will the one who contends with the Almighty correct him? Let him who argues with God give an answer." The time has come for Job to answer God's blitz quiz. Job had been accusing God of contending with him; now God turns the tables. Time for a yes or no answer, Job!

Job's Response

JOB 40:3-5

Job makes his first reply to God. (Here's your chance, Job! You've been waiting and longing for this moment to stand face-to-face with God and get the answers you feel you deserve!) Stunned and overawed at God's parade of power and wisdom in creation, Job replies,

> *"I am so insignificant. How can I answer you? I place my hand over my mouth. I have spoken once, and I will not reply; twice, but now I can add nothing."* (vv. 4-5)

Like a talkative kid in elementary school who is supposed to be doing his work quietly while the teacher is out of the room but instead talks incessantly and fails to realize the teacher has returned, Job is caught up short.

Job's response asserts two things: (1) his insignificance—his weak humanity and lowly state as a created being as compared to God's infinite wisdom and power; and (2) his inability—he has said enough and has no more to say to God. Job is beginning to see clearly that he does not see clearly. Arguing with God about justice is a no-win proposition. It is impossible for a human being to attempt to measure God's justice with puny and fallible human scales. All Job can sputter to God is the rough equivalent of "I talk too much!" and "I don't know what I'm talking about." Job had been frustrated at God's silence throughout the book. Now Job is silent.

> Job had come almost full circle—from hesitation to confront God ("How then can I answer Him?" [9:14]) through confidence ("I will answer" [13:22a]) and a final sweep of assertiveness ("Like a prince I would approach Him" [31:37]) to humbled inability to respond. (Zuck, *Job*, 175)

Yahweh's Second Speech

JOB 40:6–41:34

Job may feel that the encounter is over and there is nothing more to say. But God says, "No, I'm not done yet, Job!" God answers Job a second time from the whirlwind (v. 6): "Get ready to answer me like a man;[46] When I question you, you will inform me" (v. 7). Job is now out of options. In the game Who Wants to Contend with God?, he can't phone a friend or use 50-50; the time has come for Job to give his "final answer." Job had brought a legal suit against God, and God has offered evidence that the suit should be thrown out of court (Holbert, *Preaching Job*, 129).

The key question that gets to the heart of the problem is the one God asks Job in verse 8: "Would you really challenge my justice? Would you declare me guilty to justify yourself?" God is asking Job, "Do you have to make me wrong so you can be right?" (Holbert, *Preaching Job*, 133). Job's headlong defense of his own integrity got him into trouble. It pushed him beyond the boundary to the point that he questioned God's justice in his life. Job had boastfully contended that he understood enough about things to conclude that God was being unfair. Well, Job, if your notion of justice is superior to God's notion of justice, then you must also have the equality or superiority of power as compared to God too! "Do you have an arm like God's? Can you thunder with a voice like his?" (v. 9). With a divine chuckle, God challenges Job to an arm-wrestling contest.

Job's problem is often our problem. But do we really want to argue with God over what is fair in life? Do we really want to demand of God, "Give me what I deserve!"? Spiritually speaking, the dumbest thing we could ask God for is justice. If we got justice, we would spend eternity separated from God because of our sin. That's what we deserve. Don't ask God for justice. Ask him for mercy and grace.

A customer was unhappy with how her photograph looked, so she complained to the photographer: "This picture doesn't do me justice!" The photographer responded, "You don't need justice; you need mercy!" We don't need justice; we need mercy and grace, just like Job.

In 40:10-14 God does not ask a single question of Job. Instead, several declarative statements function semantically as interrogatives with

---

[46] The CSB's "Get ready to answer me like a man" is the rendering of the Hebrew "gird up your loins." "Although impossible to prove, it seems likely that the Lord employed the verb ['azar] 'gird up {the loins}' in a forensic sense in 38:3 (and 40:7) in order to heighten the irony of his twofold interrogation of Job. A main function of the Lord's speeches is to show the absurdity of Job's attempt to manipulate God by a 'lawsuit,' which assumed that his relationship to God is a juridical one. Consequently, the Lord virtually ignored Job's allegations of His injustice (except for 40:8)" (Parsons, "Structure and Purpose," 32).

the single intent of asking Job, "Who is omnipotent over all creation and therefore competent to criticize God's justice?"

First, God ironically suggests that Job play God and imagine himself in control of the universe. Job must dress the part and "adorn [him]self with majesty and splendor, and clothe [him]self with honor and glory" (v. 10). Next, Job must display his anger by bringing down the wicked: "Trample the wicked where they stand. . . . Imprison them in the grave" (vv. 11-13). If Job could perform this administrative function, which he had previously accused God of neglecting, then God would "confess to [him] that [his] own right hand can deliver [him]" (v. 14) (Zuck, *Job*, 176–77).

Archer summed it up well:

> If you think to contend with me about the way I deal with
> men in the light of their innocence or guilt, then you must
> demonstrate an ability on your own part of unleashing your
> judicial wrath at all the proud and compelling them to abase
> themselves before the bar of justice. Then you must crush
> them completely and consign them to the grave as retribution
> for their sin. Only when you have accomplished all of this will
> I concede your ability to justify your criticism of Me. (*Book of Job*, 106)

In the remainder of God's second speech (40:15–41:34), God takes Job to what seems a prehistoric stock show and rodeo. God singles out two animals to illustrate to Job God's control of the world: Behemoth and Leviathan. There has been much debate about the identity of these two creatures. It boils down to two alternatives: mythological chaos creatures or actual animals. If the former, God may be simply referencing cultural beliefs he himself does not affirm in terms of their actual existence. But the latter option is preferable due to how God speaks of Behemoth: "which [he] made along with [Job]" (v. 15),[47] not a likely statement if Behemoth is a mythological creature.[48]

Behemoth has often been identified as either an elephant, hornless rhinoceros (extinct), brontosaurus (extinct), water buffalo, or what I think is most likely, the hippopotamus, based on the description. His

---

[47] As also Ps 104:26; Joel 1:20.
[48] For an accessible discussion of the interpretation of Leviathan and Behemoth, consult Brown, *Job*, 394–97.

diet, strength, habitat, and fierceness point in this direction. He eats grass (feeding on the vegetation floating down from the hills), possesses great strength in his back and belly, and his thigh tendons, bones, and limbs are strong (vv. 16-18). God describes him as "the foremost of God's works; only his Maker can draw the sword against him" (v. 19). All sorts of wild animals play where Behemoth is found, where he "hides in the protection of marshy reeds"[49] and "the willows . . . surround him" (vv. 20-22). He is a fearless animal (v. 23) and almost impossible to capture (v. 24). Fear not, though, for God's pets are leashed.

The point here is for Job to understand that he cannot approach or fathom the wisdom of God in creating such a creature like Behemoth. Thus, how can Job be qualified to determine issues of justice for himself or anyone else?

As if things couldn't get any stranger, in chapter 41 God introduces Job to another of his magnificent creations: Leviathan. Here again, theories abound as to the identity of this great creature. Some see Leviathan as a mythological creature[50] such as the dragon; a seven-headed sea monster in Ugaritic mythology, the whale, the dolphin, or a marine dinosaur that survived the flood. But to me it seems more likely that Leviathan is a reference to a crocodile or some similar reptile. Evidence exists that the crocodile was once an inhabitant of the Levant.

Most descriptive characteristics of Leviathan would fit the crocodile: he cannot be domesticated (vv. 2-6), and it is virtually impossible to capture or kill him (vv. 1,7-9).

In verses 10-11 God interrupts his description to make an application for Job:

> "No one is ferocious enough to rouse Leviathan; who then can stand against me? Who confronted me, that I should repay him? Everything under heaven belongs to me." (vv. 10-11)

God's syllogistic reasoning is simple: Job, I created Leviathan. You cannot control him or challenge him. Therefore, you cannot control or challenge me.

---

[49] Hippopotami were known to lie hidden among the lotuses and reeds of the Jordan River in ancient times (Archer, *Book of Job*, 107). An adult hippo can weigh in excess of eight thousand pounds.

[50] Leviathan is the only creature in God's list not explicitly described as a creation of God in his speech, but the text and context make this evident.

In verses 12-34 God continues his detailed description of Leviathan in two parts: his anatomy (vv. 12-25) and his inability to be captured by hunters and their equipment (vv. 26-34). Both sections conclude with a statement about humanity's fear of the creature.

Verses 18-20, I think, are examples of poetic language in describing a crocodile and do not lend support to the theory that this is some mythical creature: "His snorting flashes with light, while his eyes are like the rays of dawn. Flaming torches shoot from his mouth; fiery sparks fly out! Smoke billows from his nostrils as from a boiling pot." When the crocodile snorts spray through his nostrils, the water particles appear to flash light in the bright sun. The small eyes with their catlike slits for pupils are the first part of the animal one sees when it slowly emerges from the water. The author compares this to the sun's rays at dawn. In Egyptian hieroglyphics, the eye of the crocodile represents dawn.

Verse 25 speaks of the fear people have when the creature begins to thrash about in the water.

The crocodile was virtually impossible to capture in Job's day (vv. 26-29). When he swims, the crocodile churns up the water, and as he moves swiftly through the water, "he leaves a shining wake behind him" such that the whitecaps on the water's surface appear like grey hair (vv. 30-32).

Finally, God concludes Job's tour of Leviathan in 41:33-34: "He has no equal on earth—a creature devoid of fear! He surveys everything that is haughty; he is king over all the proud beasts."[51]

From Behemoth and Leviathan, and indeed from all of God's creatures, Job has been listening to God lecture to this point.[52] Job is to infer that if God can make, care for, and control all these creatures, then God is beyond the capability of Job to attempt to hold him accountable to a mere human assessment. God's infinite capacity to govern all of nature makes clear Job is in no position to question God about his own suffering. He may not understand, but he must not presume to judge God.

---

[51] "Not many people know that a whole chapter of the Bible is devoted to a description of a crocodile, and fewer still that—in one way or another—the crocodile is the key to the meaning of the universe" (Clines, "Coming to a Theological Conclusion," 216).

[52] "This God loves the detail, and even when he is taking the broadest view, he only ever works with examples" (Clines, "Coming to a Theological Conclusion," 211). Here is God the Aristotelian—he loves the particulars.

Anyone who cannot undertake God's works has no right to undermine God's ways. And anyone who trembles at the sight of fierce beasts is unwise in boldly contending with the beasts' Maker. (Zuck, *Job*, 183)[53]

Just as the natural order involves things that escape Job's knowledge, so the moral order is beyond his power to comprehend. Game. Set. Match. Many find God's response to Job in these four chapters puzzling and troubling. Puzzling because on the surface it doesn't appear God addresses the issue of Job's suffering at all. Troubling because, well, God doesn't appear to address Job's suffering at all. However, if God is too harsh on Job, he might appear to endorse the views of the three friends. If he is too soft, then Job might not hear what God wanted him to hear. "The playful irony of the Yahweh speeches preserves a right balance" (Wilson, "Job, Book of," 386).

At first God refused to answer. Chapter after chapter in Job concludes without a single syllable from God. As Brueggemann noted,

He remains inscrutably remote from the polemics. This remoteness is treated not as silence but as majestic mystery. Finally, God does answer. It is not, however, a user-friendly answer, and it concedes nothing to Job. God refuses to enter into discussion with Job about justice, reliability, or covenantal symmetry. God's speech is one of overwhelmingness, not engagement. (*Theology of the Old Testament*, 390)

God refuses to be domesticated.

Along with Job, we must ever learn the lesson that God owes us nothing, including an explanation for our suffering. We must all come to the place in our Christian lives where we learn total trust and total

---

[53] "To be sure, God's examples from nature are exhibitions of His power, but they are also exhibitions of His wisdom and His providence for His creatures (38.27; 39.1-4; 26). Through nature, God reveals Himself to Job as both purposive and nonpurposive, playful and uncanny, as evidenced by the monsters He created. To study nature is to perceive the complexity, the unity of contraries, in God's attributes, and the inadequacy of human reason to explain His behavior, not the least in His dealings with man" (Greenberg, *Book of Job*, xix–xx). "Job has no right to an explanation for his suffering, any more than he has a right to have the purpose of crocodiles explained to him. . . . The order of creation sets the standard for the moral order of the universe; and that is, that God must be allowed to know what he is doing, and lies under no obligation to give any account of himself" (Clines, "Shape and Argument," 138).

dependence on our heavenly Father. Our example of total trust in God and total dependence on God is Jesus. In John's Gospel I am struck by how many times Jesus says things like, "I have come to do the will of my Father who sent me"; "I always do those things that please the Father"; "I don't speak of myself, but I speak what the Father has told me to say." Like Job, we must learn the path of total trust and obedience in the sovereign Lord who orders and sustains nature and who will order and sustain our lives. Through his many unanswerable questions to Job, God taught Job who is in charge. Job is not capable of understanding the ways of God or of operating God's world. Neither are we. Our attitude should be that of Jesus's mother Mary at the wedding feast in Cana recorded in John 2. She said to the servants, "Do whatever he tells you." He is ultimately in charge, and only he has the sovereign power to do what needs to be done. This should always be our attitude toward the Lord, no matter what is happening in the world or in our personal lives that we cannot understand. "Do whatever he tells you."

Reflect and Discuss

1. What does God charge Job with in his two speeches?
2. How does Job respond to God's first speech?
3. Why do you think God peppers Job with questions about his knowledge of nature?
4. Why do you think God does not directly answer Job's questions about his suffering and the justice of God?
5. Do you think Behemoth and Leviathan are literal creatures or mythological creatures? Why?

God Is All You Need—Job's Response to God

JOB 42:1-6

Main Idea: In light of God's presence and revelation to Job, Job repents of accusing God of injustice and submits himself to God.

I.   God's Omnipotence and Sovereignty (42:2)
II. Job's Ignorance (42:3)
III. Job's Revelation (42:4–5)
IV. Job's Repentance (42:6)

Have you ever felt speechless in the presence of a famous person? In the movie *The Christmas Story*, Ralphie can't seem to convince his mother that she should let him have a Red Ryder BB gun for Christmas. Running out of options as Christmas approaches, Ralphie hits on the idea of asking Santa Claus for it. When he finally gets to sit in Santa's lap, he freezes and can't think of what to ask Santa for. Santa says, "How about a nice football?" Ralphie, still in a mental fog, manages a nod and a faint yes. As Santa's elf puts Ralphie on the slide to slide down from Santa's elevated platform and chair, Ralphie descends about six feet, then puts his feet out and suddenly stops. Turning around, he climbs back up the slide, looks at Santa, and informs him of the desired Christmas present. Santa looks down silently for a moment, then says, "You'll shoot your eye out, kid!" And with a "Ho, Ho, Ho!" and the sole of his boot, he gently gives Ralphie a nudge and down the slide he goes.

With the intensity and eagerness of Ralphie, Job has longed for an audience with God concerning his suffering. When Job finally gets his wish, he is dumbfounded in the presence of almighty God. In the face of God's rapid-fire questions about how the universe is run, Job is left with a stupefied silence. He can't think of a thing to say. "God's questions aren't intended to teach; they are intended to stun. They aren't intended to enlighten; they are intended to awaken. They aren't intended to stir the mind; they are intended to bend the knees" (Lucado, *Eye of the Storm*, 162).

Now at the end of God's four-chapter Q&A session with Job, illustrating God's omnipotence and sovereignty, Job is left with only two things to say: (1) an admission of his own ignorance, and (2) repentance of his foolishness.

The key to understanding what God is up to may be found in Job's response to God in 42:1-6, which concludes the entire poetic section of Job (3:1–42:6). These six verses record Job's final response to Yahweh:

> *I know that you can do anything and no plan of yours can be thwarted. You asked, "Who is this who conceals my counsel with ignorance?" Surely I spoke about things I did not understand, things too wondrous for me to know. You said, "Listen now, and I will speak. When I question you, you will inform me." I had heard reports about you, but now my eyes have seen you. Therefore, I reject my words and am sorry for them; I am dust and ashes."*

Job begins by acknowledging the ultimate authority of God, including his ultimate sovereignty. He continues by acknowledging his own ignorance and his sin. Finally, Job confesses his sin before God and acknowledges his finitude. In the midst of it all, God destroyed Job's pride but not his personhood. All his self-pity, frustration, and anger evaporate in the presence of God.

Job's suffering for no apparent reason caused him to question God's orderly universe. There must be a breakdown in the system somewhere. God refutes that charge with his two speeches. There is a plan; Job just doesn't know what it is.

Furthermore, the world is not about Job or what Job does. Job never gets an answer to his question or learns details about his suffering, much less about the divine encounter in the heavenly council described in chapters 1–2. During Job's encounters with the three friends, he expressed his desire to take God to court. God obliged by putting Job on the witness stand and questioning him.

God's response is not intended to answer Job's question, at least not the way Job expected an answer. God's response was intended to reorient Job to God himself primarily by a combination of natural theology (the tour of nature) and special revelation (God revealed himself to Job and conducted the tour). The result? Job is satisfied. There is something about firsthand experience with God that trumps secondhand experience: "I had heard reports about you, but now my eyes have seen you" (v. 5).

There is some question about exactly what Job means by what he says in 42:6. Literally, the text reads, "I reject [with no direct object] and

I repent concerning dust and ashes." Many translations insert "myself" as the direct object. Others, like the CSB, translate, "I reject my words and am sorry for them." Others suggest the direct object should be his attitude of pride and even rebellion against God.

Though most translations render Job's last statement in verse 6 as "I *repent* in dust and ashes," the CSB renders it "I *am* dust and ashes" (emphasis added). Either way one approaches the text, the point remains the same: Job repented. In 40:4-5 Job made his first response to God's speech. There he said in essence, "I will say no more." Now in 42:6 Job not only says no more but repents of what he had said. Job has "seen" God by receiving his words. "Truly to see God is to hear God" (Fyall, *Now My Eyes Have Seen You*, 179). In seeing God, Job sees himself in relation to God in a way he had never seen before.[54]

God's message in the form of these many questions broke through to Job. "Job is a peasant, telling the King how to run the kingdom. Job is an illiterate, telling e. e. cummings to capitalize his personal pronouns. Job is the bat boy, telling Babe Ruth to change his batting stance. Job is the clay, telling the potter not to press so hard" (Lucado, *Eye of the Storm*, 163).

Job has learned many lessons. He learned about God's omnipotence (v. 2). He learned about God's sovereignty (v. 2). He learned about his own ignorance and God's superior knowledge and wisdom (v. 3). The main point behind God's extended object lesson in Job 38–42 is the ultimate fact that the universe is theocentric. If Job cannot understand how God governs the natural world, which he certainly cannot, then he cannot be expected to comprehend how God governs humanity. The world is like the periodic chart of the elements. There is order but not completely predictable order. Not everything fits neatly into place, nor does it have to.

> God's challenge to Job is not directed toward Job's integrity
> or his suffering, but toward Job's level of discernment about
> the design of the universe (38:2). Job's innocence is not in
> question, but his understanding of the design of the universe is
> deficient. God's speeches make it clear that one cannot deduce
> from the laws of the universe that the wicked will inevitably be
> punished or that the innocent will be immune from suffering.

---

[54] As F. Buechner expressed it, "By comparison he was no more than a fleck of dust on the head of a pin in the lapel of a dancing flea" (*Peculiar Treasures*, 38).

There is no eternal principle of natural justice inherent in the natural order. (Habel, "Literary Features," 119)

Job learned that sometimes we truly encounter God only through great suffering. This may well be the reason for your own suffering right now. You've heard about God. Now God wants you to "see" him, to experience him in a new way as Job did. Job got to the place where he didn't *need* answers anymore. God himself was answer enough.

It is important to notice that Job repented while he was still suffering and with no knowledge that God would ever restore his health and wealth. Job submitted to God, confessed his ignorance of God and his ways, silenced himself before God (vv. 3-4), and repented (v. 6). The motifs of Job's response serve as a model to us all. Submission and resignation, followed by humility, followed by silence (ceasing from arguing with God about it), followed by confession and repentance, resulting in what some call the "beatific vision" in verse 5, the goal of human existence (Ryken, "Job, Book of," 454).

Job finally faced his real problem: his self-defensiveness. Job rightly refused to settle for a false solution to the mystery of his suffering. Job's three friends did their best to brainwash Job to accept the lie that his own hidden sins had brought about his suffering. But in the pressure of his pain, Job was guilty of accusing God of injustice for allowing such extreme suffering. In a sense this misjudgment on Job's part caused him to fall into the same grave fallacy into which his three critics had fallen. They too misjudged God on the basis of mere appearances. Job's criticism was similar to the three friends': he misjudged God and accused him of injustice like Job's three friends misjudged Job and accused him of sin he did not commit (Archer, *Book of Job*, 106).[55] For several

---

[55] Greenberg's assessment is worth the lengthy quotation: "What had Job known of God in his former happy state? He had known Him as a conferrer of order and good. Basking in His light, Job's life had been suffused with blessings (29.2-5). No later evidence to the contrary could wipe out Job's knowledge of God's benignity gained from personal experience. Job calls that former knowledge of God a 'hearing,' while his later knowledge, earned through suffering, is a 'seeing' (42.5); that is, the latter knowledge gained about God is to the former as seeing is to hearing—far more comprehensive and adequate. Formerly, Job had only a limited notion of God's nature—as a benign, constructive factor in his life, 'good' in terms of human morality. At that time, any evidence that ran against this conception of God was peripheral: it lay outside Job's focus. He assumed that it too could somehow be contained in his view of the divine moral order, but nothing pressed him to look the uncongenial facts in the face.

chapters, Job asked God, "Are you really just?" When he responded to Job, God essentially asked, "Seriously?"

> There are two truths that collide in the book of Job. Suffering is common to all people. Suffering is sometimes punitive, corrective, exemplary, vicarious. From one angle, suffering is inflicted by God in justice. From another angle, it can be accepted by persons in love. Scripture is clear; God is no respecter of persons. He pays back every man according to his deeds. This is where justice begins: but it is not where love ends. These two truths do not cover all the facts. They do not apply to Job. (Anderson, "Problem of Suffering," 186–87)

No doubt discerning readers have wondered why God did not reveal or explain to Job the nature of the test involved in his suffering as he did with Abraham. God told Abraham, "Now I know that you fear God" (Gen 22:12). The text never answers this question. Greenberg seems right:

> From the epilogue, it is clear that God's vindication of Job's honesty, proven in his passionate recriminations against God and against his friends' simplistic theories, is more important for Job than knowing the reason for his suffering. The epilogue shows Job satisfied by the divine assurance that his friends' arguments were specious, as he had always asserted (13.7-10; 19.22-29; 42.7-9). Beyond that, God does not go in revealing to Job the cause of his suffering. (*Book of Job*, xxi)

Job dared carry the question of human justice into the danger zone of God's holiness. But as Brueggemann noted, "There is a terrible mismatch between human justice and God's sovereign holiness" (*Theology of the Old Testament*, 392).

One final point is worth making. God's answer to the problem of suffering does not include reincarnation. As Hebrews 9:27 states, "It is appointed for people to die once—and after this, judgment."

"But misfortune moved the periphery into the center, and the perplexity that ensued is a testimony to Job's piety, for he was not transformed by senseless misfortune into a scoffer—a denier of God—but, instead, thrown into confusion. His experience of God in good times had left on him indelible conviction of God's goodness that clashed with the new, equally strong evidence of God's enmity. Though one contradicted the other, Job experienced both as the work of God, and did not forget the first (as did his wife) when the second overtook him" (Greenberg, *Book of Job*, xx).

Job's final word to God is in beautiful contrast with much
of his former unmeasured utterances. It breathes lowliness,
submission, and contented acquiescence in a providence
partially understood. (Maclaren, *Esther, Job*, 64)

1. Job acknowledges God's omnipotence. "There had been frequent recognitions of that attribute in the earlier speeches, but these
had lacked the element of submission and had been complaint rather
than adoration" (Maclaren, *Esther, Job*, 65). We learn a lesson from this:
"The very same thought of God may be an argument for arraigning and
for vindicating his providence" (ibid.).

2. Job acknowledges his incapacity for judging God's providence.
God's rebuke of Job 38:2 has now become Job's confession.

"Job had been a critic; now he is a worshiper. He had tried to
fathom the bottomless and had been angry because his short
measuring line had not reached the depths." (Ibid., 66)

[In verse 4 Job] had tried to solve his problem by . . .
sometimes barely reverent thinking. He had racked brain
and heart in the effort, but he has learned a more excellent
way. . . . Prayer will do more for clearing mysteries than
speculation, however acute, and it will change the aspect of
the mysteries which it does not clear from being awful to being
solemn—veils covering depths of love, not clouds obscuring
the sun. (Ibid., 67)

The center of all Job's confession is in verse 5 [—a sense of
God's nearness.] That change was the master transformation
in Job's case, as it is for us all. Get closer to God, realise His
presence—life beneath His eye and with your eyes fixed on
Him—and ancient puzzles will puzzle no longer, and wounds
will cease to smart, and instead of angry expostulation or
bewildered attempts at construing His dealings, there will
come submission, and with submission, peace. (Ibid., 67–68)

The cure for questions of his providence is experience of
his nearness. (Ibid., 68)

A man who has learned his own sinfulness will find few
difficulties and no occasions for complaint in God's dealings
with him. If we would see aright the meaning of our sorrows,
we must look at them on our knees. Get near to God in

heart-knowledge of Him, and that will teach our sinfulness, and the two knowledges will combine to explain much of the meaning of sorrow, and to make the unexplained residue not hard to endure. (Ibid., 68)

Job's words came scalding hot from his heart. (Ibid., 69)

[Truth may be] spoken heartlessly, . . . and flung at sufferers like a stone, rather than laid on their hearts as a balm. (Ibid., 69)

It would be harder for some of us to offer sacrifices for our Eliphazes than to argue with them. (Ibid., 69)

It was "when Job prayed for his friends" that [he was healed.] The turning point was not merely the confession, [but his action.] In ministering to others, one's own griefs may be soothed. (Ibid., 70)

Our light affliction is working out an eternal weight of glory.

What mountains of words could not achieve, the presence of God to Job achieved. We who know Christ are "in him" and he dwells in us. Jesus said, "I am with you always" (Matt 28:20). The Greek word order of this wonderful statement of our Lord illustrates his nearness. Literally, the word order reads, "I with you am." Jesus, the great "I am," God in human flesh, brackets your life. As long as you realize that the "with you" is between "I" and "am," you will have the victory over suffering. As Paul said in Romans 8:35, nothing can "separate us from the love of God which is in Christ Jesus our Lord."

Job began to learn the important lesson we all must learn: "For our momentary light affliction is producing for us an absolutely incomparable eternal weight of glory" (2 Cor 4:17). Profound. We are coheirs with Christ. We share in his sufferings now; we will share in his glory then. We learn from Job that our hope is placed in what is yet to come. Our comfort in the midst of suffering comes from what is yet to come.

Both Job and Paul prayed many times for relief from their suffering. Job cried out to God over and over but to no avail. The heavens were brass. Paul prayed for God to remove his "thorn in the flesh" three times, an idiom expressing many times of concerted prayer but to no avail (2 Cor 12:8). Both Job and Paul received God's silent treatment. Unanswered prayer is God's silent treatment. Job mistook the silence of God for the indifference of God and told him so! But finally God answered Job. Paul waited some time before he received God's standing answer to his request for the removal of the thorn. Here is the lesson: never mistake the silence of God for the indifference of God! The prayers of God's people are never unheard or unheeded. God will answer in his time. He will either give us what we ask in Jesus's name, or he will give us what we need. Either way, he has not abandoned us.

Both Job and Paul received a direct answer from God. God himself appeared to Job. God himself responded to Paul. Paul's request is reported in indirect speech. God's answer is reported in direct speech: "he has said" (author's translation), perfect tense in Greek—God's standing answer to Paul that continues to ring in his ears—"My grace is sufficient for you" (2 Cor 12:9)! This reply was permanently valid. Paul's multiple prayer sessions and Job's extended whining sessions all led to one powerful lesson for both men. Both got a standing answer from God: God and his grace are all you need.

We must learn the difference between means and ends in prayer. Job desired relief from his suffering. Paul desired relief from his thorn. Both thought the means to their desired end was removal of suffering. But Job and Paul needed something much more than the removal of their suffering. Each needed an encounter with the living God. Their requests were denied, but their prayers were answered. The Lord sometimes refuses to give us what we ask in order to give us what we need. Like Job, sometimes we are so busy telling God what we think he ought to do, we cannot hear what he wants to do!

When Job encountered God, he never received from God an actual answer to his question about suffering. But Job's response in 42:1–6 reveals that God's answer was his own presence, which Job found sufficient: "I had heard reports about you, but now my eyes have seen you." God in his grace met Job, and Job found God's grace was enough. When Paul finally heard from God concerning his thorn, he did not receive what he desired—removal of the thorn. Rather, God said, "My grace is sufficient!" Job and Paul both learned that sufficient grace means all of the resources of God are on our side. Put all the needs of every human being on the planet together, and God's grace is sufficient to supply every one. God never has to make deposits to replenish his grace account. His account is never overdrawn or depleted. Both Job and Paul experienced God's sufficient grace for suffering. Sufficient grace—God's pillow for you to lay your head on in suffering.

Like Job, Paul too experienced God's power and grace in the midst of his weakness. Job came to the end of himself when he came face-to-face with God. Paul came to the end of himself when he realized his impotence before God. Both Job and Paul learned that weakness that knows itself to be weakness is strength.

Job and Paul both learned that pain is the medium of God's power. There is a certain quality to life that only suffering can bring. Were it all privilege, it would bring pride; were it all pain, despair. It is both—to bring power. Pain can be creative. It can transform character. It can deepen and sweeten us. Sorrow becomes a chisel in the hand of the Master Craftsman, and the result is Christlikeness. Credentials without grace equals bankruptcy. The suffering embittered Job until he came face-to-face with God. Then all of his bitterness drained out of him. The thorn may have tempted Paul to be bitter. But by the time he wrote 2 Corinthians, Paul's thorn had become useful. Paul's thorn blossomed! At the *throne* of grace, Job and Paul came to understand the meaning of the *thorn* of grace.

God is able to make more use of you thorned than thornless. "Free me from this suffering, and I will be more useful!" we cry. But if you were freed from suffering, you would be useless. You cannot drink the grapes; they have to be crushed. A. W. Tozer said, "God never uses a man greatly until he has hurt him deeply." God used Job greatly—he is a hero in the Old Testament, the poster child for patience. God used Paul greatly—he is a hero in the New Testament, the poster child for sufficient grace.

There are three ways you can pray about your suffering. You can pray to *escape* it. That's what Job prayed. That's what Paul prayed. You can pray to *endure* it. Or you can pray to *enlist* it. In his play *The Angel that Troubled the Waters*, Thornton Wilder vividly portrays the scene at the pool of Bethesda in Jerusalem where the sick, the maimed, and the blind are waiting eagerly for the troubling of the waters, believing that when an angel comes to stir the pool, healing is made available for those who immediately step into the waters. A physician with an infirmity steps forward and begs for the chance to be healed. The angel who presides over the healing waters answers: "Without your wound where would your power be? In Love's service, only the wounded soldiers can serve. Draw back" (*Collected Plays*, 54–56).

Job and Paul learned the value of being a wounded warrior who serves. Authentic ministry is God's power in your weakness. When suffering is combined with grace, the result is humility, dependence, and usability. Both Job and Paul learned to stop praying for pain's removal and experience pain's conversion by the presence of God in their lives. Paul said, "When I am weak, then I am strong." Job said, "I had heard reports about you, but now my eyes have seen you. Therefore, I reject my words and am sorry for them." Both Job and Paul changed their groaning into glorying.

Missionary Amy Carmichael wrote a moving short poem, "Hast Thou No Scar?"

> Hast thou no scar?
> No hidden scar on foot, or side, or hand?
> I hear thee sung as mighty in the land;
> I hear them hail thy bright, ascendant star.
> Hast thou no scar?
>
> Hast thou no wound?
> Yet I was wounded by the archers; spent,
> Leaned Me against a tree to die; and rent
> By ravening wolves that compassed me, I swooned.
> Hast thou no wound?
>
> No wound? No scar?
> Yet, as the Master shall the servant be,
> And pierced are the feet that follow Me.
> But thine are whole; can he have followed far
> Who has nor wound nor scar? (*Mountain Breezes*, 173)

Job responded correctly to his suffering and to God in the end. Earlier he had done what many of us do all too often when we suffer: he played the blame game. Our first inclination is to blame somebody. Sometimes we blame Satan. Sometimes we blame God. Second, we engage in a pity party. Self-pity comes when we focus on ourselves rather than God. The result is often anger and bitterness. Both are self-destructive.

Here are some practical ways to respond to your suffering, compliments of Charles Stanley:

1. Reaffirm your position in Christ.
2. Ask God to remove the adversity.
3. Reaffirm the promise of God's sustaining grace.

4. Thank God for the unique opportunity to grow spiritually.
5. Receive adversity as if it were from God.
6. Read and meditate on Scriptures describing the adversities of God's servants.

Stanley concluded his book *How to Handle Adversity* with these helpful words:

> Suffering is unavoidable. It comes without warning; it takes us by surprise. It can shatter or strengthen us. It can be the source of great bitterness or abounding joy. It can be the means by which our faith is destroyed. Or it can be the tool through which our faith is deepened. The outcome hinges not on the nature or source of our adversity, but on the character and spirit of our response. Our response to adversity will for the most part be determined by our reason for living, our purpose for being on this earth, as we see it.
>
> If you are a child of God whose heart's desire is to see God glorified through you, adversity will not put you down for the count. There will be those initial moments of shock and confusion. But the man or woman who has God's perspective on this life and the life to come will always emerge victorious. (Quoted in Stanley, *Victory*, 363–64)

Reflect and Discuss

1. What is the nature of Job's repentance before God?
2. What has changed for Job in light of his encounter with God?
3. What does Job mean when he says in the past he has "heard" of God but now he has "seen" him?
4. What do you think Job means when he says he rejects his words and is sorry for them?
5. Where was Job right and where was Job wrong?

All's Well that Ends Well—
God's Grace and Blessings

JOB 42:7-17

Main Idea: God condemns and restores Job's three friends and restores Job with blessings of physical healing, material wealth, and children.

I. **Condemnation and Restoration of Eliphaz, Bildad, and Zophar (42:7-9)**

II. **Blessing and Restoration of Job (42:10-17)**

All fairy tales have one thing in common: a happy ending. No matter how much pain and suffering occur in a story, no matter how many evil stepmothers or wicked witches there are, in the end somebody lives "happily ever after." The book of Job is no fairy tale. It is a true account about a real man named Job who experienced in one short time span enough loss, grief, pain, and suffering to last a dozen lifetimes. Still, it has a happy ending.

So the poetic section of Job ends, and the prose section, abandoned at the end of Job 2, is now taken up once again.

> This extreme moment of engagement is like a stunning artistic
> performance . . . and then one must leave the auditorium
> and go back to real life. . . . Or it is like the intensity of
> sexual interaction . . . and then one must do the dishes.
> (Brueggemann, *Theology of the Old Testament*, 392)

Many people are unhappy with the happy ending of Job. They think it undoes the basic premise of the book. Not so. The happy ending of Job reinforces our eternal hope in God. God is good—more so than we can ever imagine. Whatever comes our way, we believers live with holy confidence that our present light affliction is working for us an eternal weight of glory (2 Cor 4:7).

Condemnation and Restoration of
Eliphaz, Bildad, and Zophar
JOB 42:7-9

God has not forgotten about Job's three friends. The question arises, Just exactly what did they get so wrong?[56] The text never says. We can surmise that their sin included falsely accusing Job of sin based on their false assumption that the retribution principle was always a valid one-size-fits-all theology. The answer to suffering in Job is as much stated in the negative, what it is not, as the positive. God says, "I am angry with you and your two friends, for you have not spoken the truth about me, as my servant Job has" (v. 7). The answer is not retributive justice. It is not tit for tat. It is not even, "As you sow, that shall you reap," though that biblical principle is generally true.

Perhaps a part of the answer to the question of the error of Job's friends resides in their rigid orthodoxy. They lacked a compassionate approach to Job's suffering. They should have moved beyond Job's "verbal transgressions" of his accusations against God. They should have approached Job from the spirit of the law rather than the letter of the law. As Brown stated, the friends should have focused . . .

> on Job's spiritual pain rather than being put off by his
> violation of godly decorum.
> In contrast, a too-rigid orthodoxy sees a drunken man
> lying in his own vomit and condemns him as a vile sinner
> without first asking, "How did this poor soul get into such
> a broken condition?" It judges a prostitute to be an evil
> seductress without wondering, "Perhaps she herself is a victim
> of sex trafficking or some other form of sexual abuse?" This
> kind of religious attitude is careful to keep every last jot and
> tittle of the Law—like the Levite and the priest in the parable
> of the Good Samaritan who could not risk being defiled by
> tending to a beaten and bloodied man—in contrast with
> the religious outsider (the Samaritan!) who is moved by
> compassion to help (see Luke 10:25-37). (*Job*, 368)

---

[56] Andrew Zack Lewis summarizes and discusses five theories in answering this question (*Approaching Job*, 104–8).

But we might also ask, What did Job get right? First, Job knew he was not guilty of sin, and he maintained his innocence. Second, Job sought to engage God even when God was silent. Third, Job repented where he was guilty: trying to justify himself before God. God required Job's three friends to seek Job out and offer burnt offerings in Job's presence. Such a large sacrifice indicated the gravity of their sin. Then Job interceded for his friends in prayer, and God responded by forgiving their sin. Job prays to God consistently in the prologue and epilogue. The book of Job has prayer for its bookends (1:5 and 42:8). Job functions as a priest in both places.

Zuck's point is important: Job "had maligned God and was forgiven when he repented; now it was his turn to forgive those who had maligned him and were repenting" (*Job*, 187). Interestingly, God calls Job "my servant" four times in verses 7-9. Also interesting is that God never speaks of Elihu, so we are left to guess as to whether God considered his words to Job to be good or bad.

Blessing and Restoration of Job
JOB 42:10-17

The remainder of Job 42 comprises three sections: 10-11, 12-15, and 16-17. In verses 10-11, after Job had prayed for his friends, "the LORD restored his fortunes and doubled his previous possessions" (v. 10).[57] All of Job's brothers, sisters, and former acquaintances came to Job's home and dined with him. They sympathized and comforted him "concerning all the adversity the LORD had brought on him" (v. 11). Each brought him a gift of "a piece of silver" and "a gold earring" (v. 11).

"The LORD blessed the last part of Job's life more than the first" (v. 12). Given the fact that Job was immensely blessed by God prior to his suffering, this is saying a lot! The remainder of verse 12 tabulates the livestock that Job over time was able to acquire. Job was blessed with ten more children—seven sons and three daughters (v. 13). It is

---

[57] David Wolfers (*Deep Things*, 103) remarks about the meaning of this verse, "The meaning of this (42:10) is: *And the Lord turned the captivity of Job*. Of all the innumerable indications of a national and historical allegorical meaning to the Book of Job, this is the most explicit and impossible to deny, but it is nevertheless universally denied. The customary solution is to translate the phrase: *And the Lord restored the fortunes of Job* but in thirty Biblical contexts the phrase with slight variations recurs always with the meaning of return from captivity." Wolfers wants to see in this verse a post-exilic provenance for Job.

unusual that the narrator gives so much attention to Job's three daughters, informing us of their names (which he did not do for the sons) (v. 14), their rare beauty as compared to all the women in the land, and that Job "granted them an inheritance with their brothers" (v. 15).

On first glance, this restoration of property, wealth, and children would seem to confirm the notion of divine retribution, which is the operative theology of Job and his three friends. Job is like a man innocent but who serves prison time. Afterward, he is compensated for the state's error.

However, this restoration was not a reward or payment. It was God's gift based solely on God's sovereign grace. If one were to infer this action by God were indeed something of a reward or compensation for Job's suffering, the text itself does not state it or even hint at it.

When we face adversity as did Job, we need to learn the lesson of the lodgepole pine tree.

> An unusual evergreen is the lodgepole pine that is seen in great numbers in Yellowstone Park. The cones of this pine may hang on the tree for years and years, and even when they fall they do not open. These cones can only be opened when they come in contact with intense heat. But God has a reason for planning them this way. When a forest fire rages throughout parks and forests all the trees are destroyed. At the same time, however, the heat of the fire opens the cones of the lodgepole pine; and these pines are often the first tree to grow in an area that has been burned by fire. (Browne, *Illustrations*, in Swindoll, *Tardy Oxcart*, 22)

Or consider a lesson from industry. Machine shops often have what is called the "heat treat" department. When metal is heated, it gets so hot that it turns white. Across the top of the white-hot liquid, surface particles of slag or dross form. This is the impurity that was trapped in the metal but now released by the heat. Workers in asbestos suits wipe away the slag to make the metal as pure as possible (Swindoll, *Tardy Oxcart*, 579).

When we face the fire of adversity, we can rest assured that some things in our lives can only be unlocked by the intense heat of our suffering. God always has a purpose, even if we don't know what it is.

The narrator concludes the book of Job with a summary statement in verses 16-17. Job lived an additional 140 years after his great trial of suffering. This would place Job near the age of two hundred when he died. This advanced age indicates an early patriarchal setting for Job. These extended years of life allowed Job to see his children, grandchildren, and great-grandchildren "to the fourth generation" (v. 16). The book of Job ends with the sentence "Then Job died, old and full of days." D. A. Carson offers a helpful summary of the purpose of Job's happy ending:

1. We must beware of our own biases. In the contemporary world, ambiguity is morally revered whereas moral certainty is despised. Job ends with moral certainty.
2. Job has served God from a pure heart. God has made his point with the devil.
3. Though the ending is happy, the suffering was real.
4. The book of Job has no interest in praising mystery without restraint. The book of Job does not disown all forms of retribution; it disowns simplistic definitions and application of retribution. Job still does not have all his answers, but he has learned to trust God.
5. Job's blessings at the end are not cast as rewards for good behavior. They are gifts of God's grace.
6. God's "wager" with Satan is not frivolous or capricious. God is not toying with the lives of people like a cat with a plaything. God's purposes in Job's suffering are serious. There is a spiritual struggle between God and Satan, but the Lord always comes out on top.
7. Job denies neither God's sovereignty nor his justice in the end. Job passes the test with flying colors. First Corinthians 10:13 is an important New Testament verse to understand in the light of Job: "he will not let them be tempted beyond what they can bear. But when they are tempted, he will always provide a way out so that they can stand up under it" (Carson, *How Long?* 154–56).

James speaks of suffering in James 1:2-4:

Consider it great joy, my brothers and sisters, whenever you experience various trials, because you know that the testing of your faith produces endurance. And let endurance have its full effect, so that you may be mature and complete, lacking nothing.

Suffering is a form of testing of our faith that works to produce endurance in us. This endurance leads to spiritual maturity. Here we learn that one of the purposes of our suffering is endurance and spiritual maturity. Job is a book about this.

James 5:10-11 specifically mentions Job in connection with suffering.

Brothers and sisters, take the prophets who spoke in the Lord's name as an example of suffering and patience. See, we count as blessed those who have endured. You have heard of Job's endurance and have seen the outcome that the Lord brought about—the Lord is compassionate and merciful.

The word translated "endured" here is the same Greek word in James 1:2-4. The key point to observe here in connection with Job is James's reference to "the outcome that the Lord brought about." Here it would seem that the Lord's purpose in Job's suffering was to refute the slander of Satan and to vindicate Job's faith. But the final outcome in Job 42:7-17 is God's blessings on Job, which in light of what is said here in James may be considered the result of God's "compassion" and "mercy" in light of all that Job endured during his sufferings. Calvin's statement is on target: "Afflictions ought ever to be estimated by their end" (*Catholic Epistles*, 352).

James teaches us that we "should respond to our suffering with joy, faith, perseverance, hope, and caution. And we should respond to the suffering of others with ministry, encouragement, love, and prayer" (Morgan, *Theology of James*, 76). The book of Job teaches us this as well.

The only time the New Testament names Job, it singles out his steadfastness and perseverance (Jas 5:11). In this way he is a type of Christ who endured the sufferings of the cross for us. This is an important connection between the book of Job and Jesus that needs to be expressed in our preaching.

That the Lord Himself has embraced and absorbed the underserved consequences of all evil is the final answer to Job and to all the Jobs of humanity. As an innocent sufferer, Job is a companion of God. (Anderson, "Problem of Suffering," 188)

George Foreman struggled to find his way as a troubled teenager. With a menacing manner and imposing physique, Foreman became a bully. Through Job Corps he met Charles "Doc" Broadus, a counselor and boxing coach, who inspired Foreman to pursue boxing. Incredibly, in less than two years Foreman became the world heavyweight amateur champion as a gold medalist at the 1968 Olympics in Mexico City. Turning professional in 1969, Foreman racked up a stunning 37–0 record by 1972. His big moment came on January 22, 1973, in Kingston, Jamaica, when he defeated Smokin' Joe Frazier to become the heavyweight champion of the world.

On October 30, 1974, Foreman stepped into the ring in Kinshasa, Zaire, against the 4–1 underdog Muhammad Ali in the now famous "Rumble in the Jungle." To the surprise of most, Ali sent the undefeated world heavyweight champion to the canvas in the eighth round. After months of sulking over the loss, Foreman returned to post a five-straight-knockout comeback in 1977 but succumbed to Jimmy Young in a twelve-round fight in Puerto Rico that nearly led to Foreman's death.

In the midst of his despair, Foreman turned to Christ and found salvation. Immediately he was a changed man. He gave up boxing and started preaching in his hometown of Houston. He planted his own church in 1980 and later built and founded the George Foreman Youth and Community Center for at-risk kids and troubled teens.

When his financial fortune dwindled, Foreman realized he must make the greatest "comeback" of his life to keep his Youth Center and ministry alive. Out of shape, and with his friends thinking he was out of his mind, he decided to box again.

In November 1994, the world witnessed the greatest comeback in boxing history as forty-five-year-old George Foreman sent twenty-seven-year old Michael Moorer to the canvas—out cold.

Foreman retired from boxing in 1997 with a 76–5 career record. His new celebrity status led to the launch of a new career in television marketing. Over the years he sold millions of his George Foreman Lean Mean Grilling Machines and then sold millions of mufflers for Meineke Car Care Centers (Hale, "George Foreman").

Job made perhaps the greatest comeback in history. But he did not do it on his own. Like his victory, your victory over Satan and self is not possible without divine help. Jesus Christ and his cross secures that victory.

In 1987, little eighteen-month-old Jessica McClure playfully dangled her feet over an innocent-looking eighteen-inch-wide hole in her aunt's backyard in Midland, Texas. But when Jessica tried to stand up, she slipped into the hole and fell down the pipe of an abandoned water well until she was wedged one leg up and one leg down, twenty-two feet below the surface. An anxious nation riveted to their televisions watched with bated breath to see whether little Jessica would be rescued. Rescuers drilled a twenty-nine-foot shaft parallel to the well and then bored a five-foot horizontal tunnel through solid rock in an attempt to reach Jessica. All the while, medics were worried that dehydration and shock would take her life before the rescuers could get there. The rescue attempt took far longer than anyone expected. The solid rock, plus equipment failure, meant that it took fifty-eight hours to reach little Jessica. She was wedged in the pipe so tightly that they couldn't move her. Medical personnel hooked up monitors to her, and they discovered the worst—her life was ebbing away. She had little time left. That critical point between life and death had arrived. Robert O'Donnell went down the parallel shaft and then across to little Jessica in an effort to free her and pull her to safety. A voice from above echoed down the shaft to O'Donnell: "Robert! Pull hard, Robert! You may have to break her in order to save her." He pulled so hard that he scarred her face. She lost one toe. Yet when Robert O'Donnell emerged from the ground with little Jessica in his arms, no one accused him of child abuse. Everyone knew if he had not scarred her, he could not save her.

With reverent pen I write in hope that with reverent eyes you read these words. On the cross, in the midst of extraordinary physical and spiritual suffering, Jesus cried, "My God, why have you forsaken me?" It is as if God responded to that cry by saying, "My beloved Son, I have to break you in order to save them." Could this be a glimpse of what Isaiah 53:5 means: "We are healed by his wounds"? The Gospel writers inform us that after the resurrection of Jesus, when he appeared to the disciples in the upper room, the only tangible evidences on the resurrected and glorified body of Jesus were the scars from the cross. The book of Revelation informs us that Jesus in heaven is "like a slaughtered lamb." Where there is a scar, there has been a healing. Jesus is the wounded healer!

This is how Job must be read—through the crimson lens of the cross. The problem of suffering is not solved by anthropology, sociology, psychology, or philosophy. It can only be solved by theology proper (the doctrine of God), Christology, and soteriology. "In Christ, God was reconciling the world to himself" (2 Cor 5:19). The problem of suffering is only solved by the Suffering Servant by whose wounds we are healed.

Reflect and Discuss

1. How does the ending of Job compare with the prologue of Job? Why do you think Satan is not mentioned?
2. What do you think the friends had not spoken correctly about God?
3. Why does God instruct the three friends to ask Job to pray for them?
4. How do you feel about the fact that nowhere in the book does God explain to Job about the conversation between God and Satan or about why Job is suffering?
5. What does the life and teaching of Jesus say to us in the context of Job?

Conclusion

One day many years ago, the students of the University of Glasgow were introduced to their guest speaker, the great missionary David Livingstone. When Livingstone stood up and walked to the front of the platform to speak, the students observed the tangible effects on his body of the many years of living in Africa: an emaciated form from the ravages of jungle fever, his right arm dangling at his side as a result of the attack of an African lion. In silent awe and respect, the student body rose to their feet.

Somehow I feel this should be our posture at the end of the book of Job. Job has traveled a path most of us will never travel, at least not to the extremes Job traveled. We should stand in silence before this man and the book that describes his journey and listen carefully to the still, small voice that speaks to us.

Assessing the book of Job is quite a task. Not a few readers have been left with that awkward feeling of scratching their heads and not quite getting it. Although Job ends well for Job himself, the same cannot be said for many others who suffer. Sufferers who come to Job seeking answers may well feel that God provides none—at least none directly.

If we approach Job asking the question *why*, we will not get our question answered directly. That may be because Job is teaching us that we are asking the wrong question. The proper question is not so much *why* but *who*. Ultimately Job dropped the *why* question when he came to understand the *who* question. Job learned what we must learn—we are never going to comprehend God's ways; we must learn to trust his character.

Another important aspect of the book of Job is the focus on speech throughout. "Words are the key to the book of Job. . . . Words are also the structure of the debate and the means of its resolution" (Adam, *Hearing God's Words*, 56). The poetic section of Job unfolds in a series of speeches. Throughout these speeches, motifs of speech, listening, etc. are redolent. A prominent theme throughout both the prose and poetic sections of Job is Job's refusal to sin against God with his speech. The three friends are brought to account by God for their incorrect speech. Job himself is brought to account by God for his incorrect speech as well. In his pain Job wanders to the edge of blasphemy at times, but he never crosses the boundary.

Before moving on to the question of divine justice, we need to remind ourselves of the prologue to the book of Job. There we learned of the two rival claims about Job's character and faith. Satan claimed Job was a fake in that he only obeyed God because of the blessings God had given him. In response, God claimed that Job served him because he loved God wholeheartedly. How are these two competing claims to be adjudicated? Job's sufferings. In this sense, the book is not about suffering but about Job's character and faith, along with God's character (divine justice).

The question is, Who is right, Satan or God? Actually, the question is settled in the prologue. In Job 1:20-22 Job settles the dispute between God and Satan in favor of God. But Satan refuses to give in and says to God that Job will cave if he is allowed to suffer physically. Yet even though Job is plagued with physical suffering, he does not curse God. Once again, in Job 2:10, Job settles the dispute between God and Satan in favor of God. Does Job trust God even without physical health and in the face of great physical suffering? The answer is yes!

We cannot leave the prologue without exploring once again the relationship of God and Satan in light of evil and suffering. Several points are clear. First, God possesses all power to prevent evil. Second, sometimes God acts to prevent evil. Third, often God permits evil. These three facts lead ineluctably to two questions: Why does God permit some evil to occur? and Why does God not prevent all evil? In his article "Rules of Engagement: God's Permission of Evil in Light of Selected Cases of Scripture," John Peckham offers a partial solution to this problem.

> The *satan's* objection that God has quote "put a fence around" Job itself indicates that the *satan* was restricted from bringing the harm that, he alleged, would manifest that Job was not really upright and loyal as God had declared (Job 2:10-11). This, in turn, indicates that there were some existing limits or parameters in place relative to Job: rules of engagement which, in response to the *satan's* allegations before the heavenly council, were modified in both scenes.
> . . . While God possesses the sheer power to contravene such rules of engagement, insofar as God agrees before the heavenly council to extend the *satan's* jurisdiction, God cannot *morally* prevent the *satan* from exercising his power within that

jurisdiction. . . . (1) The *satan* brings allegations against Job
and God's character, (2) there were parameters that restricted
the *satan* from harming Job—which, the *satan* alleged,
prevented him from proving the allegations true, (3) those
parameters were twice changed before the heavenly council
in response to the *satan*'s appeals, and (4) such parameters
might, as such, be thought of as rules of engagement, which
not only restrict the *satan*'s action but also *morally* restrict
God's action. ("Rules of Engagement," 251; emphasis in
original)

Peckham's approach would seem to offer insight into the question
of why God permitted Satan to afflict Job. This, in turn, sheds light on
the broader picture of evil in the world and why God sometimes restricts
evil and suffering and why he sometimes permits evil and suffering.

Regarding this question, given a rules-of-engagement
framework, the cosmic conflict can be understood not as
a conflict of sheer power but as a conflict over character
wherein God allows creatures the freedom to oppose
his moral government, within specified and limited, but
consistent, parameters. ("Rules of Engagement," 257; emphasis
in original)

Turning to the poetic middle section of the book, the reader wonders whether Job can withstand the pressure and not cave in and curse
God. In the face of withering criticism from the three friends and deafening silence from God, Job does not falter. He maintains his integrity
and refuses to do two things: confess his sin and curse God. In this section Job's familiar theological categories were expanded. Job came to
the conclusion that it might be the case that he would be vindicated after
death (14:13-22; 19:23-29). Second, recognizing the difficulty of arguing
his case before God, Job expressed his desire for a mediator who could
stand with him in his encounter with God (9:33; 33:23). Edward Curtis
perceptively noted, "Neither idea plays a role in the solution given in
Job or elsewhere in the Old Testament, but the New Testament reveals
that both possibilities imagined by Job are true" (*Interpreting*, 59).

At the end of the poetic section, where Job responds a second time
to God's speeches, we come full circle. Job 42:6 is the resolution to the
question as to who is correct about Job, God or Satan. While Job is still

suffering on his ash heap, and before there is any promise of God's blessings on the other side of his suffering, Job submits himself in trust and resignation to God. Satan's accusations in the prologue are now demonstrated to be false. Job does what Satan said he would never do—Job submits to God and serves him for who he is and not for what he can get out of him.

In Harriet Beecher Stowe's famous novel *Uncle Tom's Cabin*, Uncle Tom had been wrenched from his old Kentucky home and put on a steamship headed for an unknown place. It was a terrible moment of crisis for him. F. W. Borham describes the scene:

> Uncle Tom's faith was staggered. It really seemed to him that in leaving Aunt Chloe and the children and his old companions he was leaving God. Falling asleep, the slave had a dream. He dreamed that he was back again and that little Eva was reading to him from the Bible. He could hear her voice, "When thou passeth through the waters, I will be with thee, for I, the Lord thy God, the Holy One of Israel, I am thy Savior." A little later poor Tom was writhing under the cruel lash of his new owner. But the blows fell only on the outer man and not, as before, on the heart. Tom stood submissive, and yet the master named Legree could not hide from himself the fact that his power over his victim had gone. As [Tom] disappeared in his cabin and Legree wheeled his horse suddenly round, there passed through the tyrant's mind those vivid flashes that often send the lightning of conscience across the dark and wicked soul. He understood full well that it was God who was standing between him and Tom. (Boreham, *A Casket of Cameos*, quoted in Swindoll, *Tardy Oxcart*, 23)

We are not told what Satan thought or said about the outcome of Job's trial. Satan is not mentioned again in the book after his appearance in the prologue. Perhaps Satan learned in the end that it was God himself standing between him and Job. Job certainly learned that it was God himself standing between him and his suffering even if he had no knowledge of the role of Satan in the ordeal.

So, what is the meaning of Job? So many interpretations have been suggested. Some say education comes to Job through being overwhelmed. Job is shown the complexity and mystery of the universe, which exceeds his comprehension and competency to govern. Others say the meaning of Job is that God's justice is greater than human justice. God gives to each one that which is appropriate. Still others, like Robert Gordis, argue that the beauty of the world becomes an anodyne to suffering (*God and Man*, 133). But as Tsevat noted, "Would anyone propose that the demands of justice are met by the administering of an anesthesia to the victim of an unjust sentence?" ("Meaning," 208). Some say the meaning of Job is not the issue of why the righteous suffer but what the proper conduct is when you suffer. Each of these suggestions perhaps tells part of the story, but none tells the whole story.

The book of Job broaches the question of divine justice. Ultimately, the book teaches us that divine justice cannot be measured by an abstract code, much less by human standards. It is *sui generis* and therefore beyond comprehension (Murphy, *Tree of Life*, 46). "It is always dangerous to write the script for divinity to be bound by" (ibid., 40).

Job reminds us that reason is a good guide among the facts of life, but it simply does not and cannot explain all those facts. This is the lesson Job and his three friends had to learn. When it comes to suffering, we simply have to learn to live with mystery. God confronts Job, in the words of G. K. Chesterton, with "indecipherable mystery." God may be inscrutable, but he is neither capricious nor inconsistent. He is and remains a just God because that is his unchangeable nature. What at first appeared to Job as senseless calamity gave way to his firm conviction in the end that all things are pervaded by the presence of God, though that does not mean that all things are necessarily sensible or intelligible (Greenberg, *Book of Job*, xix).

Suffering is penal, remedial, redemptive, but never meaningless. Job teaches us that suffering is one of God's tools to refine us and fit us to a greater walk with him and greater service for him. One of the key verses that illustrates this truth is Job 23:10: "Yet he knows the way I have taken; when he has tested me, I will emerge as pure gold." Suffering is not always punitive, but it is always educative. This poem illustrates:

> I walked a mile with Pleasure; She chatted all the way;
> But left me none the wiser For all she had to say.
> I walked a mile with Sorrow, And ne'er a word said she;
> But, oh! The things I learned from her, When Sorrow walked
>   with me. (Robert Browning Hamilton, "Along the Road")

Curtis summarized well the primary themes of the addresses in the book of Job:

- Job explores the relationship between God and humanity.
- Job shows humanity's limited understanding of God's work and purposes.
- Job shows that God accepts the honest cries of his hurting people.
- Job shows that people should serve God for who he is rather than for the benefits he provides.
- Job teaches important lessons about God.
- Job shows how God's people should respond to circumstances that call into question God's justice and goodness. (Curtis, *Interpreting*, 58–63)

Paul began his second letter to the church at Corinth with these words:

Blessed be the God and Father of our Lord Jesus Christ, the Father of mercies and the God of all comfort. He comforts us in all our affliction, so that we may be able to comfort those who are in any kind of affliction, through the comfort we ourselves receive from God. For just as the sufferings of Christ overflow to us, so also through Christ our comfort overflows. If we are afflicted, it is for your comfort and salvation. If we are comforted, it is for your comfort, which produces in you patient endurance of the same sufferings that we suffer. And our hope for you is firm, because we know that as you share in the sufferings, so you will also share in the comfort. (2 Cor 1:3-7)

I have no doubt that one of the purposes of Job for us is that we may be comforted by Job's sufferings and that through this book God himself may comfort us in our sufferings. Then, because of this comfort, God will be able to use us to comfort others in their times of suffering as well.

I am reminded of the two books published on the subject of suffering by the great C. S. Lewis. *The Problem of Pain* appeared in 1940 and is Lewis's attempt at a theodicy that at least gets at a partial answer for suffering in the world. Twenty-one years later Lewis published *A Grief Observed*. The circumstances of this book were quite different. Lewis's wife of only three years died of bone cancer. The book is a collection of his reflections on suffering from the vantage point of personal experience. Lewis let his hair down in this second book, so much so that he feared his honesty might be problematic, so he published the book under the pseudonym N. W. Clerk. Only after so many of his friends presented him with copies of the book to help him in his own suffering did Lewis relent and allow the book to be published under his own name.

As in Lewis's case, Job's suffering quickly shifted the focus from the theoretical to the practical and personal. Like Job, Lewis concluded that his suffering brought him into a closer walk with God and into a greater understanding of his Maker. In this way, the book of Job goes a long way toward informing us how we are supposed to suffer; that is, what do I do when I suffer? In what way am I supposed to suffer? Or what am I to do when I am suffering? The question of *why* may not be answered. But between what God says and what Job says and does, we learn how to face suffering in our lives. Immanuel Kant got it right when he argued that the mystery of evil will not yield to an intellectual solution but only to a moral response ("On the Failure," 283–97). Job teaches us about faith and trust. The hardest thing Job had to learn was to trust God in the midst of his suffering.

> To trust God when we understand Him would be a sorry triumph for religion. To trust God when we have every reason for distrusting Him, save our inward certainty of Him, is the supreme victory of religion. (Peake, *Problem of Suffering*, 88)

Faith does not hinder knowledge but liberates it. Until Job was left with nothing but God, he could never know what kind of faith he had. When Job was not sure where God was or what he was doing, he maintained his faith in God (Wiersbe, *Why Us?*, 42–43). When a person has a "commercial" faith—an I'll-serve-God-for-what-I-can-get-out-of-it kind of faith—he has only two options when suffering comes to his life: bargain with God to persuade him to change the circumstances or blame God for breaking the "contract" and thus refuse to have anything else to do with God. Job's friends illustrate the first approach, and Job's wife illustrates the second. His friends urged Job to negotiate with God, to bargain his way back into God's blessings. His wife told him to "curse God and die!" (2:9). Satan would have been happy with either response. But Job chose neither (Wiersbe, *Why Us?*, 44). While Job's friends were looking for explanations for his suffering, Job learned to quit looking for explanations and rather look for a relationship with God. Job finally came to learn that he must live by promises not by expectations. Job questioned God, even accused God of injustice, but he never lost his faith in God.

The purpose of the book of Job is . . .

to show that there is a benevolent divine purpose running
through the sufferings of the godly, and that life's bitterest
enigmas are reconcilable with this benevolent divine purpose,
did we but know all the facts. (Baxter, *Poetical Books*, 26)

The issue that gives the book of Job the key to its meaning is the fact
that Job did not know why he was suffering and the fact that he *was not
meant to know why.*

Between the prologue, which shows how Job's trial *originated*
in the councils of heaven, and the epilogue, which shows how
Job's trial *eventuated* in enrichment and blessing, we have a
group of patriarchal wiseacres theorizing and dogmatizing
from incomplete premises and deficient data. They knew
nothing about the councils of heaven which had preceded
Job's trial: and they knew nothing about the coming epilogue
of compensation. They were philosophising in the dark. It is
in this that the book has its message to us. We are meant to
see that there *was* an explanation, even though Job and his
friends did not know it, so that when baffling affliction comes
to ourselves we may believe that the same holds good in our
case—that there is, indeed, a purpose for it in the councils of
heaven, and a foreknown outcome of blessing. (Baxter, *Poetical
Books*, 27; emphasis in original)

There are some things that God chooses not to reveal to us because, if
he did, it would thwart his purposes for our ultimate good.

The Scriptures are as wise in their *reservations* as they are in
their *revelations.* Enough is revealed to make faith intelligent.
Enough is reserved to give faith scope for development.
(Baxter, *Poetical Books*, 27; emphasis in original)

God has put enough rationality in the universe to make faith reasonable, but he has left enough out to make faith necessary.

When Job is fully digested (as if that were possible), we come to the
realization that in a true sense Job is ultimately not about suffering; the
problem is not suffering but God. Thus, not surprisingly, God himself
becomes the answer. This is Job's final and most enduring lesson for

us. For Job suffering is not so much a mystery; it is a revelation of God himself! When we are suffering, we don't need an explanation; we need a revelation of God himself. The key question in Job is not, Why do the righteous suffer? but, Do we worship a God who is worthy of our suffering? (Wiersbe, *Why Us?*, 49). This is really the single question that the more than three hundred questions in the book of Job—many of which Job himself asked—are trying to get us to answer. But at the end, when Job meets God face-to-face, all his questions are silenced. "How can I answer you? I place my hand over my mouth" (40:4).

Job was able to move on! And so must we. Whether you have suffered, are suffering, or will suffer, in any case, good or bad, sink or swim, live or die, you have to move on. And as Job discovered, the Lord will be there. As Jesus said, "And remember, I am with you always, to the end of the age" (Matt 28:20).

Preaching Job

Job is one of the more difficult books of the Old Testament from which to preach. Here are several things from Edward Curtis to keep in mind:

1. We must do justice both to Job's suffering and to his faith.
2. We must reflect the book's narrative and poetic genres in our preaching.
3. We must proclaim Job with an awareness of and sensitivity to people and their suffering (*Interpreting*, 157–59).

At the end of his book, Curtis offers suggestions on preaching Job 4–6 (*Interpreting*, 167–85). One of the strengths of Curtis's approach is his attempt to keep a narrative unit together in preaching (Job 4–6 has to do with Eliphaz's first speech and Job's response). The unit coheres linguistically. Another strength is Curtis's attention to genre and exegesis. A third strength is the effort to apply the text to daily life.

However, there are two shortcomings in Curtis's approach. First, Job's response to Eliphaz ends with Job 7, not Job 6. Curtis should add Job 7 so the complete linguistic unit, Job 4–7, is considered.

Second, Curtis suggests the topic for the sermon from this text is an example of the practice of friendship, specifically, the failure of Eliphaz to act toward Job as a friend should act—showing loving-kindness (*chesed*). All of this is well and good, but the problem is this—friendship or friendship gone wrong is not the main point of this text or even a secondary or tertiary point. This becomes evident when the text is compared and read in the context of the prologue, as Curtis rightly affirms should be done. There may be some legitimate application of failed friendship that perhaps could be made from this text, but many other points and applications should be made before anything to do with friendship.

The irony of this is that Curtis's comments on the meaning of the text via his exegesis and theological reasoning are on target and well done. He tries to force the real point or points that can be derived from the textual structure into the mold of friendship, a move that misses the point. However, preachers of this text will benefit greatly from Curtis's exegesis and theological analysis.

Here is a short, nonexhaustive list of helpful works that are mostly sermons by preachers who have preached through the book of Job:

Ash, Christopher. *Job: The Wisdom of the Cross.* Preaching the Word. Wheaton: Crossway, 2014.

Blair, J. Allen. *Living Patiently: A Devotional Study of the Book of Job.* Neptune, NJ: Loizeaux, 1966.

Brown, Michael. *Job: The Faith to Challenge God.* Peabody, MA: Hendrickson, 2019. (Preachers will find lots of help in this book. Brown includes commentary, a new translation, a series of theological reflections helpful for preaching, and exegetical essays shedding light for preaching on key passages in Job.)

Calvin, John. *Sermons on Job.* Edinburgh: Banner of Truth, 1993.

Durham, James. *Lectures on Job.* 2nd ed. Dallas, TX: Naphtali Press, 2003. (Durham [1622–1658] was a Scottish Presbyterian preacher. His work on Job was not published until 1759. His exposition is solid, coupled with good application as well.)

Green, Jay, ed. *Treasury of Job.* Vol. 1. Marshallton, DE: The National Foundation for Christian Education, 1970. (Includes William Henry Green, *The Argument of the Book of Job* under the title *Job's Triumph over Satan*; and an abridgment of Joseph Caryl's first three volumes of his *An Exposition with Practical Observations upon the Book of Job.* To my knowledge, the planned volumes 2 and 3, which would have completed the abridgment, were never published. Caryl's work on Job, begun in 1647, stretched to twelve volumes for a total of 8,700 pages and was completed in 1666.)

Jeremiah, David. *Tried, Tested, & Triumphant: The Book of Job.* 2 vols. San Diego, CA: Turning Point, 2010.

Lawson, Steven. *When All Hell Breaks Loose.* Colorado Springs, CO: NavPress, 1993. (This book contains lots of help homiletically on Job. Lawson writes vividly and with verve.)

Stedman, Ray C. *Let God Be God: Life-Changing Truths from the Book of Job.* Grand Rapids: Discovery House, 2007.

Swindoll, Charles. *Job: A Man of Heroic Endurance.* Great Lives from God's Word 7. Nashville: Thomas Nelson, 2004.

Preaching Job in the Light of Suffering in the New Testament

The New Testament has much to say about the subject of suffering. Jesus spoke about suffering persecution for his name's sake in Matthew 5. In Luke 13:1-5 Jesus spoke to the issue of retributive justice:

*At that time, some people came and reported to him about the
Galileans whose blood Pilate had mixed with their sacrifices. And he
responded to them, "Do you think that these Galileans were more sinful
than all the other Galileans because they suffered these things? No,
I tell you; but unless you repent, you will all perish as well. Or those
eighteen that the tower in Siloam fell on and killed—do you think they
were more sinful than all the other people who live in Jerusalem? No, I
tell you; but unless you repent, you will all perish as well."*

In John 9:1-3 Jesus was asked about a man who had been born blind:

*As he was passing by, he saw a man blind from birth. His disciples
asked him, "Rabbi, who sinned, this man or his parents, that he was
born blind?"*
    *"Neither this man nor his parents sinned," Jesus answered. "This
came about so that God's works might be displayed in him.*

In other words, there are clearly some cases where the retributive principle of justice does not come into play. These passages in the New
Testament can be used when illustrating the error of Job's three friends
who asserted the retribution principle of justice and/or when illustrating the truth of Job's denial of the same.

With respect to the cross of Christ, Luke records that Jesus connected his death on the cross with that of the Suffering Servant of
Isaiah 53, as can be seen in comparing Luke 4:16 with Luke 22:37,
where Jesus said to the disciples at the Last Supper, "For I tell you,
what is written must be fulfilled in me: **And he was counted among
the lawless.** Yes, what is written about me is coming to its fulfillment."
The bolded quotation is directly from Isaiah 53:12 (see Allen, *The
Atonement*, 36–49, 66).

When preaching Job, we are able to see in the man Job a type of
God's great Suffering Servant, who by his death on the cross provides
salvation. This is an important link to make when concluding sermons
on Job.

The letters of Paul are replete with passages that speak of the suffering of Christians. For example, texts like Romans 8:28-39 would
be important to weave into your preaching of Job. Likewise consider
2 Corinthians 1:3-7:

> *Blessed be the God and Father of our Lord Jesus Christ, the Father*
> *of mercies and the God of all comfort. He comforts us in all our*
> *affliction, so that we may be able to comfort those who are in any kind*
> *of affliction, through the comfort we ourselves receive from God. For*
> *just as the sufferings of Christ overflow to us, so also through Christ*
> *our comfort overflows. If we are afflicted, it is for your comfort and*
> *salvation. If we are comforted, it is for your comfort, which produces*
> *in you patient endurance of the same sufferings that we suffer. And*
> *our hope for you is firm, because we know that as you share in the*
> *sufferings, so you will also share in the comfort.*

Here Paul reminds us that from our suffering comes a ministry to others
who suffer. Job's comforters failed him miserably. God himself became
Job's comforter. As God comforts us in our suffering, we become his
instruments to comfort others. This text is important to remember
when preaching Job.

Paul also addresses the issue of suffering in Philippians 3:10-11:

> *My goal is to know him and the power of his resurrection and the*
> *fellowship of his sufferings, being conformed to his death, assuming*
> *that I will somehow reach the resurrection from among the dead.*

Part of what we as Christians should desire to "know" is the "fellowship of [Christ's] sufferings." Even if this suffering leads to death, we
as Christians have the promise of a glorious resurrection, just as Jesus
was raised from the dead. Job longed for resurrection in the famous
passage in Job 19:25-26:

> *"But I know that my Redeemer lives, and at the end he will stand on*
> *the dust. Even after my skin has been destroyed, yet I will see God in*
> *my flesh."*

Here Job affirms that though his suffering result in his physical death,
he will yet see God in the resurrection.

In Colossians 1:24 Paul writes,

> *Now I rejoice in my sufferings for you, and I am completing in my flesh*
> *what is lacking in Christ's afflictions for his body, that is, the church.*

In this remarkable passage Paul could rejoice in suffering because
he knew that the end result redounded to God's glory. Paul's own
personal suffering was because of Christ and also on behalf of fellow

believers. Paul is not suggesting that his suffering makes up something lacking in the cross of Christ and its power. Rather, he considers his persecution a service, both to Christ and to the church—a service that Christ left for his followers to fulfill. This perspective on the suffering of Christians is vital to connect with the preaching of Job.

The author of Hebrews has much to say about suffering as well. The suffering of Jesus connects him with those for whom he suffered:

> But we do see Jesus—**made lower than the angels for a short time** so that by God's grace he might taste death for everyone—**crowned with glory and honor** because he suffered death.
>
> For in bringing many sons and daughters to glory, it was entirely appropriate that God—for whom and through whom all things exist— should make the pioneer of their salvation perfect through sufferings.
> (Heb 2:9-10; emphasis in original)

Again, in Hebrews 5:8-9 the author uses the term "perfected" to describe the results of Christ's suffering in relation to himself:

> Although he was the Son, he learned obedience from what he suffered. After he was perfected, he became the source of eternal salvation for all who obey him.

In what sense was Jesus "perfected"? The author gives no hint that Jesus previously was in some way lacking morally or otherwise. Rather, the perfecting had to do with qualifying him to be the leader of salvation through human suffering, the focus being on his suffering on the cross that accomplished the atonement and salvation. The sinlessness of Jesus in Hebrews is presented against the backdrop of his humanity and susceptibility to temptation. The fact that he was tempted in all points as we are (4:15) is a part of the perfecting process the author had in mind. The use of the word "learned" in 5:8 sheds light on the use of "perfected" in 5:9. The two are seen as parallel: through suffering Jesus learned obedience, and through suffering he was made perfect. Additionally, the perfection of Christ includes an aspect of fulfillment. Through the sufferings of Christ culminating in the cross, Jesus fulfilled everything needed to make him the author of our salvation.

In Hebrews 12:11 the author speaks of suffering through discipline; it is not pleasant at the time. "Later on, however, it yields the peaceful fruit of righteousness to those who have been trained by it." This important principle, that suffering works in our lives to produce the fruit of right living, should be incorporated when preaching Job to illustrate this principle in Job's life. However, it should be noted that this is not the major focus of Job, and Job was living righteously before his suffering.

James speaks of suffering in 1:2-4:

> *Consider it a great joy, my brothers and sisters, whenever you experience various trials, because you know that the testing of your faith produces endurance. And let endurance have its full effect, so that you may be mature and complete, lacking nothing.*

Suffering is a form of testing of our faith that works to produce endurance in us. This endurance leads to spiritual maturity. Here we learn that one of the purposes of our suffering is endurance and spiritual maturity.

In James 5:10-11 Job is specifically mentioned in connection with suffering.

> *Brothers and sisters, take the prophets who spoke in the Lord's name as an example of suffering and patience. See, we count as blessed those who have endured. You have heard of Job's endurance and have seen the outcome that the Lord brought about—the Lord is compassionate and merciful.*

The word "endured" here is the same Greek word as in James 1:2-4. The key point to observe here in connection with Job is James's reference to "the outcome that the Lord brought about." Here it would seem that the Lord's purpose in Job's suffering was to refute Satan's slander and to vindicate Job's faith. But the final outcome in Job 42:7-17 is God's blessing on Job, which in light of what is said here in James may be considered the result of God's compassion and mercy after all Job endured during his sufferings. Calvin's statement is on target: "Afflictions ought ever to be estimated by their end" (*Catholic Epistles*, 352).

James teaches us that we . . .

> should respond to our suffering with joy, faith, perseverance, hope, and caution. And we should respond to the suffering of others with ministry, encouragement, love, and prayer. (Morgan, *Theology of James*, 76)

The Petrine letters also speak about suffering.

Dear friends, don't be surprised when the fiery ordeal comes among you to test you, as if something unusual were happening to you. Instead, rejoice as you share in the sufferings of Christ, so that you may also rejoice with great joy when his glory is revealed. If you are ridiculed for the name of Christ, you are blessed, because the Spirit of glory and of God rests on you. Let none of you suffer as a murderer, a thief, an evildoer, or a meddler. But if anyone suffers as a Christian, let him not be ashamed but let him glorify God in having that name. . . .

So then, let those who suffer according to God's will entrust themselves to a faithful Creator while doing what is good.
(1 Pet 4:12-16,19)

Here Peter speaks of the specific suffering of persecution that comes to Christians. In this we are actually participating in the sufferings of Christ leading to an occasion for rejoicing. Furthermore, in the midst of such suffering, the Holy Spirit "rests" on those who are suffering, and this is a great encouragement and comfort. Peter says God uses suffering to purify Christians. Finally, those who suffer should "entrust themselves to a faithful Creator." This last statement dovetails with the book of Job. In Job, God is the faithful Creator who uses his creation to teach Job lessons about his suffering. At the end of the book, Job learns to entrust himself to God, the faithful Creator.

The book of Revelation demonstrates that the suffering of God's people is never wasted, and all wrongs on earth will be righted in heaven, in eternity. There will be a new heaven and a new earth. John writes,

Then I heard a loud voice from the throne: Look, God's dwelling is with humanity, and he will live with them. They will be his peoples, and God himself will be with them and will be their God. He will wipe away every tear from their eyes. Death will be no more; grief, crying, and pain will be no more, because the previous things have passed away.

Then the one seated on the throne said, "Look, I am making everything new." He also said, "Write, because these words are faithful and true." (Rev 21:3-5)

As Job discovered that the presence of God who revealed himself to Job immediately changed everything and Job no longer needed answers, so in that day all believers will be in the presence of the Lord, and he will eliminate their suffering forevermore.

Preaching Christ from Job[58]

In preaching Christ from Job, let's begin at the macro level. The book addresses issues of sovereignty, wisdom, and suffering.

God is sovereign. So is Jesus. He is the sovereign Lord of all (Phil 2:9-11). He is the sovereign Creator and Sustainer of the universe (Heb 1:2-3). In his earthly miracles of nature, Jesus demonstrates his sovereignty. When we find references in Job to God's sovereignty over nature, whether from Job himself, his three friends, Elihu, or God in his final speeches of the book, we can correlate that with New Testament passages that teach and demonstrate this concerning Christ.

Job is a wisdom book. Job 28 is a key chapter on the source of wisdom. Job searched for wisdom to understand why he was suffering and came up short. Wisdom can only be found in God. In the New Testament, Christ is the embodiment of wisdom. First Corinthians 1:30 says those of us who are believers are "in Christ Jesus" who is the "wisdom from God." In Colossians 2:3 Christ is the one in whom "are hidden all the treasures of wisdom and knowledge." "The fear of the LORD is the beginning of wisdom" is a favorite refrain in the Old Testament, especially in Psalms (111:10) and Proverbs (9:10). Christ is our wisdom. When we come to Christ, we have his wisdom to guide us day by day. He is the "Wonderful Counselor" of Isaiah 9:6. He provides an answer to our question, a solution to our problem, and salvation for our souls. In this way, whenever we come to anything wisdom-related in Job, we can turn the application to Christ in our preaching.

Job suffered. He suffered physically, mentally, emotionally, and spiritually. Job is the quintessential human example of suffering. Job's suffering is not punitive, as the book makes clear. Job's suffering is educative and exemplary. In this way Job is singled out in the New Testament as an example of patience in the midst of suffering. In all these ways, the suffering of Christ on the cross can be compared to that of Job. Christ was not suffering for his own sins. In that sense his suffering was not punitive. He was innocent in the midst of his sufferings. Christ's suffering on the cross was certainly educative and exemplary for all humanity.

But there is one crucial difference between the suffering of Job and the suffering of Jesus: Job's suffering was not redemptive. Christ's

---

[58] For a helpful study of preaching Christ from Job, see O'Donnell, *Beginning and End*.

suffering on the cross was redemptive. Christ's death on the cross provides atonement for the sins of all humanity. Through the cross of Christ, reconciliation with God takes place. On the grounds of the cross of Christ, all who repent of sin and believe in Jesus are justified by their union with Christ through faith, their sins are forgiven, and they are reconciled to God.

Job was an innocent sufferer who did not choose his suffering. Jesus was an innocent sufferer who chose his suffering. His suffering was voluntary. His death on the cross on our behalf was a choice motivated by his love for all humanity. Jesus is the Suffering Servant of Isaiah 53. In preaching Job, we should correlate what is said about Christ in Isaiah 53 with the New Testament revelation of Christ's death on the cross.

Job never got an explanation for his suffering. Jesus does not formally explain his own sufferings beyond their redemptive purpose. Job never dismissed the reality of his sufferings. Jesus likewise faced the reality of his suffering. Hebrews 4:15 tells us that Jesus was "tempted in every way as we are, yet without sin." As noted above, Hebrews 5:8-9 says, "Although he was the Son, he learned obedience from what he suffered. After he was perfected, he became the source of eternal salvation for all who obey him." As fully human as he was divine, Jesus experienced the full force of suffering. In the garden of Gethsemane, Jesus submitted himself to the suffering of the cross as God's will for him. On the cross Jesus endured the suffering to the end. "It is finished," the cry of victory in John 19:30, is all the explanation we need regarding the *why* of Christ's suffering. It was for us. It was necessary for our salvation. The suffering of the cross of Christ was the only means of our redemption. The salvation of every human soul that believes is the direct result of a Savior who suffered. Had he not worn the crown of thorns, I could not wear the crown of life.

In our preaching we need to point out that Job's suffering was a unique case. The prologue makes that clear. Few people have suffered to the degree Job suffered and for the reasons he suffered. In like manner, Jesus's suffering on the cross was a unique case. As the God-man, truly human and truly divine, Jesus suffered in the place of others for their sins. Unlike Job's, Jesus's suffering is redemptive. I remember hearing Stephen Olford say, "That which is not incarnational is not redemptive, and that which is not redemptive is not life transforming." The incarnation of Jesus was the necessary precursor to his death on the cross for our sins. By means of his death, we experience life transformation.

The final word of the suffering of the cross was not death. The final word of suffering is the resurrection. Job hints at the resurrection in Job 19:25-26; but what Job could only dream of, Christ has made abundantly real. He arose! Job spoke many times of his impending death caused by his suffering. He spoke of the Pit, of the grave, of dust, of worms, and of bodily destruction. But the other side of the coin is the resurrection of Christ. By his cross and resurrection, Christ became the victor over sin, death, and the grave.

The pastoral implications of Job are evident. Job persevered and endured his suffering by faith. So must we. The supremacy of Christ over nature—his victory over suffering and death at the cross and the empty tomb—is the clarion call to us to persevere by faith. It is a call to run our race—the arduous marathon that comprises this oft beleaguering life we live—with patient endurance,

> *keeping our eyes on Jesus, the pioneer and perfecter of our faith. For the joy that lay before him, he endured the cross, despising the shame, and sat down at the right hand of the throne of God.*
> *For consider him who endured such hostility from sinners against himself, so that you won't grow weary and give up.* (Heb 12:2-3)

The only time the New Testament names Job, it singles out his steadfastness and perseverance (Jas 5:11). In this way he is a type of Christ, who endured the sufferings of the cross for us. This is an important connection between the book of Job and Jesus that needs to be expressed in our preaching.

> That the Lord Himself has embraced and absorbed the underserved consequences of all evil is the final answer to Job and to all the Jobs of humanity. As an innocent sufferer, Job is a companion of God. (Anderson, "Problem of Suffering," 188)

Christopher Ash demonstrates the connection between Job and Jesus:

> However deep our suffering, it is unlikely that our experience can ever do more than very approximately mirror Job's. We have neither been so great as Job, nor so fallen, neither so happy, nor so lonely, neither so rich, nor so poor, neither so pious, nor so cursed. All of which points to a fulfillment greater and deeper than your life or mine. Job in his extremity is actually but a shadow of a reality more extreme still, of a

man who was not just blameless but sinless, who was not just the greatest man in a region, but the greatest human being in history, greater even than merely human, who emptied himself of all his glory, became incarnate, and went all the way down to the degrading, naked, shameful death on the cross, whose journey took him from eternal fellowship with the Father to utter aloneness on the cross. The story of Job is a shadow of the greater story of Jesus Christ. (*Job*, 54)

WORKS CITED

Adam, Peter. *Hearing God's Words: Exploring Biblical Spirituality.* New Studies in Biblical Theology 16. Downers Grove: InterVarsity Press, 2004.

Alexander, J. W. *A Dictionary of Thoughts.* Edited by Tryon Edwards. Detroit, MI: F. B. Dickerson, 1908.

Allen, David. *The Atonement: A Biblical, Theological, and Historical Study of the Cross of Christ.* Nashville, TN: B&H Academic, 2019.

Allen, J. "Job 3: History of Interpretation." Pages 361–71 in *Dictionary of the Old Testament: Wisdom, Poetry, and Writings.* Edited by Tremper Longman III and Peter Enns. Downers Grove: IVP Academic, 2008.

Alter, Robert. *The Wisdom Books: Job, Proverbs, and Ecclesiastes.* New York: W. W. Norton, 2010.

Andersen, Francis. *Job: An Introduction and Commentary.* TOTC. Downers Grove: IVP Academic, 1976.

———. "The Problem of Suffering in the Book of Job." Pages 181–88 in Roy Zuck, ed., *Sitting with Job: Selected Studies on the Book of Job.* Grand Rapids: Baker, 1992.

Andrews, Arun. "Yesterday and Today, or Forever?" http://discerningmusic.wordpress.com/2009/04/09/yesterday-today-or -forever-by-arun-andrews. Accessed July 6, 2021.

Aquinas, Thomas. *The Literal Exposition on Job: A Scriptural Commentary Concerning Providence.* Classics in Religious Studies 7. Translated by Anthony Damico. Atlanta, GA: Scholars Press, 1989.

Archer, Gleason L. *The Book of Job: God's Answer to the Problem of Undeserved Suffering.* Grand Rapids: Baker, 1982.

Ash, Christopher. *Job: The Wisdom of the Cross.* Preaching the Word. Wheaton: Crossway, 2014.

Aurandt, Paul, ed. *More of Paul Harvey's The Rest of the Story.* New York: Bantam, 1980.

Ballentine, Samuel. *Job*. Smyth & Helwys Bible Commentary. Macon, GA: Smyth & Helwys, 2006.

Baxter, J. Sidlow. *Explore the Book*, vol. 3, *Poetical Books (Job to Song of Solomon): Isaiah, Jeremiah, Lamentations*. Grand Rapids: Zondervan, 1973.

Beck, H. F. "Shuhite." Page 341 in volume 4, *Interpreter's Dictionary of the Bible*. 4 vols. Edited by George Arthur Buttrick, John Knox, Herbert Gordon May, Samuel Terrien, and Emory Stevens Bucke. Nashville, TN: Abingdon, 1962.

Beuken, W. A. M., ed. *The Book of Job*. BETL 114. Louvain: Leuven University Press and Peeters, 1994.

Blair, J. Allen. *Living Patiently: A Devotional Study of the Book of Job*. Neptune, NJ: Loizeaux Brothers, n.d.

Brooks, Thomas. *The Mute Christian under the Smarting Rod: With Sovereign Antidotes against the Most Miserable Exigents*. Eighth edition, corrected. London: John Hancock, 1684. https://www.preachtheword.com/bookstore/mute-christian.pdf. Accessed February 8, 2021.

Brown, Michael. *Job: The Faith to Challenge God*. Peabody, MA: Hendrickson, 2019.

Browne, Benjamin P. *Illustrations for Preaching*. Nashville: Broadman, 1977.

Brueggemann, Walter. *Theology of the Old Testament: Testimony, Dispute, Advocacy*. Minneapolis, MN: Fortress, 1997.

Buechner, Frederick. *Peculiar Treasures: A Biblical Who's Who*. New York: Harper & Row, 1979.

Calvin, John. *Commentaries on the Catholic Epistles*. Translated and edited by John Owen. Grand Rapids: Eerdmans, 1948.

———. *Sermons from Job*. Selected and translated by Leroy Nixon. Grand Rapids: Eerdmans, 1952.

———. *Sermons on Job*. Translated by Arthur Golding. Edinburgh: Banner of Truth, 1993.

Carlyle, Thomas. *On Heroes, Hero-Worship, and the Heroic in History*. London: Chapman and Hall Limited, 1901.

Carmichael, Amy. *Mountain Breezes: The Collected Poems of Amy Carmichael*. Fort Washington, PA: CLC Publications, 1999.

Carson, D. A. *How Long Oh Lord? Reflections on Suffering and Evil*. 2nd ed. Grand Rapids: Baker, 2006.

Chappell, Clovis. *Sermons from Job*. Nashville: Abingdon, 1957.

Cheney, M. *Dust, Wind, and Agony: Character, Speech, and Genre in Job.* ConBOT 36. Stockholm: Almqvist and Wiksell, 1994.

Ciholos, Paul. *Consider My Servant Job.* Peabody, MA: Hendrickson, 1998.

Clines, D. J. A. "The Arguments of Job's Three Friends." Pages 265–78. in Roy Zuck, ed., *Sitting with Job: Selected Studies on the Book of Job.* Grand Rapids: Baker, 1992.

———. "A Brief Explanation of Job 1–3." Pages 249–52 in Roy Zuck, ed., *Sitting with Job: Selected Studies on the Book of Job.* Grand Rapids: Baker, 1992.

———. "Coming to a Theological Conclusion: The Case of the Book of Job." Pages 209–23 in *The Centre and the Periphery: A European Tribute to Walter Brueggemann.* Edited by Jill Middlemas, David J. A. Clines, and Else Holt. Hebrew Bible Monographs 27. Sheffield: Sheffield Phoenix Press, 2010.

———. *Job 1–20.* Word Bible Commentary. Nashville: Thomas Nelson, 1989.

———. "The Shape and Argument of the Book of Job." Pages 125–40 in Roy Zuck, ed., *Sitting with Job: Selected Studies on the Book of Job.* Grand Rapids: Baker, 1992.

Course, J. E. *Speech and Response: A Rhetorical Analysis of the Introductions to the Speeches of the Book of Job (Chaps. 4–24).* Catholic Biblical Quarterly Monograph Series 25. Washington DC: Catholic Biblical Association, 1994.

Crowner, David, Gerald Christianson, and August Tholuck, eds. *The Spirituality of the German Awakening.* New York: Paulist, 2003.

Curtis, Edward M. *Interpreting the Wisdom Books: An Exegetical Handbook.* Handbooks for Old Testament Exegesis. Grand Rapids: Kregel Academic, 2017.

Davis, Creath. *Lord, if I Ever Needed You, It's Now.* Grand Rapids: Baker, 1987.

Dunham, Kyle C. *The Pious Sage in Job: Eliphaz in the Context of Wisdom Theodicy.* Eugene, OR: Wipf & Stock, 2016.

Durham, James. *Lectures on Job.* Edited by Christopher Caldwell. 2nd ed. Dallas, TX: Naphtali Press, 2003.

Estes, Daniel J. *Handbook on the Wisdom Books and Psalms.* Grand Rapids, MI: Baker Academic, 2005.

———. *Job.* Teach the Text Commentary Series. Grand Rapids: Baker, 2013.

Fokkelman, Jan P. *The Book of Job in Form: A Literary Translation with Commentary*. Studia Semitica Neerlandica 58. Leiden: Brill, 2012.

Fox, Michael V. "God's Answer and Job's Response." *Biblica* 94.1 (2013).

Fyall, Robert. *Now My Eyes Have Seen You: Images of Creation and Evil in the Book of Job*. New Studies in Biblical Theology 12. Downers Grove: InterVarsity, 2002.

Gariepy, Henry. *Portraits of Perseverance*. Wheaton: Victor, 1989.

Gibson, John C. L. *Job*. Old Testament Daily Bible Study Series. Philadelphia: Westminster, 1985.

Goldingay, John. *Israel's Life*. Volume 3 of *Old Testament Theology*. Downers Grove: IVP Academic, 2009.

Good, Edwin M. "Job 31." Pages 335–44 in Roy Zuck, ed., *Sitting with Job: Selected Studies on the Book of Job*. Grand Rapids: Baker, 1992.

Gordis, Robert. *The Book of God and Man*. Chicago: University of Chicago, 1965.

Green, Jay, ed. *Treasury of Job*. Vol. 1. Marshallton, DE: The National Foundation for Christian Education, 1970.

Greenberg, Moshe. *The Book of Job: A New Translation according to the Traditional Hebrew Text*. Philadelphia: The Jewish Publication Society of America, 1980.

Gregory the Great. *Morals on the Book of Job*. Translated by Charles Marriott. A Library of Fathers of the Holy Catholic Church, vols. 18, 21, 23, 31. Oxford: John Henry Parker, 1844–1850. Migne, *Patrologia Latina*, vols. 75–76.

Habel, Norman C. *The Book of Job*. The Cambridge Bible Commentary on the New English Bible. Cambridge: Cambridge University, 1975.

———. "Literary Features and the Message of the Book of Job." Pages 97–123 in Roy Zuck, ed., *Sitting with Job: Selected Studies on the Book of Job*. Grand Rapids: Baker, 1992.

Hale, Ron. "George Foreman: Fighting the Good Fight." *The Message*. August 11, 2016. https://baptistmessage.com/george-foreman -fighting-good-fight. Accessed June 27, 2021.

Hamilton, Robert Browning. "Along the Road." *Poetry Nook*. https:// www.poetrynook.com/poem/along-road. Accessed February 8, 2021.

Harris, R. Laird. "The Doctrine of God in the Book of Job." Pages 151–80 in Roy Zuck, ed., *Sitting with Job: Selected Studies on the Book of Job*. Grand Rapids: Baker, 1992.

Hartley, J. E. *The Book of Job*. New International Commentary on the Old Testament. Grand Rapids: Eerdmans, 1988.

————. "Job 2: Ancient Near Eastern Background." Pages 346–61 in *Dictionary of the Old Testament: Wisdom, Poetry, and Writings*. Edited by Tremper Longman III and Peter Enns. Downers Grove, IVP Academic, 2008.

Henry, Matthew. *Job to Song of Solomon*. Vol. 3 of *Matthew Henry's Commentary on the Whole Bible*. Peabody, MA: Hendrickson, 1991.

Holbert, John. *Preaching Job*. Saint Louis: Chalice, 1999.

Holden, J. Stuart. *Chapter by Chapter through the Bible*. 4 vols. London: Marshall Brothers, n.d.

House, Paul. *Old Testament Theology*. Downers Grove: InterVarsity Press, 1998.

Hunt, June. *Hope for Your Heart: Finding Strength in Life's Storms*. Wheaton: Crossway, 2011.

Inch, Morris. *My Servant Job: A Discussion on the Wisdom of Job*. Grand Rapids: Baker, 1979.

Jeremiah, David. *Tried, Tested, & Triumphant: The Book of Job*. 2 vols. San Diego: Turning Point, 2010.

"Job, Book of." Pages 452–54 in *Dictionary of Biblical Imagery*. Edited by Leland Ryken, James C. Wilhoit, and Tremper Longman III. Downers Grove, IL: InterVarsity Press, 1998.

Kant, Immanuel. "On the Failure of All Attempted Philosophical Theodicies." Translated by Michel Despland. Pages 283–97 in *Kant on History and Religion*. Montreal: McGill-Queen's University Press, 1973.

Keener, Craig S., and John H. Walton, eds. *NIV Cultural Backgrounds Study Bible*. Grand Rapids: Zondervan, 2016.

Keil, Karl Friedrich, and Franz Delitzsch. *Job*. Keil and Delitzsch Commentary on the Old Testament. Originally published in German, 1866. English translation by Francis Bolton. Grand Rapids: Wm. B. Eerdmans, 1956. Kindle edition.

Lawson, Stephen J. *Job*. Holman Old Testament Commentary. Nashville: Broadman & Holman, 2004.

————. *When All Hell Breaks Loose: You May Be Doing Something Right*. Colorado Springs, CO: NavPress, 1993.

Lewis, Andrew Zack. *Approaching Job*. Cascade Companions 33. Eugene, OR: Cascade, 2017.

Lewis, C. S. *Mere Christianity*. New York: Harper Collins, 2001.

Littleton, Mark R. "Where Job's 'Comforters' Went Wrong." In Roy Zuck, ed., *Sitting with Job: Selected Studies on the Book of Job*. Grand Rapids: Baker, 1992. Pages 253–60.

Longman, Tremper. "Job 4: Person." Pages 371–74 in *Dictionary of the Old Testament: Wisdom, Poetry, and Writings*. Edited by Tremper Longman III and Peter Enns. Downers Grove: IVP Academic, 2008.

Lucado, Max. *In the Eye of the Storm*. Dallas: Word, 1991.

Maclaren, Alexander. *Esther, Job, Proverbs, Ecclesiastes*. In vol. 3 of *Expositions of Holy Scripture*. 17 vols. Grand Rapids: Baker, 1974 reprint.

Mara, M. G. "Job." Pages 414–15 in vol. 2 of *Encyclopedia of Ancient Christianity*. 3 vols. Edited by Angelo Di Berardino, Thomas C. Oden, Joel C. Elowsky, and James Hoover. Downers Grove: IVP Academic, 2014.

Mason, Mike. *The Gospel according to Job: An Honest Look at Pain and Doubt from the Life of One Who Lost Everything*. Wheaton: Crossway, 1994.

McGee, J. Vernon. *Poetry (Job)*. Thru the Bible Commentary Series, vol. 16. Nashville: Thomas Nelson, 1991.

Morgan, Christopher. *A Theology of James: Wisdom for God's People*. Phillipsburg, NJ: P&R Publishing, 2010.

Morgan, G. Campbell. *The Answer of Jesus to Job*. 1935; repr. Eugene, OR: Wipf & Stock, 2013.

Muggeridge, Malcolm. *A Twentieth Century Testimony*. Nashville: Thomas Nelson, 1978.

Murphy, Roland E. *The Tree of Life: An Exploration of Biblical Wisdom Literature*. The Anchor Bible Reference Library. New York: Doubleday, 1990.

Newsom, Carol. "Job, Book of." Pages 813–14 in *Eerdmans Dictionary of Early Judaism*. Edited by John J. Collins and Daniel C. Harlow. Grand Rapids: Eerdmans, 2010.

Nicholson, Martha Snell. *Treasures*. Chicago: Moody, 1952.

O'Donnell, Douglas Sean. *The Beginning and End of Wisdom: Preaching Christ from the First and Last Chapters of Proverbs, Ecclesiastes, and Job*. Wheaton: Crossway, 2011.

O'Neill, George. *The World's Classic, Job*. Milwaukee: The Bruce Publishing Co., 1938.

Owen, G. Frederick. "The Land of Uz." Pages 245–47 in Roy Zuck, ed., *Sitting with Job: Selected Studies on the Book of Job*. Grand Rapids: Baker, 1992.

Parsons, Greg. "Guidelines for Understanding and Proclaiming Job." *Bibliotheca Sacra* 151 (1994): 393–413.

———. "The Structure and Purpose of the Book of Job." In Roy Zuck, ed., *Sitting with Job: Selected Studies on the Book of Job.* Grand Rapids: Baker, 1992. Pages 17–33.

Peake, Arthur. *The Problem of Suffering in the Old Testament.* 1904, repr. London: The Epworth Press, 1947.

Peckham, John. "Rules of Engagement: God's Permission of Evil in Light of Selected Cases of Scripture." *Bulletin for Biblical Research* 30:2 (2020): 243–60.

Perdue, L. G., and W. C. Gilpin, eds., *The Voice from the Whirlwind: Interpreting the Book of Job.* Nashville: Abingdon, 1992.

Peterson, Eugene. *Job: Led by Suffering to the Heart of God.* Colorado Springs, CO: NavPress, 1996.

Scherer, Paul. "The Book of Job." Page 974 in vol. 3 of *The Interpreter's Bible.* Edited by George Buttrick. 12 vols. Nashville: Abingdon, 1954.

Schreiner, Susan. *Where Shall Wisdom Be Found? Calvin's Exegesis of Job from Medieval and Modern Perspectives.* Chicago: University of Chicago Press, 1994.

Seow, C. L. *Job 1–21: Interpretation and Commentary.* Illumination Series. Grand Rapids: Eerdmans, 2013.

Spurgeon, Charles. "Songs in the Night." Pages 548–53 in vol. 6 of *A Treasury of Great Preaching.* Edited by Clyde Fant and William Pinson. 13 vols. Dallas: Word Publishing, 1971.

Stanley, Charles. *Victory over Life's Challenges.* New York: Inspirational Press, 1995.

Stedman, Ray C. *Let God Be God: Life-Changing Truths from the Book of Job.* Grand Rapids: Discovery House, 2007.

Stewart, James. *The Message of Job.* London: Independent Press, 1959.

Stott, John. *The Message of the Sermon on the Mount (Matthew 5–7): Christian Counter-Culture.* The Bible Speaks Today: New Testament Series. Downers Grove: InterVarsity Press, 1985.

Swindoll, Charles. *Job: A Man of Heroic Endurance.* Great Lives from God's Word 7. Nashville: Thomas Nelson, 2004.

———. *The Tale of the Tardy Oxcart.* Nashville: Word, 1998.

Thomas, David. *Problemata Mundi: The Book of Job, Exegetically and Practically Considered.* James & Klock Publishing, 1976 reprint (originally published in 1884).

Tsevat, Matitiahu. "The Meaning of the Book of Job." Pages 189–218 in Roy Zuck, ed., *Sitting with Job: Selected Studies on the Book of Job.* Grand Rapids: Baker, 1992.

van der Lugt, P. *Rhetorical Criticism and the Poetry of the Book of Job.* Old Testament Studies 32. Leiden: Brill, 1995.

Walton, John. "Job 1: Book of." Pages 333–46 in *Dictionary of the Old Testament: Wisdom, Poetry, and Writings.* Edited by Tremper Longman III and Peter Enns. Downers Grove, IVP Academic, 2008.

Washington, James, ed. *A Testament of Hope: The Essential Writings and Speeches of Martin Luther King, Jr.* San Francisco: HarperSanFrancisco, 1986.

Westermann, Claus. *The Structure of the Book of Job: A Form-Critical Analysis.* Philadelphia: Fortress, 1977.

Wharton, James. *Job.* Westminster Bible Companion. Louisville: Westminster/John Knox, 1999.

Wiersbe, Warren. *Why Us? When Bad Things Happen to God's People.* Ada, MI: Revell, 1984.

Wilcox, Ella Wheeler. In *Masterpieces of Religious Verse.* Edited by James Dalton Morrison. New York: Harper & Brothers, 1948.

Wilder, Thornton. *Collected Plays & Writings on Theater.* New York: Library of America, 2007.

Wilson, Lindsay. "Job, Book of." Pages 384–89 in *Dictionary for Theological Interpretation of the Bible.* Edited by Kevin J. Vanhoozer. Grand Rapids: Baker Academic, 2005.

Wolfers, David. *Deep Things Out of Darkness: The Book of Job, Essays and a New English Translation.* Grand Rapids: Eerdmans, 1995.

Yancey, Philip. *Disappointment with God: Three Questions No One Asks Aloud.* Grand Rapids: Zondervan, 1988.

———. "A Fresh Reading of the Book of Job." Pages 141–50 in Roy Zuck, ed., *Sitting with Job: Selected Studies on the Book of Job.* Grand Rapids: Baker, 1992.

———. *Where Is God When It Hurts?* Grand Rapids, MI: Zondervan, 1977.

Zuck, Roy. "The Certainty of Seeing God: A Brief Exposition of Job 19:23-29." Pages 279–82 in Roy Zuck, ed., *Sitting with Job: Selected Studies on the Book of Job.* Grand Rapids: Baker, 1992.

———. *Job.* Everyman's Bible Commentary. Chicago: Moody, 1978.

———, ed. *Sitting with Job: Selected Studies on the Book of Job.* Grand Rapids: Baker, 1992.

SCRIPTURE INDEX